The BEST of
Reader's Digest

Reader's
Digest
New York, NY / Montreal

A READER'S DIGEST BOOK

ISBN 978-1-62145-472-4 (retail hardcover)
ISBN 978-1-62145-474-8 (hardcover)
ISBN 978-1-62145-502-8 (undated hardcover)
ISBN 978-1-62145-473-1 (e-pub)

We are committed to both the quality of our products and the service we provide to our customers. We value your comments, so please feel free to contact us.

Reader's Digest Adult Trade Publishing
44 South Broadway
White Plains, NY 10601

For more Reader's Digest products and information, visit our website:
www.rd.com

Printed in the United States

1 3 5 7 9 10 8 6 4 2

CONTENTS

INTRODUCTION

Reader's Digest is living history. Since its founding in 1922, *Reader's Digest* has become known for many things: curating the best reads of the day, showcasing the work of notable authors, cutting through the clutter to serve up great advice, sharing the most amusing anecdotes from readers, and telling dramatic stories of ordinary people who find themselves in extraordinary situations.

When we set out to create this series showcasing the best of *Reader's Digest*, we surveyed readers like you to ask which parts of this legacy interested them the most. The answer was clear. It wasn't the "important" articles or famous writers. They wanted the timeless stories—the ones that make you *feel* something deeply, that stick with you, just as they had stuck with readers years or decades before, when they first appeared.

So we combed the archives to find the stories that would thrill your senses, warm your heart, lift your spirits, and leave you amazed or simply grateful for your connection with your fellow humans. In this inaugural volume, you will relive the joy of parents who hear their son—diagnosed with a rare disease that left him silent and motionless—laugh for the first time. You will marvel at the courage of a teenage girl who saved her little brother's friend after they got swept out to sea. You will chuckle at humorist Rick Bragg's complete failure to catch a fish. And because variety is what you expect of us, you also will discover many of our most memorable photographs, laugh-out-loud jokes and cartoons, and truest reader stories—including some bonus material never published in the magazine itself.

Enjoy this series in the spirit that it is intended—as an oasis of optimism that will help quench anyone's thirst for positivity.

—The Editors of *Reader's Digest*

Letter in the Wallet

by Arnold Fine, from *The Jewish Press*

When a Good Samaritan tracks down the owner of a lost wallet, fate takes over.

It was a freezing day, a few years ago, when I stumbled on a wallet in the street. There was no identification inside. Just three dollars and a crumpled letter that looked as if it had been carried around for years.

The only thing legible on the torn envelope was the return address. I opened the letter and saw that it had been written in 1924—almost 60 years ago. I read it carefully, hoping to find some clue to the identity of the wallet's owner.

It was a "Dear John" letter. The writer, in a delicate script, told the recipient, whose name was Michael, that her mother forbade her to see him again. Nevertheless, she would always love him. It was signed, Hannah.

It was a beautiful letter. But there was no way, beyond the name Michael, to identify the owner. So I called information to see if the operator could help.

"Operator, this is an unusual request. I'm trying to find the owner of a wallet I found. Is there any way you could tell me the phone number for an address that was on a letter in the wallet?"

The operator gave me her supervisor, who said there was a phone listed at the address but that she could not give me that number. However, she would call and explain the situation. Then, if the party wanted to talk, she would connect me. I waited a minute, and she came back on the line. "I have a woman who will speak with you."

I asked the woman if she knew a Hannah.

"Oh, of course! We bought this house from Hannah's family."

"Would you know where they could be located now?" I asked.

"Hannah had to place her mother in a nursing home years ago. Maybe the home could help you track down the daughter."

The woman gave me the name of the nursing home. I called and found out that Hannah's mother had died. The woman I spoke with gave me an address where she thought Hannah could be reached.

"Yes, Michael Goldstein was his name. If you find him, tell him I still think of him often. I never did marry."

I phoned. The woman who answered explained that Hannah herself was now living in a nursing home. She gave me the number. I called and was told, "Yes, Hannah is with us."

I asked if I could stop by to see her. It was almost 10:00 p.m. The director said that Hannah might be asleep. "But if you want to take a chance, maybe she's in the dayroom watching television."

The director and a guard greeted me at the door of the nursing home. We went up to the third floor and saw the nurse, who told us that Hannah was indeed watching TV.

We entered the dayroom. Hannah was a sweet, silver-haired old-timer with a warm smile and friendly eyes. I told her about the wallet and showed her the letter. The second she saw it, she took a deep breath. "Young man," she said, "this letter was the last contact I had with Michael." She looked away, then said pensively, "I loved him very much. But I was only 16, and my mother felt I was too young. He was so handsome. You know, like Sean Connery, the actor."

We both laughed. The director then left us alone. "Yes, Michael Goldstein was his name. If you find him, tell him I still think of him often. I never did marry," she said, smiling through tears that welled up in her eyes. "I guess no one ever matched up to Michael. . . ."

I thanked Hannah, said good-bye, and took the elevator to the first floor. As I stood at the door, the guard asked, "Was she able to help you?"

I told him she had given me a lead. "At least I have a last name. But I probably won't pursue it further for a while." I explained that I had spent almost the whole day trying to find the wallet's owner.

While we talked, I pulled out the brown-leather case with its red-lanyard lacing and showed it to the guard. He looked at it and said, "Hey, I'd know that anywhere. That's Mr. Goldstein's. He's always losing it. I found it in the hall at least three times."

"Who's Mr. Goldstein?" I asked.

"He's one of the old-timers on the eighth floor. That's Mike Goldstein's wallet, for sure. He goes out for a walk quite often."

I thanked the guard and ran back to the director's office to tell him what the guard had said. He accompanied me to the eighth floor. I prayed that Mr. Goldstein would be up.

"I think he's still in the dayroom," the nurse said. "He likes to read at night. . . . A darling man."

We went to the only room that had lights on, and there was a man reading a book. The director asked him if he had lost his wallet.

Michael Goldstein looked up, felt his back pocket, and then said, "Goodness, it is missing."

"This kind gentleman found a wallet. Could it be yours?"

The second he saw it, he smiled with relief. "Yes," he said, "that's it. Must have dropped it this afternoon. I want to give you a reward."

"Oh, no thank you," I said. "But I have to tell you something. I read the letter in the hope of finding out who owned the wallet."

The smile on his face disappeared. "You read that letter?"

"Not only did I read it, I think I know where Hannah is."

He grew pale. "Hannah? You know where she is? How is she? Is she still as pretty as she was?"

I hesitated.

"Please tell me!" Michael urged.

"She's fine, and just as pretty as when you knew her."

"Could you tell me where she is? I want to call her tomorrow." He grabbed my hand and said, "You know something? When that letter came, my life ended. I never married. I guess I've always loved her."

"Michael," I said. "Come with me."

The three of us took the elevator to the third floor. We walked toward the dayroom where Hannah was sitting, still watching TV. The director went over to her.

"Hannah," he said softly. "Do you know this man?" Michael and I stood waiting in the doorway.

She adjusted her glasses, looked for a moment, but didn't say a word.

"Hannah, it's Michael. Michael Goldstein. Do you remember?"

"Michael? Michael? It's you!"

He walked slowly to her side. She stood, and they embraced. The two of them sat on a couch, held hands and started to talk. The director and I walked out, both of us crying.

"See how the good Lord works," I said philosophically. "If it's meant to be, it will be."

Three weeks later, I got a call from the director, who asked, "Can you break away on Sunday to attend a wedding?"

He didn't wait for an answer. "Yup, Michael and Hannah are going to tie the knot!"

It was a lovely wedding, with all the people at the nursing home joining in the celebration. Hannah wore a beige dress and looked beautiful. Michael wore a dark-blue suit and stood tall. The home gave them their own room, and if you ever wanted to see a 76-year-old bride and a 78-year-old groom acting like two teenagers, you had to see this couple.

A perfect ending for a love affair that had lasted nearly 60 years.

Originally published in the September 1985 issue of *Reader's Digest* magazine.

A MEANINGLESS DIAGNOSIS

Most would not smile in my position. I sat across from the psychiatrist, holding my wife's hand as our two-year-old son played inattentively in the background. "The severity of your son's autism will likely prevent him from ever being independent. It is very possible that he will never speak or have friends. The comorbidity of mental retardation will compound these challenges." The psychiatrist paused and examined our expressions. My wife clenched my hand a little tighter, but she too smiled because we knew firsthand that the diagnosis was meaningless: at age three, a psychologist told my parents the same thing about me.

—Brian Mayer *Antelope, California*

I HATED MY PARENTS

I hated my parents. I hated them with all the bile that could be generated by a seven-year-old. I convinced my little brother to hate them too. To exact revenge, we would run away. We ate breakfast, made peanut butter sandwiches, and took cookies, summer sausage, and thermoses of juice. We went first to the creek and watched the minnows swim for our lunch crumbs. Then we went to the dairy farm, helped the farmer pen his calves, stall and milk his cows, feed his cows. . . . We sat in the shade under the dilapidated buckboard, examined our empty thermos, and decided that we were cruel. We went home expecting police cars and tears. Our parents were still in bed.

—Fran Samuelson *Liberty Hill, Texas*

In Over His Head

by Doug Colligan

Willie Stewart had no business kayaking the Colorado River. But he went for it anyway.

Willie Stewart loves to tell the story of his first day kayaking through the Grand Canyon. He carried his brand-new purple-and-blue plastic boat to the water, strapped on his helmet and life vest, slipped into the cockpit and shoved off. In a matter of minutes, he was getting bounced around in the roughest white water he had ever seen. But there was nothing the river threw at him he couldn't handle. A quick flick of a paddle blade here, an executed turn there, and he glided through the churning waters with ease.

Pleased with himself, he turned to his buddies—experienced river rats all—and said, "Great run."

They looked at him, totally baffled. "What are you talking about?" someone said. "We haven't gotten to the rapids yet."

"That was the biggest stuff I had ever seen," Stewart laughs. "I remember thinking: I'm dead."

He's the first to admit that his situation was crazy; there he was in a 40-pound boat, with only a few months of training—and one arm. Strapped to his left shoulder was a prosthetic limb that he'd had for just about a week. The plan was to paddle for 20 days over 227 miles of some of the roughest white water in the United States. What took place was one of the most remarkable adventures the Grand Canyon has ever seen.

It started with a casual phone call in the spring of 2005. A good friend, Mike Crenshaw, finally got a permit from the National Park Service to lead a private party of 16 boaters down the Colorado River that coming August. He had a slot open for Willie. Was he interested?

"It was the chance of a lifetime," Stewart says. He had been waiting years for this trip to happen. "How could I refuse?"

But before they shoved off, he had a couple of things to take care of. He had to get a white-water kayak, learn how to use it and get an arm.

For most of his life, the rugged 45-year-old has lived with only his right arm intact. He lost the left in a horrible accident when he was 18. Fresh out of high school, Stewart was working a summer construction job in Washington, D.C. The trailing end of a rope he was carrying got entangled in an industrial fan. Before he could react, the fan reeled in the rope taut and severed his arm just above the elbow.

He became a bitter young man, angry at the unfairness of what had happened, getting into brawls. When asked if one story told about him is true—that he got into a bar fight the day he got out of the hospital—Stewart looks off to the side. "A lot of fights, but it's nothing to be proud of."

In time, he learned to channel his rage into sports. He joined a rugby team, established a reputation as a fearless player and eventually was elected captain. He became a medal-winning Paralympic skier, a marathon runner and a triathlete, even an Ironman competitor (he's done seven of them). Stewart discovered that his intensity and tremendous stamina made him a natural for endurance competition. His days of rage long gone, he found peace and purpose in his life. As he explains, "Sports makes me whole."

The trip was still about four months off and Stewart figured he had time to master the needed skills for white-water kayaking. As for the arm, he had a friend who could hook him up. Michael Davidson runs the prosthetics lab at Loma Linda University Medical Center, where Stewart coordinates a sports program for the disabled called PossAbilities. Davidson's team built

Stewart a prototype prosthesis, basically a length of plastic pipe laminated with carbon fiber. After watching Stewart practice with it, they crafted a second, shorter carbon-fiber-and-resin limb with an extratight shoulder strap to hold it on in the punishing rapids of the Colorado.

Stewart spent hours practicing in the university pool and in a creek down the road from his house. Over and over, he flipped himself upside down so he could work on his Eskimo roll—a self-rescue technique in which he uses his paddle and a little hip action to flip himself upright. Finally, figuring he was as ready as he'd ever be, Stewart headed for the Grand Canyon.

Even with all his training, he was barely prepared for the adventure. At the first significant rapids, a middling run of white water called Badger Creek, Stewart was thrown out of his boat. He recalls how demoralized he felt as he swam to shore. Farther downriver at a place called House Rock, he was knocked over four times. He made it through mostly because he'd mastered one good move: the Eskimo roll.

At another set of rapids, Horn Creek, he got sucked into a violent implosion of water

"I was upside down, backward—basically, I was bounced down the river like a rubber ball."

that held him in a swirling maelstrom for several terrifying seconds. At the next, Hance, which was full of rocks, Stewart says, "I was upside down, backward—basically, I was bounced down the river like a rubber ball." He was figuratively, and literally, in over his head.

Stewart decided that to even pretend he knew what he was doing would be pure suicide. From then on, he followed more experienced paddlers through the thundering waters and relied on his Eskimo roll for emergencies. "I can't tell you how many times I was saying, 'Guys, I'm not really good at this.'" The rugged outdoorsmen who had watched Stewart battle his way through figured he was just being modest.

Up until now, even after his injury, Stewart had dominated just about every competition he entered. Here in the canyon, he realized, he might have met his match.

* * *

Dwarfed by the killer rapids of Lava Falls, one of the river's roughest stretches, Willie Stewart and his buddy Timmy O'Neill fight their way through tons of icy water.

The Colorado can be a brutal adversary. It flows at the rate of anywhere from 10,000 to 30,000 cubic feet—that's as much as 950 tons of water—every second. It has roughly 100 named, or significant, rapids and a dozen smaller ones, all more than capable of trashing Stewart and his little plastic boat. And then there is the cold. Water temperature seldom gets above the high 40s. Some stretches are so chilly, hikers and boaters are warned not to swim in them at all. The shock of immersion can cause muscle exhaustion and drowning, even a heart attack.

After about a week and a half, Stewart had made it 90 miles. "I couldn't believe I was still alive," he admits. "It was pure luck." His luck was about to change.

He had been dreading the huge rapids called Crystal. Rapids in the Grand Canyon are rated one to ten in degree of difficulty, ten being the meanest. Crystal was a ten, so terrifying some who survive it have ABC—Alive Below Crystal—parties. Stewart began his attack by dodging an enormous whirlpool. Paddling frantically, he slipped past a wall of waves powerful enough to flip a boat twice the size of his, and skirted what one guide called a "raft-ripping rock."

But he still wasn't finished. There was a second half to navigate, a treacherous, boulder-strewn run euphemistically called the Rock Garden. To Stewart's relief, he wove through it all without getting tipped over once.

Shortly afterward, the river took a sharp left turn where he had to negotiate a little set of white water, coincidentally called Willies Necktie. The danger here is the way the current drives boats into the crook of the turn on the right side. The way to avoid it is to stay on the left. Stewart knew that, but he dropped his guard, making a deadly mistake. He drifted right.

Before he could make the correction, his boat slammed into a boulder and flipped. Tons of rushing water pinned him against the canyon wall. He tried to do his Eskimo roll, but his right arm—the one he always used to pull himself up—was jammed against the rock. Somehow he had to get himself vertical using his prosthesis.

Stewart fought hard, pushing up again and again, each time getting a few gasps of air before being submerged. Exhausted, freezing, running out of room to breathe, he thought he had one more try left in him. Gathering his last bit of energy, he lunged for the surface. This time, his paddle blade caught just right, and he pulled himself upright.

After a little less than a minute, the current spun him around and slammed him into a rock. Before he'd even caught his breath, Stewart was underwater again.

Luckily, this time someone saw him go down. Timmy O'Neill was an experienced kayaker on his fifth Canyon run. He quickly paddled across the river to help, arriving just in time to see Stewart's kayak pop to the surface. Several long seconds later, Stewart bobbed up. As he reached for O'Neill's kayak, they were both sucked into a hole of churning water—"getting Maytagged," kayakers call it.

Finally, the river spit them out, and Stewart discovered he had a new problem. His paddle, strapped to his prosthesis, was acting like an anchor, dragging him toward the next set of rapids. He had to decide: Keep the arm and drown, or cut it loose.

Frantic, he clawed at the tight straps, finally getting them free. Then he felt the current drag everything away. "My arm," he gasped. It was gone.

"I was devastated," Stewart recalls. Here he was at the 100-mile mark, less than halfway, and for all practical purposes the trip was over. How much more can you take before your luck runs out? he'd wondered. Now he had his answer.

Eerily, just the day before, his wife Lynnsey had asked him to quit. An athlete and Ironman competitor herself, she had joined the group for the first half of the trip, riding on one of the support rafts. She had to return to her job as a physician at Loma Linda, and as she turned to say good-bye to her husband, she urged, "Don't go back. You're going to die down there."

Stewart was jolted by her plea. "She's seen me do a lot of dumb things," he says, "so maybe she was right." Then he remembered the other arm. As an afterthought, he had tucked the prototype into a bag, thinking it might come in handy for parts.

For the next couple of days, Stewart worked on it, rigging a makeshift shoulder harness from duct tape and spare straps. He spent a day on the river, fussing and adjusting and tinkering, fully aware that he had to get it right. Finally, he decided to try it out at the next big stretch of rapids.

He remembers the moment well, as he headed toward the roaring water: "I felt like I was paddling to my suicide."

To Stewart's relief, the arm held. And so, every morning for the next 127 miles, he would strap it on and set out to battle the Colorado, with

In Over His Head

Timmy O'Neill guiding him through the killer rapids. The trip became an ongoing workshop in adaptation. Stewart learned that to get a tighter fit, he could slip the prosthesis over a waterproof shirt called a "dry top." When one of the straps pulled free, he drilled holes through it with a Swiss Army knife and used string and duct tape to reattach it.

The arm, like its owner, took a beating but never quit. When Michael Davidson heard that the prototype worked beyond expectations, he refused to take credit. "It's a tribute to the guy who wore it," he says. "Willie probably could have made it with a broom handle."

On the very last day of the trip, Stewart paddled off by himself, not truly believing he had made it. He'd been beaten up, suffocated in water cold enough to kill, come close to drowning at least twice, was terrified almost every day, and lost an arm.

"Right up to the very last 20 seconds, it was stressful," he admits. "And, boy, was it fun."

Originally published in the April 2007 issue of *Reader's Digest* magazine.

Willie Stewart lives in Boise, Idaho, and still competes in triathlons. He was named to the Disabled Snow Sports Hall of Fame in 2018.

Splish Splash

Even tigers need to beat the heat. Fortunately, eight-year-old Akasha has a backyard pool—her yard being located at Six Flags Discovery Kingdom in Vallejo, California. Tigers are actually the rare large felines that like to swim (those scaredy-cat lions generally avoid the water). In this 2012 photograph, when her trainer supplies a fleshy incentive, Akasha dives with her ears tucked, teeth bared, and wide-open eyes on the prize. *Photograph by Justin Sullivan/ Getty Images*

Humor Hall of Fame

Cartoon by Jim Benton

When a man placed a package of cookies on my supermarket checkout counter, one end opened and the cookies tumbled out. "That was the last package!" he said. "It's all right. We can give you a store credit," I assured him. "No, I'll take these," he said, picking up the stray treats. "I promised my donkey cookies, and I can't go home without them."

—JOHN FLYNN
MARSHALL, NORTH CAROLINA

My collection of vintage kitchen utensils includes one whose intended purpose was always a mystery. It looks like a cross between a metal slotted spoon and a spatula, so I use it as both. When not in use, it is prominently displayed in a decorative ceramic utensil caddy in my kitchen. The mystery of the spoon/spatula was recently solved when I found one in its original packaging at a rummage sale. It's a pooper-scooper.

—PATTY BROZO GREEN VALLEY, ARIZONA

Not a Moment to Spare

by Kevin Harter

Eleven children face death by fire . . . and their rescuers have run out of options.

When he heard the school bus coming down South Curtis Road around 11 a.m., 49-year-old Wayne Barrett headed out the door. By staggering their work schedules, he or his wife always managed to be home for their five-year-old son, Spencer. Now, on the cold morning of March 6, 1996, the yellow bus loaded with kindergartners from the rural Winn Elementary School near Mt. Pleasant, Michigan, pulled into their driveway. With a wave to his friends, Spencer jumped into his father's arms.

"I'll just get the mail," Barrett said, shooing his son into the house. He walked down the driveway, then crossed the road to his mailbox. Several yards away from the road stood a 50-foot-tall utility pole, and hidden in the knee-deep snow-bank at its base was a metal guy wire that steadied the old wooden structure.

The bus started backing out of the driveway. Then it stopped, as 65-year-old substitute driver Richard Childs scanned the roster to see which child would be dropped off next. "Is Kory Kenny aboard?" he asked.

"Yes," chimed in several youngsters, referring to the freckled-nosed boy in the first seat across from Childs. Seated a few rows behind Childs was Megan Martinez. Two seats over from Megan sat Dennis James Sexton, known to all as D.J., whose twin sister, Nikki, was across the aisle. There were 11 kids in all.

As the bus slowly resumed moving, the sound of shattering wood ripped the air. Barrett looked up to see the bus's bumper pushing at the guy wire. The wooden pole snapped. One of the power lines hung harmlessly off to the side. The other snaked over the bus's emergency hatch on the roof. It carried 46,000 volts.

Inside the bus, however, the noise of the ripping wood was muffled by the chatter of children, static on the bus radio and the blowing heater. Childs moved his foot to accelerate.

"Stop!" Barrett shouted, frantically waving his hands to alert Childs. "There's a live wire. Don't get off the bus! I'll call 911."

Childs reached for his two-way radio to alert school officials. Then, to reassure the children, he said, "We've just got to stop for a moment. Don't worry. I won't let anything happen to you."

Barrett sprinted toward his house, remembering what he'd learned years before as a fireman. The kids should be fine as long as they stayed put and didn't touch the bus and the ground at the same time, or anyone who was touching the ground. But any child stepping off the bus risked electrocution.

Barrett raced inside and called 911. He spat out his address, saying, "The school bus just snagged a power line. Call the power company and get somebody out here."

Barrett told his son to stay inside, then ran out again. The rear tires, he saw, were smoking. Sparks were jumping off the roof—the result of electricity being conducted across the rear axle.

Inside the bus the frightened faces of the children were pressed against the windows. Next to Megan, her best friend, Austin Fisher, began to sob.

Barrett quickly explained the situation to Childs. Nobody could safely touch the vehicle and ground at the same time, he said.

But as they talked, Childs noticed smoke building in the air vents and seeping through the floorboards. The bus's wiring and insulation were smoldering. Meanwhile, the current began menacing the bus with a loud buzzing.

Childs had an idea. Hoping to slip the bus out from under the line, he eased his foot onto the gas pedal to move the bus forward. But he heard a metallic screech and felt a growing tension on the bus, like a giant rubber band pulled so taut it might snap. The power line had hooked firmly on to the emergency hatch.

Childs stopped, realizing that he risked pulling down the electrical line, which might bring down more poles and further ensnarl the bus. Better to stay put, he thought.

Now Barrett noticed flames leaping from the bus's rear tires. Once more he sprinted for his phone and dialed 911. Firefighters were on the way, he was told. But in the rural area it was unclear how long it would take for the power company, Consumers Energy, to cut the line.

Barrett rushed outside, remaining about six feet away from the bus. He knew Childs couldn't have seen the guy wire with the snow piled up. All those years, he thought. It was an accident waiting to happen.

*　　*　　*

The children saw smoke rising in the back of the bus, and some noticed that the seat frames were getting hot. Megan squeezed her stuffed toy bird, Flint. Then seeing tears streaming down Austin's cheeks, she reached for her hand.

"I'm scared," Austin stammered.

"We'll be okay," Megan said, repeating what Childs had told them. "Spencer's dad will help us too." Then the girls began coughing.

For about ten minutes now, electricity had coursed through the bus. Flames started to swirl from the rear tires.

Childs thought about the location of the bus's fuel tanks—fortunately up front. Diesel has a high ignition point, so he knew an explosion wasn't imminent. In the meantime, however, the smoke was building up inside and the kids were coughing more. It was time to act.

Childs opened the bus door. "We've got to get the kids off," he called to Barrett.

"Yes," Barrett yelled back. "Right now." Their eyes locked. The men feared that death by smoke inhalation or fire could be just minutes away. They had only one option—but it involved a deadly gamble. Childs would throw each youngster through the narrow bus door toward Barrett.

"Get up," Childs told the school kids. "Leave everything. Line up single file behind me." He instructed them on the importance of not touching anything. They had to go out face first with their arms tucked in, not brushing the door on the way out. If a child fell to the ground, then reached back to grab the door or another child on the bus, he could be electrocuted.

Childs wanted to catapult each youngster at least five feet from the front door, a difficult task from inside the tight entrance of the bus. "You'll all be safe," Childs promised. Barrett would quickly collect each child.

Kory, standing nearest Childs, would go first. The six-foot, 187-pound bus driver hooked the 45-pound boy under the arms. Almost as if coaching himself on what to do, he said to himself, "Grab them under the arms and give it all you've got."

Childs tossed Kory out the door with a great heave. The boy hit the snow about five feet out and continued to roll. Barrett yanked Kory to his feet and pushed him toward the porch. "Run to the house," he said.

Next in line was Austin, her blue eyes filled with fright. Childs slung her out the door. Megan watched as her friend landed in the snow and was picked up by Barrett. She tried to stuff her toy bird, Flint, into her backpack. But the zipper had broken, and Flint kept falling out.

Reaching firmly for Megan, Childs got a good grip and sent her sailing out of the bus. But Flint dropped to the floor near the door. As Barrett grabbed for Megan, she took a step toward the vehicle to retrieve her toy.

"No!" Childs yelled as Barrett seized Megan. "I'll get your bird later," Barrett promised. "Now run for the porch."

As Childs turned for the next child, Nikki Sexton tried to move past him toward the steps, attempting to grab her friend's stuffed bird. "No!" the kids yelled.

Childs grabbed Nikki, and out the door she went. Three more girls flew out on the heels of each other. Four children remained.

Sirens now pierced the air. From the north a blue Michigan State Police cruiser roared down the road, while from the south a motorcade of firefighters arrived on the scene. They could see flames and thick black smoke, while the electricity from the hot wire caused a crackle of bright blue-white sparks.

On the bus, D.J., next in line, was beginning to rock like a sprinter preparing to race. Suddenly he bolted toward the door. "I can do it myself," he said. "I can jump."

Childs admired the young boy's courage. "You can jump another time," he said as he grasped the child under the shoulders. Out the door went number eight.

Childs tossed out two more girls. Finally there was Kory's cousin, ponytailed Kayla Kenny. Childs picked her up and heaved her into the snowbank. It appeared that the last child was safe.

Still worried that he might have missed someone, Childs searched the bus, calling out for children. Choking on the thick, rubbery-smelling smoke, he patted the seats and felt around on the hot floor. He found only books, toys and snow pants.

Returning to the front door, he planted his work boots and pushed hard off the top step, landing breathless in the snowbank next to Barrett. Within several minutes utility workers shut off the power. The fires were extinguished before anyone was hurt.

Three weeks later, in front of the kindergartners at Winn Elementary, Consumers Energy presented Richard Childs and Wayne Barrett with an award for saving the children's lives. Tribute of a different sort for Barrett came some months after the mishap. He was sitting in a booth at a local restaurant and heard a small voice call out. "That's one of the men who saved me," said Megan Martinez, pointing out Barrett to her parents. Smiling, she added, "He's my hero."

Originally published in the October 1998 issue of *Reader's Digest* magazine.

13 THINGS I'LL TELL MY DAUGHTER (SOMEDAY)

1. It's OK to date frogs; they'll help you recognize your prince. 2. Confidence is the best accessory. 3. Even if you have unlimited texts, call. 4. Heartbreak doesn't last forever, but it sure can feel like it. 5. Your life will not end because we don't buy a car when you turn 16. 6. Work like a dog in your 20s. 7. Know one good dirty joke and one good clean one and the right times to tell each. 8. Read more than you watch TV. 9. If you're ever in A LOT of trouble, ask me to tell you the Aunt Sarah story. This will only work once. 10. Making mistakes is easy. Admitting them is difficult. 11. Vulnerable doesn't equal weak. 12. Go to college, even if it's just for the life experience (but we're only paying for the first four years). 13. I love you unconditionally.

—Aimee Harris *Atlanta, Georgia*

TWO SHOES

I was having the time of my life with the incredible fifth-grade class I had this year. They were full of compassion and creativity. One day a student raised her hand and asked if I had realized I was wearing two different shoes. Laughter filled the room and I blushed with embarrassment. The next gesture is the part I will never forget. The students proceeded to trade shoes with each other to match my crazy situation.

—Teresa Kiefer *Genoa City, Wisconsin*

Stowaway!

by Armando Socarras Ramirez, as told to
Denis Fodor and John Reddy

*Two teens risk their lives in a daring
attempt to escape Cuba and find
freedom in America.*

T he jet engines of the Iberia Airlines DC-8 thundered in earsplitting crescendo as the big plane taxied toward where we huddled in the tall grass just off the end of the runway at Havana's José Martí Airport. For months, my friend Jorge Pérez Blanco and I had been planning to stow away in a wheel well on this flight, No. 904, Iberia's once-weekly, nonstop run from Havana to Madrid. Now, in the late afternoon of last June 3, our moment had come.

We realized that we were pretty young to be taking such a big gamble; I was 17, Jorge 16. But we were both determined to escape from Cuba, and our plans had been carefully made. We knew that departing airliners taxied to the end of the 11,500-foot runway, stopped momentarily after turning around, then roared at full throttle down the runway to take off. We wore rubber-soled shoes to aid us in crawling up the wheels and carried ropes to secure ourselves inside the wheel well. We had also stuffed cotton in our ears as protection against the shriek of the four jet engines. Now we lay sweating with fear as the massive craft swung into its about-face, the jet blast flattening the grass all around us. "Let's run!" I shouted to Jorge.

We dashed onto the runway and sprinted toward the left-hand wheels of the momentarily stationary plane. As Jorge began to scramble up the 42-inch-high tires, I saw there was not room for us both in the single well. "I'll try the other side!" I shouted. Quickly I climbed onto the right wheels, grabbed a strut and, twisting and wriggling, pulled myself into the semi-dark well. The plane began rolling immediately, and I grabbed some machinery to keep from falling out. The roar of the engines nearly deafened me.

As we became airborne, the huge double wheels, scorching hot from takeoff, began folding into the compartment. I tried to flatten myself against the overhead as they came closer and closer; then, in desperation, I pushed at them with my feet. But they pressed powerfully upward, squeezing me terrifyingly against the roof of the well. Just when I felt that I would be crushed, the wheels locked in place and the bay doors beneath them closed, plunging me into darkness. So there I was, my five-foot-four-inch, 140-pound frame literally wedged in amid a spaghetti-like maze of conduits and machinery. I could not move enough to tie myself to anything, so I stuck my rope behind a pipe.

Then, before I had time to catch my breath, the bay doors suddenly dropped open again and the wheels stretched out into their landing position. I held on for dear life, swinging over the abyss, wondering if I had been spotted, if even now the plane was turning back to hand me over to Castro's police.

By the time the wheels began retracting again, I had seen a bit of extra space among all the machinery where I could safely squeeze. Now I knew there *was* room for me, even though I could scarcely breathe. After a few minutes, I touched one of the tires and found that it had cooled off. I swallowed some aspirin tablets against the head-splitting noise and began to wish that I had worn something warmer than my light sport shirt and green fatigues.

Up in the cockpit of Flight 904, Capt. Valentín Vara del Rey, 44, had settled into the routine of the overnight flight, which would last 8 hours and 20 minutes. Takeoff had been normal, with the aircraft and its 147 passengers, plus a crew of ten lifting off at 170 m.p.h. But, right after lift-off, something unusual had happened. One of three red lights on the instrument panel had remained lighted, indicating improper retraction of the landing gear.

"Are you having difficulty?" the control tower asked.

"Yes," replied Vara del Rey. "There is an indication that the right wheel hasn't closed properly. I'll repeat the procedure."

The captain re-lowered the landing gear, then raised it again. This time the red light blinked out.

Dismissing the incident as a minor malfunction, the captain turned his attention to climbing to assigned cruising altitude. On leveling out, he observed that the temperature outside was 41 degrees F. Inside, the pretty stewardess began serving dinner to the passengers.

Shivering uncontrollably from the bitter cold, I wondered if Jorge had made it into the other wheel well, and began thinking about what had brought me to this desperate situation. I thought about my parents and my girl, María Esther, and wondered what they would think when they learned what I had done.

My father is a plumber, and I have four brothers and a sister. We are poor, like most Cubans. Our house in Havana has just one large room; 11 people live in it—or did. Food was scarce and strictly rationed. About the only fun I had was playing baseball and walking with María Esther along the seawall. When I turned 16, the government shipped me off to vocational school in Betancourt, a sugarcane village in Matanzas Province. There I was supposed to learn welding, but classes were often interrupted to send us off to plant cane.

Young as I was, I was tired of living in a state that controlled *everyone's* life. I dreamed of freedom. I wanted to become an artist and live in the United States, where I had an uncle. I knew that thousands of Cubans had got to America and done well there. As the time approached when I would be drafted, I thought more and more of trying to get away. But how? I knew that two planeloads of people are allowed to leave Havana for Miami each day, but there is a waiting list of 800,000 for these flights. Also, if you sign up to leave, the government looks on you as a *gusano*— a worm—and life becomes even less bearable.

My hopes seemed futile. Then I met Jorge at a Havana baseball game. After the game we got to talking. I found out that Jorge, like myself, was disillusioned with Cuba. "The system takes away your freedom—forever," he complained.

Jorge told me about the weekly flight to Madrid. Twice we went to the airport to reconnoiter. Once a DC-8 took off and flew directly over us; the wheels were still down, and we could see into the well compartments. "There's enough room in there for me," I remember saying.

These were my thoughts as I lay in the freezing darkness more than five miles above the Atlantic Ocean. By now we had been in the air about an hour, and I was getting lightheaded from the lack of oxygen. Was it really only a few hours earlier, that I had bicycled through the rain with Jorge and hidden in the grass? Was Jorge safe? My parents? María Esther? I drifted into unconsciousness.

> *The sun rose over the Atlantic like a great golden globe, its rays glinting off the silver-and-red fuselage of Iberia's DC-8 as it crossed the European coast high over Portugal. With the end of the 5,563-mile flight in sight, Captain Vara del Rey began his descent toward Madrid's Barajas Airport. Arrival would be at 8 a.m. local time, the captain told his passengers over the intercom, and the weather in Madrid was sunny and pleasant.*
>
> *Shortly after passing over Toledo, Vara del Rey let down his landing gear. As always, the maneuver was accompanied by a buffeting as the wheels hit the slipstream and a 200 m.p.h. turbulence swirled through the wheel wells. Now the plane went into its final approach; now, a spurt of flame and smoke from the tires as the DC-8 touched down at about 140 m.p.h.*
>
> *It was a perfect landing—no bumps. After a brief post-flight check, Vara del Rey walked down the ramp steps and*

stood by the nose of the plane waiting for a car to pick him up, along with his crew.

Nearby, there was a sudden, soft plop as the frozen body of Armando Socarras fell to the concrete apron beneath the plane. José Rocha Lorenzana, a security guard, was the first to reach the crumpled figure. "When I touched his clothes, they were frozen as stiff as wood," Rocha said. "All he did was make a strange sound, a kind of moan."

"I couldn't believe it at first," Vara del Rey said when told of Armando. "But then I went over to see him. He had ice over his nose and mouth. And his color . . ." As he watched the unconscious boy being bundled into a truck, the captain kept exclaiming to himself, "Impossible! Impossible!"

The first thing I remember after losing consciousness was hitting the ground at the Madrid airport. Then I blacked out again and woke up later at the Gran Hospital de la Beneficencia in downtown Madrid, more dead than alive. When they took my temperature, it was so low that it did not even register on the thermometer. "Am I in Spain?" was my first question. And then, "Where's Jorge?" (Jorge is believed to have been knocked down by the jet blast while trying to climb into the other wheel well, and to be in prison in Cuba.)

Doctors said later that my condition was comparable to that of a patient undergoing "deep freeze" surgery—a delicate process performed only under carefully controlled conditions. Dr. José María Pajares, who cared for me, called my survival a "medical miracle," and, in truth, I feel lucky to be alive.

A few days after my escape, I was up and around the hospital, playing cards with my police guard and reading stacks of letters from all over the world. I especially liked one from a girl in California.

"You are a hero," she wrote, "but not very wise." My uncle, Elo Fernández, who lives in New Jersey, telephoned and invited me to come to the United States to live with him. The International Rescue Committee arranged my passage and has continued to help me.

I am fine now. I live with my uncle and go to school to learn English. I still hope to study to be an artist. I want to be a good citizen and contribute something to this country, for I love it here. You can smell freedom in the air.

I often think of my friend Jorge. We both knew the risk we were taking, and that we might be killed in our attempt to escape Cuba. But it seemed worth the chance. Even knowing the risks, I would try to escape again if I had to.

Originally published in the January 1970 issue of *Reader's Digest* magazine.

Armando Socarras Ramirez is now 68 years old and lives in Virginia with his wife. He retired from the transportation industry. Ramirez and his wife have four children and 11 grandchildren. He will appear on the upcoming program "Greatest Escapes of All Time" on the History Channel.

Humor Hall of Fame

Cartoon by Mike Baldwin

"You might be overthinking it.
Sometimes a belly rub is just a belly rub."

IT'S A GOOD THING SNAKES AND DOGS DON'T
INTERBREED. NOBODY WANTS A LOYAL SNAKE.
—ROY BLOUNT JR., HUMORIST

My granddaughter loves
my puppy so much, she asked,
"When you die, can I have Romeo?"
"Of course," I said.
She was thrilled. "Oh, I can't wait!"
—**BARBARA CORREY** WOODBURY, TENNESSEE

Dogs have no money.
Isn't that amazing?
They're broke their entire lives. But they get by.
You know why dogs have
no money? No pockets.
—**JERRY SEINFELD,** COMEDIAN

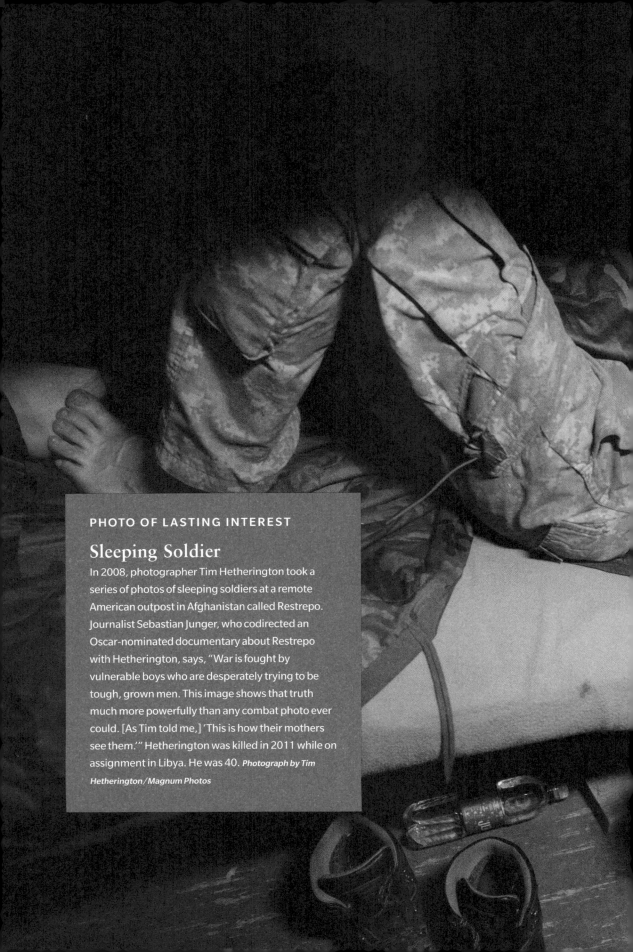

PHOTO OF LASTING INTEREST

Sleeping Soldier

In 2008, photographer Tim Hetherington took a series of photos of sleeping soldiers at a remote American outpost in Afghanistan called Restrepo. Journalist Sebastian Junger, who codirected an Oscar-nominated documentary about Restrepo with Hetherington, says, "War is fought by vulnerable boys who are desperately trying to be tough, grown men. This image shows that truth much more powerfully than any combat photo ever could. [As Tim told me,] 'This is how their mothers see them.'" Hetherington was killed in 2011 while on assignment in Libya. He was 40. *Photograph by Tim Hetherington/Magnum Photos*

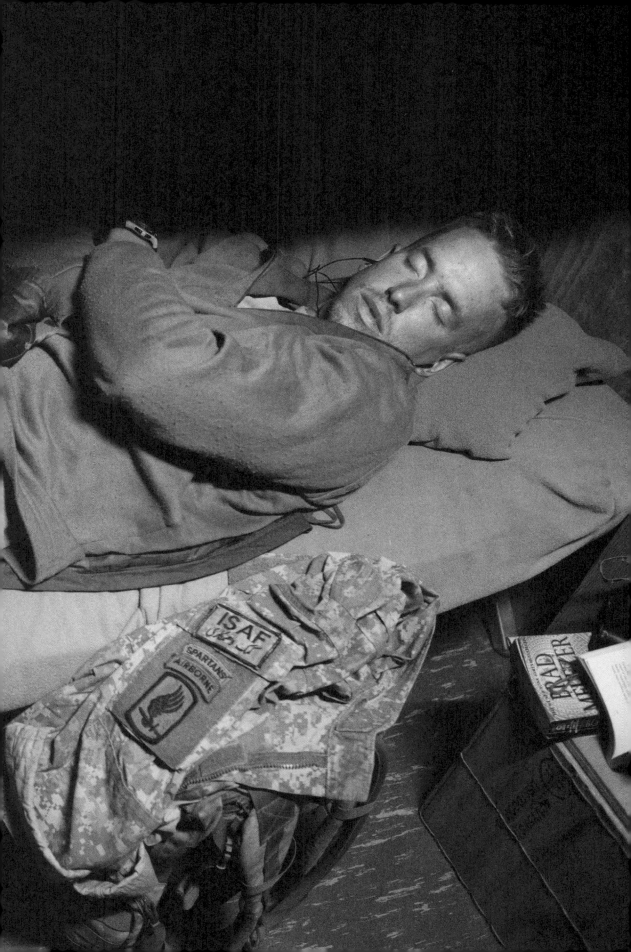

PICTURE PERFECT MOMENT

On a cool October afternoon I dropped my seventeen-year-old, Mayree, off for volleyball practice. She jogged off toward the field, then suddenly turned back, ran to the car, and leaned in through the driver's side window. "See y'all in a few," she said waving goodbye to her baby brother and sister. Standing outside the window, her ponytail swaying slowly in the breeze, bathed in the glow of the setting sun behind her, she looked like an angel encircled by a golden halo; like a Fra Angelico painting. I don't recall if I told her how much I loved her, or how proud I was of the amazing young woman she had become, before driving away that day. I never saw her alive again. But I thank God every day for leaving me with that beautiful final image of her.

—Vickey Malone Kennedy *Norman, Oklahoma*

HAPPY RETURNS

A long flight of weathered steps led to a hollow wooden door with rusty numbers beckoning us into Room 1108. Inside we barely noticed the faded wood paneling, lumpy queen-sized bed, and thin, tacky carpet. We could see the expanse of seashore from our perch and easily wander down the access path to feel the sand between our toes. We returned again and again until the burgeoning resort tore down our orange-shingled eyesore. Forty years later, my husband periodically sends me a short e-mail that declares the time: 11:08. "I love you, too," I write back.

—Laurie Olson *Dayton, Nevada*

To Do or Not to Do

by Mary Roach

She keeps lists, he doesn't. Can this marriage be saved?

There are three kinds of people in this world: 1) People who make lists, 2) People who don't make lists, and 3) People who carve tiny Nativity scenes out of pecan hulls. I'm sorry, there isn't really a third category; it's just that a workable list needs a minimum of three items, I feel. I am, as you might have guessed, a person who makes lists: daily To Do lists, long-term To Do lists, shopping lists, packing lists. I am married to a man whose idea of a list is a corner torn off a newspaper page, covered with words too hastily written to later decipher, and soon misplaced or dropped on the floor. Every now and then I'll discover one of Ed's lists in some forgotten corner of the house: *Rescrangen polfiter*, it will say. Pick up *grellion. Bregoo!* underlined twice.

It isn't entirely accurate to say that Ed has no formal To Do list. He does. It's just that it isn't Ed that makes it, it's me. It's easy enough, as the same ten or 12 items, mostly involving home-repair projects abandoned midterm, have been on it for years. I once wrote it out for him and put it on the side of the fridge. When I glanced at it some months later, nothing had been crossed off, though he'd added a few of his own: *Make violin. Cure diabetes. Split atom.*

* * *

I make lists to keep my anxiety level down. If I write down 15 things to be done, I lose that vague, nagging sense that there are an overwhelming number of things to be done, all of which are on the brink of being forgotten. Ed, on the other hand, controls his anxiety precisely by forgetting them. If they're not on some numbered piece of paper, they don't exist. So there's no reason why he shouldn't come home and turn on the game. People like me really gum up the works for people like Ed by calling them to see if they've gotten around to any of the things on the To Do list we're secretly keeping for them.

Here's the sick thing: I don't really care whether Ed has done the things on this list. I just want to be able to cross them off. My friend Jeff best summed up the joy of crossing off: "No matter how unproductive my week has been, I have a sense of accomplishment." Jeff actually tried to convince me that the adjective *listless* derived from the literal definition "having no lists."

> *I don't really care whether Ed has done the things on this list.*

It is possible, I'll admit, to go overboard. I have a list of party guests in my desk drawer. Every so often I take it out, add people we've met, cross off couples that have moved away, and then put it back in my drawer. We're never actually going to have this party; we're just going to keep updating the list—which, for people like me, is a party all by itself.

My husband is the first person I ever met who doesn't even make a shopping list. Ed prefers to go up and down the aisles, figuring he'll see the things we need. The problem is that he has no idea whether we actually need them that week, and so it is that we have six cans of water chestnuts and enough Tabasco sauce to sober up the population of Patoka, Indiana, on any given New Year's Day. It seems to be a male pride thing. "Men don't want to admit that they can't remember everything," says my friend Ron. Ron finds shopping lists limiting. "Take M&M's," he says. "Those are never going to be on the list."

Ed agrees. He says the things on lists are always chores and downers. Ed wants a To Do list that says, 1) Giants game, 2) Nap, 3) Try new cheese-steak place. Meanwhile, the polfiter sits unscrangened.

Originally published in the June 2002 issue of *Reader's Digest* magazine.

Class Action

by Lynn Rosellini

Six heroes are made as they
throw everything they've got into
protecting their teacher.

Debbie Shultz is the kind of teacher students love. At Heritage
High School in Conyers, Georgia, Mrs. Shultz makes studying Spanish
fun. To help students learn vocabulary, she cajoles them with clever
rhymes and sayings—"memory jogs," she calls them. To brighten the
trailer that houses her classroom, she spray-painted the walls vivid blue,
fuchsia and yellow, and edged the ceiling with tiny white Christmas
lights. After class, she always has time to listen when the teens bend her
ear about problems with girlfriends or boyfriends or Mom and Dad.

If the popular Spanish teacher ever had problems of her own—
an emotionally troubled husband, an impending divorce—her sunny
demeanor hid them well.

At 9:25 one morning last December, Shultz, 46, looked up from her
desk and froze. The class had just completed its Spanish II final exam,
and she was about to take the papers to the office. Then she noticed her
estranged husband, Ted, 51, a stocky man with brown curly hair and
wire-rimmed glasses, standing in the doorway.

"What are you doing here?" she asked. Shultz had taken out a
restraining order against Ted the previous week, telling police he had

Debbie Shultz and her salvadores.

been stalking her. Since their separation, Ted had attempted suicide. He'd also tried to buy a shotgun at a nearby Wal-Mart.

Now her husband of seven years removed a 12-inch butcher knife that had been hidden under his jean jacket. As students looked up, uncomprehending, Ted lunged for his wife, the knife pointed at her chest.

"Go get help!" she screamed. "Dial 911!" She grabbed her husband's right arm and pushed his knife hand toward the floor. But it was too late. The blade slashed deep into her thigh, laying open her jeans, cutting through muscle and severing a vein. But Shultz kept struggling. The next swipe of the knife landed a gash nearly three inches long across her thumb.

Austin Hutchinson, 16, jumped to his feet. Around him, students were screaming and running from the classroom. Hutchinson, a bear of a boy at six feet, 215 pounds, hesitated. *Should I run? No—I can't just leave her!* Scott Wigington, 17, a starting lineman for the Heritage High Patriots, was on his feet too. Son of the county sheriff, Wigington thought: *I'm gonna save her!*

Debbie Shultz was losing her grip on her husband's hand. Ted would have the weapon free any minute.

In a blur of motion, Wigington grabbed Ted's right arm. Hutchinson took his left side.

Then Nimesh Patel, 17, a slender, bookish boy who prefers science to sports, leapt on Ted's back, grabbing desperately at the man's collar. Together the three boys pulled him off their teacher, flung him against the wall and wrestled him to the floor. Three more boys piled on.

But Ted, a muscular five feet, ten inches and 190 pounds, was not about to give up. Gripping the knife, he struggled to get free. With a sudden burst of strength, Wigington bent Ted's arm back, and then pried his fingers from the knife. He flung it toward the door, where another student, Matt Battaglia, scooped it up.

"Mrs. Shultz, get out!" Wigington yelled. But the teacher, bleeding profusely, refused to leave her students. "Not until help gets here," she gasped.

Within moments, Capt. Ray Girardin, the school ROTC instructor, barged through the door and jumped on the pile, followed by the school security officer. The police soon arrived and arrested Ted Shultz, charging him with aggravated assault and stalking.

"An hour later, it hit me what actually happened," said Patel. Like the other boys, he said instinct and adrenaline took over in the classroom fight, and he felt no fear. "But afterward, I was shaking."

The next day, with her leg and thumb stitched, Debbie Shultz stopped at school. Although she had to lean heavily on a friend to walk, she hugged and thanked every one of her students. "I wanted them to see me in the flesh, smiling," she said.

Her husband, Shultz explained, had recently checked into a psychiatric hospital in nearby Atlanta. Unknown to her, after a week in its alcohol detox program, he had walked out. She said that if Ted arrived 40 minutes later—when her class ended—she would have been alone in the classroom. "I'd probably be dead now," she said.

After the incident, the six boys—Hutchinson, Wigington, Patel and Battaglia, as well as John Bailey, Jr., 16, and Andy Anderson, 17—were honored by the governor and the Georgia house of representatives.

As for their teacher, Debbie Shultz, she's back in the classroom, once again using her favorite "memory jogs" to drill vocabulary words. The Spanish verb for "to help" is *ayudar*. "Help, help, are you there (a-yu-dar)?" she recites rhetorically to her students. On a chilly morning last December, their answer was: Absolutely.

Originally published in the April 2004 issue of *Reader's Digest* magazine.

Ted Shultz served six-and-a-half years in prison for aggravated assault, cruelty to children and possession of a weapon at school. He was released in 2010 and now lives in Georgia.

Friends for Life

by Ellen Sherman

Two men choose to embrace how alike they are instead of focusing on their differences.

T he 77-year-old image is faded but familiar: 42 third-graders from Cincinnati's North Avondale Elementary School. A small child in the third row stands out; John Leahr is the only black boy in the class.

"Almost everything was segregated then," recalls Herb Heilbrun, an 84-year-old real estate broker, "so we didn't play together. I wasn't a racist, but I didn't have black friends. I just thought that's the way the world was supposed to be."

Little did Herb imagine that he and John would be inextricably linked for the next three-quarters of a century—that one of them would be instrumental in saving the other, and that a lesson in friendship would be taught.

*　　*　　*

More than a decade after the class picture was snapped, World War II broke out. The two men went their separate ways, never really knowing each other. Herb became a bomber pilot assigned to B-17 Flying Fortresses, and John, also wanting to do his part for his country, joined the Tuskegee Experiment.

"I'd always had dreams of flying, but there was no place for black pilots," John remembers. In response to a lawsuit brought by a student

Herb Heilbrun (above right) and John Leahr became friends 69 years after standing close together in their 1928 third-grade class photo.

petitioning to fly, a program to train black pilots was started. "The military thought they'd show we couldn't do it, and close it." But the Tuskegee Airmen surprised everyone, flying cover for hundreds of missions. Still, it wouldn't be until 1995, when HBO produced a film about the unit, that the world would hear of the brave exploits of these pilots.

The thrill of flying outweighed the disappointment John felt over the treatment he and his fellow airmen received. "On our first day of training at Moton Field in Tuskegee," he remembers, "our officer said, 'You boys came down here to fly airplanes, not to change social policy. If anybody gives you a hard time off base, you're on your own. The Army isn't going to protect you; your life is in your hands.'" White men in training to serve their country wouldn't be greeted so callously, John thought. "It was like he was saying, 'This is the South, and you're still black men. Your lives don't matter to anyone.'"

*   *   *

During the war, Herb flew 35 combat missions over Europe. "Once, in December 1944, I was flying over Czechoslovakia," he recalls. "Eight hundred and fifty flak guns were aimed at us, and I was hit 89 times. But I made it home because I had great cover from our planes."

Those planes were piloted by black airmen. "Though the bases were segregated, we'd meet in the sky," John says. In more than 200 escort missions, only about five bombers were lost to enemy fighters.

*　　*　　*

After the war, Herb returned to Cincinnati, married and started a family. He rarely thought about his time in battle. But one cold day in 1997, he read in the newspaper that his town was honoring the Tuskegee Airmen. "I just wanted to give them a big hug for keeping those German fighter planes away from me," Herb explains.

He headed over to the reception and began asking the men who'd gathered whether any of them might have flown at the same time he did. They pointed to a distinguished-looking man in the corner. It was John Leahr.

Leahr (left, in 1945) in his military uniform. Heilbrun (right) posed next to his WWII B-17 bomber after flying his 35th mission in April 1945.

"This lanky, white fellow comes up and puts his arms around me," John recalls. "I didn't know what was going on." But after comparing mission books, John learned that he had actually flown cover for Herb on two missions in 1944. In fact, John's plane was among those that helped Herb make it home on that frightening December day.

"These guys were fighters, but they were told not to be aces—just protect the bombers at all costs," Herb says. "And they did. It was amazing to be able to thank him."

As John and Herb talked, they realized they'd worked at the same aeronautics plant before the war and at the same Air Force base after. John had gone on to become a stockbroker, but the two men had lived only minutes apart—a few miles from where they attended elementary school.

Herb went home after the reception and began looking for his old class photos. "I got out my third-grade picture, called John up and said, 'If this little black guy in the third row is you, then this is getting really scary.'" Indeed, it was John, standing almost shoulder to shoulder with Herb.

"I couldn't go through life hating people just because of the color of their skin. I couldn't not forgive."

The men began spending time together. Herb learned about John's homecoming after the war—so different from his own. While parades were given for white servicemen, John and his fellow airmen went uncelebrated. Sometimes they were even targets for scorn. Once, in Memphis with three fellow officers, John suffered a beating. "A guy came along," John remembers, "and said, 'I've killed niggers before, but I've never killed no nigger officers.' Two white policemen came up and just drove on. Luckily a sailor passed by and stopped the guy. If it wasn't for him, I'd be dead."

"If I had gotten killed," John told Herb, "not a thing would have been said. They would have just sent my body home. It was a terrible thought to have about the country that you'd been willing to die for."

But to counter any resentment he might feel toward whites after the war, John joined a multiracial church. "I couldn't go through life hating people just because of the color of their skin," he says. "I couldn't not forgive." And through his wife, a teacher, he began giving talks at schools about his war-time experiences and the importance of overcoming prejudice.

John invited Herb to come to one of his talks. "I knew people faced racism," Herb admits, "but it never hit home until I heard John speak. And I felt a certain complicity. I hadn't done anything to make it worse, but I hadn't done anything to make it better."

When John asked Herb to join him at the lectern, Herb saw it as a way to make good on a debt he owed to his new friend—and to hundreds like him, who'd been unsung heroes of the war.

"The kids are fascinated hearing John talk," Herb explains. "Then he introduces me. We give each other a hug. When we show them the picture of our class, they cheer."

In the fall of 2003, the pair received the Harvard Foundation medal for encouraging racial diversity. "Having Herb tell people how grateful and proud he is of us makes me realize I could have had this relationship for 77 years, not just eight," says John. "Because of racism, he stayed in his world and I stayed in mine. We don't want that to happen to two other little boys."

"Adlai Stevenson once praised Eleanor Roosevelt because she'd rather 'light a candle than curse the darkness, and her glow has warmed the world,'" says Herb. "Johnny and I aren't about to warm the world, but I think our story has certainly lit a few candles."

Originally published in the March 2005 issue of *Reader's Digest* magazine.

John Leahr died at the age of 94 in March 2015. Herb Heilbrun celebrated his 99th birthday in October 2019 in Cincinnati, where he still lives. In 2017, he marked his 97th birthday by taking a spin in a restored B-17 bomber that took off from Lunken Field at the Cincinnati Municipal Airport.

Humor Hall of Fame

"I told you the tank was half empty, but oh no, you said it was half full."

After finishing our Chinese food, my husband and I cracked open our fortune cookies. Mine read, "Be quiet for a little while." His read, "Talk while you have a chance."

—**CAROL BURKS** PROVIDENCE, RHODE ISLAND

At dinner, my six-year-old niece told her father, "Dad, when I grow up, I'm gonna marry you." I laughed until her mom said to her, "Don't make the same mistake I did."

—**ISAIAH INMAN,** RD READER

The Prisoner and the Encyclopedia Editor

by Daniel A. Gross, from newyorker.com

When an encyclopedia misprint brings two book lovers together, the only thing that stands between them is the bars of a Maryland prison.

One day in mid-2016, Robin Woods drove seven hours from his home in Maryland to visit a man named Mark Stevens in Amherst, Massachusetts. The two had corresponded for years, and they'd spoken on the phone dozens of times. But they had never met in person. Woods, who is bald and broad shouldered, parked his car and walked along a tree-lined street to Stevens's house. He seemed nervous and excited as he knocked on the door. A wiry man with white hair and glasses opened it.

Within a few minutes, Woods, 54, and Stevens, 66, were sitting in the living room, talking about books. The conversation seemed both apt and improbable: When Woods had first written to Stevens, in 2004, he was serving a 16-year prison sentence in Jessup, Maryland, for breaking and entering.

And yet it was a book that had brought them together.

At Jessup, Woods had bought and begun reading *Merriam-Webster's Collegiate Encyclopedia*, a nearly five-pound tome that starts with an entry on the German city of Aachen and ends with zymogen, an inactive protein precursor to enzymes. He hoped to read all its alphabetical entries, which exceeded 25,000, and he spent hours flipping through the pages. One day, he was puzzled to read an entry stating that the 11th-century ruler Toghril Beg had entered Baghdad in 1955. He quickly realized that it should have been 1055. "I read it several times to make sure," he says. Then he turned to the masthead, which listed the editor, Mark A. Stevens.

"Dear Mr. Stevens," Woods wrote in a letter. "I am writing to you at this time to advise you of a misprint in your FINE!! Collegiate Encyclopedia." He described the error and offered his thanks for Merriam-Webster's reference books. "I would be lost without them," he wrote, unsure whether he'd ever get a response.

What Woods didn't mention in his first letter to Stevens was that the encyclopedia represented the culmination of his self-education. Woods grew up in a housing project in Cumberland, Maryland. Cumberland was once an industrial center but has become one of the poorest metropolitan areas in America. Woods was first sent to prison at 23, for firing his grandfather's rifle through an apartment window after a drug-related dispute. He was young, embittered, and almost completely illiterate. "I had never read a book in my life," he says.

Woods remembers enjoying first grade, but he says he was bullied because of his light skin. (Woods was raised by his mother, who was African American. His father was of mixed race.) In second grade, he developed an antagonistic relationship with his teacher, who made him sit in a coat closet whenever he annoyed her. Eventually, the school transferred him to a special education program. As he progressed through the grades, instead of learning to read and write, he was given chores such as collecting attendance slips and stacking milk in the cafeteria refrigerator. These tasks earned him mostly A's and B's. "Of course, I didn't learn nothing," he says. "They say it takes a community to raise a child. It takes one to destroy a child too." Woods ultimately dropped out of high school.

During his first stint in prison, Woods began his own course of study. He was sent to a notoriously harsh prison in Hagerstown, Maryland.

Stevens (right) asked the prison to return Woods's books, vouching for his character.

He resented authority figures and often directed outbursts at the guards, who responded by putting him on lockup. For 23 hours at a time, and sometimes longer, Woods would be alone in a cell that had no television or radio. One day, a man with a cart of books wound his way through the lockup tiers, shouting, "Library call!" Woods wasn't interested at first, but his boredom won out: He decided to borrow *The Autobiography of Malcolm X* and *The Sicilian*, a Mafia novel by Mario Puzo.

The autobiography proved "too complicated," and *The Sicilian* was only slightly easier. Still, Woods persisted. "Many, many words I had to skip over because I couldn't read them," Woods recalls. Each page took him about five minutes but left him with a glow of accomplishment. By the time he got to the end, about a week had passed. "I remember that I wept," Woods says—not because of what he had read but because he had succeeded in reading.

Woods soon bought his first dictionary at the prison commissary and began etching words into his memory by copying them down and reading them aloud. He read into the early hours of the morning. "Even though I was confined in a cell, my mind was free," Woods says. "I could escape."

"Even though I was confined in a cell, my mind was free, I could escape."

For a brief time, Woods also regained his physical freedom. In 1987, he finished his sentence and moved back to Cumberland, where he lived in a shack and worked occasionally for a man who cleaned offices. Books had expanded Woods's world, but they hadn't made it any easier for him to stay out of trouble. One night, Woods says, he drove to one of the offices he'd helped clean, knocked out a window, and stole several thousand dollars' worth of equipment.

The next day, he went to a local club and, over a game of pool, tried to sell some of the equipment. When a group of state troopers walked in the side door, he didn't put up a fight. Not even two years had passed since his release, and Woods was once again incarcerated at the prison in Hagerstown—an institution he had come to detest. Because of his prior record, Woods received a harsh sentence: 16 years for two counts of breaking and entering. In 1991, after Woods got caught up in a prison riot, his sentence was extended by seven years.

There are a few ways that books enter prisons. They're sold at prison commissaries and lent by prison libraries; nonprofits also distribute donated books to prisoners. There are state and federal restrictions, of course: In some institutions, hardcover books may be sent to an inmate only if they're from a publisher, a book club, or a bookstore; the U.S. Bureau of Prisons also prohibits texts that are "detrimental to the security, good order, or discipline of the institution" or that "may facilitate criminal activity." Many prisons also add their own idiosyncratic rules.

Even so, Woods managed to assemble a small library in his cell. "A lot of prisoners put emphasis on how many Nike shoes they have," he says. "I would wear a pair of prison tennis shoes if necessary, but I had eight or nine hundred dollars' worth of books." Woods ordered his encyclopedia through the mail after reading about it in a catalog. When it arrived, he says, it was carefully inspected for contraband.

* * *

In late November 2004, when Mark Stevens received his first letter from Robin Woods, he responded on Merriam-Webster, Inc., letterhead. "I believe you're the first to have spotted the error in the Toghrïl Beg entry; by 1955 Toghrïl was no longer exactly in his prime," Stevens wrote. "Please stay on the lookout for more." Woods was thrilled, and soon he wrote again, highlighting errors in the entries for Edward the Confessor and 'Uthmn ibn 'Affn—"not as a critic, but as a friend," he explained in his letter. "For I believe that M.W.I. is the crème de la crème. I would like to help it to stay that away [sic]!"

Over the next two years, Stevens sent 18 letters to Woods; Woods sent several dozen to Stevens. They discussed the life of Cleopatra and the self-education of Malcolm X, but Woods barely discussed his criminal record, and Stevens never asked. "They were perfectly executed letters, and very courteous," Stevens says. "It still seems astonishing to me." One letter concluded, "I have the honor to be, Sir, your most obedient servant."

But in 2005, it seemed as if all of that was about to change. Woods learned that he would be transferred, without a clear explanation, to a supermax prison in Baltimore. Officials told him he wouldn't be allowed to bring his books.

Woods protested. Within days of arriving at his new cell, he went on a hunger strike. "I've gone crazy and will not eat until they allow me to keep my books," he wrote to Stevens. Several weeks later, he wrote another letter, this one short and despondent: "I look like walking death. But I'm hardheaded and shall not give up." Locked in a single room, Woods lost about 70 pounds.

One day, as Woods remembers it, he saw a shadow on the wall of his cell. It was the Maryland commissioner of corrections, who asked about his health. "He had a very curious look on his face," Woods recalls. Finally, the commissioner asked, "Who is this Mark Stevens?"

Woods remembers thinking, How does he know Mr. Stevens? As it turns out, Stevens had written to two prison wardens, and eventually word had gotten to the commissioner, who called him. They spoke about Woods and the encyclopedia. Not long after that, the commissioner offered Woods a deal. If he would end his hunger strike and follow the rules for a year, the commissioner would cut short the extended sentence and send Woods home. In the meantime, his books would be restored to him.

"I feel like a kid getting out of high school," Woods wrote to Stevens near the end of 2006. "The whole world is waiting for me!" In January 2007, 18 years after the start of his incarceration and five years before the scheduled conclusion of his extended sentence, Robin Woods was discharged from prison. He had about $50 to his name, the minimum required by law.

Woods once more moved back to Cumberland, where he was given housing by a local pastor. Every few months, he called Stevens. The calls continued for a decade before they finally arranged to meet.

When Woods visited Stevens at his home in Amherst in June 2016, they were soon acting like old friends. "I never met you until today, but I love you very much," Woods told Stevens. "You're a good man." They took hikes, went to a play, and visited the home of Emily Dickinson, where a plaque quotes her lines: "There is no Frigate like a Book / To take us Lands away." On Sunday, after a goodbye hug, Woods began the long drive home.

Woods rarely reads anymore—partly, he says, because it takes considerable effort just to pay the bills and keep clear of the law. But he still keeps a copy of *Merriam-Webster's Collegiate Encyclopedia* close.

"While my body is here in prison, my mind has seen the world," Woods once wrote to Stevens. "There are a lot of places that I hope to see that I have read about in my many books." Stevens responded by quoting another book, T. H. White's *The Once and Future King*.

"The best thing for being sad," Merlyn says in the novel, "is to learn something. That is the only thing that never fails."

Originally published in the December 2017/January 2018 issue of *Reader's Digest* magazine.

Killer on Call

by Max Alexander

Terror takes the form of a caretaker
in this chilling tale of a disturbed
man's true crime.

Helen Dean was one of those lucky people who had managed to grow old gracefully. At 91 she was still active in the Eastern Star order, a sister group to the Masons. She was alert, quick to laugh, and looked much younger than her years. "She didn't have a lot of wrinkles," says her niece Sharon Jones.

In late August 1993, she was enjoying a smooth recovery from colon surgery at Warren Hospital in Phillipsburg, New Jersey, when a thin, sharp-featured male nurse entered her room. The nurse told Helen's son Larry to leave; when he finished his work and Larry returned a few minutes later, Helen angrily announced, "He stuck me!"

Larry thought that was odd, as his mother wasn't scheduled to receive any medications. Strange, too, was the location of the shot—on her inner thigh, where it was very hard to see. Just to be certain, Larry whipped out his Swiss Army knife and trained the magnifying glass on the spot. Sure enough, there was a tiny puncture wound in the skin. Later that day, the same nurse came in to clear dishes. "That's the man who stuck me!" Helen said again. Larry told his mother's doctors and other nurses, but beyond questioning some hospital staffers, they did nothing.

The next day, Helen began vomiting inexplicably, delaying by several hours her discharge to a nursing home, where she was to receive physical therapy before going home. It came as a tremendous shock to her relatives when she died of heart failure that afternoon.

That night, Helen's son called the local prosecutor and told him that she'd been murdered. He had a suspect in mind. It was the male nurse who gave Helen the mysterious injection, and he knew his name—Charles Cullen.

* * *

Sharon Jones had remembered the nurse's name because Helen Dean's middle name happened to be Cullen. But not much else about Charlie Cullen stood out. An emotionally withdrawn man who could barely bring himself to converse with his own wife, Cullen had hidden in plain sight for years—blending in and getting by, despite a history of bizarre behavior.

Cullen was born in 1960 in West Orange, New Jersey, a densely populated blue-collar enclave of double-decker houses and winding streets. He was the youngest of eight kids—five of them girls—in a tight-knit Roman Catholic household that included his parents—Florence and bus

The Liberty Nursing and Rehabilitation Center in Allentown, Pennsylvania, one of the many facilities where Cullen worked.

driver Edmond—and an aunt. When Charlie was almost seven months old, his father died of an undisclosed illness, at age 56.

Growing up without a father in a large family consisting mainly of women, Charlie developed into an awkward kid who kept to himself. When neighbors can place him, they vaguely recall a boy who didn't have much to say. Robert Hull remembered that Cullen seldom responded with anything more than a perfunctory "fine" when asked how he was doing. In fact, things weren't so fine. When Charlie was 17, his mother was killed in a car accident.

Exactly how Cullen handled the loss of his second parent is unclear— but soon afterward he joined the Navy, serving as a technician for ballistic missiles on the *Woodrow Wilson*, a nuclear submarine.

> *"Charlie was one of those people everyone picked on."*

All new sub recruits endure a period of "hazing," but shipmates say Petty Officer Second Class Charles Cullen was singled out for his flinching, geeky demeanor. "Charlie was one of those people everyone picked on," says Marlin Emswiler, his bunkmate.

Still, Emswiler says Cullen was basically a nice guy. "Charlie would give you the shirt off his back," he says. He was particularly helpful to the ship's doctor, according to Emswiler, who remembers Cullen volunteering to give vaccinations when sailors lined up for shore leave.

But Cullen's interest in medicine took a bizarre turn one day when Petty Officer First Class Michael Leinen found Cullen manning the missile controls while wearing a surgical gown, mask, and gloves. At the time, Leinen thought Cullen was just trying to be funny, but years later, he came to believe Cullen had been deeply troubled. "He didn't have a grasp on reality," he says. Eventually, Cullen was transferred out of sub duty, but his problems continued. Leinen heard Cullen attempted suicide a few years later, which may have led to his discharge in 1984. (Citing privacy rules, Navy officials will not confirm a suicide attempt.)

After his release, Cullen enrolled in the Mountainside Hospital School of Nursing, located just a few miles from where he grew up. He graduated in May 1987—two months after his brother James died suddenly at age 31, possibly from a drug overdose. A week later, Cullen married Adrienne Taub, a computer programmer, who has refused to speak to the press about her former husband. Shortly thereafter, Charles Cullen, RN, landed his first nursing job at Saint Barnabas Medical Center in Livingston, New Jersey.

Chief burn technician Jeanne Hackett worked with Cullen in a Saint Barnabas unit for severely burned patients. "His job was to make sure they were comfortable during their bandage change," she says. "It's the hardest time for the patients, and Charlie seemed very appropriate. He didn't have the warm, coddling part in him, but there weren't too many guys who did."

Home was a subject that rarely came up, says Hackett. "He never talked about his family life. I worked with him for a while before I found out that he had a wife and children." (Charlie and Adrienne's two daughters are now 16 and 12.) The male nurse certainly never shared his problems—including the breakup of his marriage.

*　　*　　*

In divorce papers filed in January 1993, Adrienne Cullen described a dysfunctional relationship in which her sullen, remote husband slept on the couch for three years and never took her out. Instead he immersed himself in his work. "He consistently works 12 to 36 hours of overtime each week," she wrote. "When I approach him about working less overtime, he implies that I am being unreasonable and selfish."

At home, Adrienne claimed that her husband repeatedly turned the heat off in winter—and when she complained, he retaliated by cranking the thermostat to 80. While his wife and daughters roasted in their bedrooms, "He sleeps in the living room with the window open," Adrienne charged.

Cullen apparently reserved much of his anger for the family's two Yorkshire terriers. "I was awakened many nights by the screams of these dogs," Adrienne said. Cullen once zipped a misbehaving pup into a bowling bag.

He was also losing it on the road, racking up tickets and fender benders left and right. In 1989 he was pulled over for speeding. In 1990 he ran a stop sign in Phillipsburg and caused a minor accident. Less than five months later, he ran another stop sign. By the time of his arrest, his driving record showed three accidents and three speeding tickets.

The ride was getting bumpy at work too. The nursing agency through which Cullen was then working at Saint Barnabas fired him in January 1992 for undisclosed reasons, and a month later he was hired at Warren Hospital in Phillipsburg. There, shortly after Adrienne filed for divorce, Cullen became obsessed with a nurse named Michelle Tomlinson, buying her an engagement ring after just one dinner date. One morning, soon after Tomlinson got back together with her old boyfriend, she woke up to find the glass smashed out of her back door and evidence that someone had entered her Palmer Township, Pennsylvania, home during the night. Later that morning, Cullen called and admitted to the break-in.

"I wanted to check on you," he told Tomlinson. "You know, to make sure you were okay, that you did not try anything—like suicide." Tomlinson was so shaken that she pressed charges.

When police called Cullen, says Palmer Township Police Chief Bruce Fretz, "he came right in and admitted to everything." After being fingerprinted, photographed, and arraigned, Cullen left and attempted suicide—ending up a patient in the same intensive-care unit where he worked at Warren Hospital. He was later admitted to Greystone Park Psychiatric Hospital in Parsippany, New Jersey.

Less than five months later, Cullen pleaded guilty to misdemeanor trespassing in the Tomlinson incident and was sentenced to a year's probation. At his plea hearing, Cullen said, "I have never in my life intentionally tried to inflict any distress or harm on anyone." Days later he appealed, representing himself and filing pages of handwritten motions detailing his assertion that he had not been stalking Tomlinson. "Their [sic] was a sexual, intamate [sic] relationship between Michelle Tomlinson and myself," he scrawled on one document to the court. Court and police papers show that Warren Hospital officials were well aware of Cullen's arrest and suicide attempt. Yet two months after breaking into Tomlinson's home and while still undergoing treatment for depression, he was back working long hours.

In an April 2014 plea agreement, Cullen pleaded guilty to murdering 13 patients.

Cullen definitely needed the money: In his pretrial application for a public defender, he listed monthly expenses of $1,460 for child support, $300 for psychiatric treatment, and $346 in minimum-balance credit card payments. (In 1998 he filed for bankruptcy.) But his enthusiasm for work apparently went beyond compensation. Exactly three weeks after his conviction, Cullen walked into Helen Dean's hospital room and asked her son to leave.

An autopsy on Dean was inconclusive, but because no injection had been ordered by a doctor, the hospital made Cullen take a lie detector test. He passed—then quit his job. The matter was dropped.

* * *

Cullen next stepped onto a merry-go-round of short-term positions, working at eight more hospitals or nursing homes in the next nine and a half years. He favored the hard-to-fill night shift, a time when nurses are less supervised. Meanwhile, his private life continued to spiral. In 1997, during a brief period when he was unemployed after being fired for poor performance from Morristown Hospital in New Jersey, Cullen was back as a patient in Warren's emergency room, being treated for a depression-related illness that may have been another suicide attempt.

He was working the night shift at the Liberty Nursing and Rehabilitation Center in Allentown, Pennsylvania, on May 7, 1998, when an elderly patient received an unauthorized dosage of insulin and eventually died. The man, Francis Henry, had been in a car accident and appeared to be in severe pain—barely able to mouth "I love you" to his wife. The nurse in charge of Henry, Kimberly Pepe, was fired over the incident.

Pepe claimed that the nursing home should have instead suspected Cullen, who had a patient in the same room and was already being monitored by the pharmacy for stealing drugs, including morphine and digoxin, a medication that is used to regulate the heart and can cause cardiac arrest if administered improperly. The nursing home denies Cullen was under investigation at the time, but Liberty eventually did fire him in late 1998 for failing to follow guidelines on medication delivery. Less than a week later, Cullen landed a job at Easton Hospital in Easton, Pennsylvania.

Kristina Toth had a bad feeling about the gaunt-looking male nurse who wheeled her 78-year-old father, Ottomar Schramm, out of Easton's emergency room. "I thought he was real cold," Toth recalls. "He didn't show any emotion." In his hand was a hypodermic needle. "What's that for?" Toth asked.

"In case his heart stops," replied the nurse.

Schramm's heart did indeed stop three days later, the last day of 1998. An autopsy revealed a digoxin overdose. Schramm, a retired steelworker, had been admitted after experiencing seizures; there was no medical reason for the digoxin in his system. Although the pathologist concluded the death was accidental, Toth suspected otherwise. By then Cullen was living in a basement apartment on a tidy block in Phillipsburg. "He kept to himself," says Charles Cook, who lived two doors down. "He was a nice neighbor; in the summer he kept his yard beautiful. On weekends sometimes his kids would visit."

But there were no children around on the morning of January 3, 2000. Upstairs neighbor Karen Ziemba woke to the smell of a strong fuel odor coming from the basement. When Cullen didn't come to the door, she called the police. Officer Bernie Kelly arrived, forced his way in, and found a charcoal hibachi grill burning in the bathtub. Cullen had removed batteries from smoke detectors and blocked heat vents with insulation. "He wouldn't admit it was a suicide attempt," says Kelly. "He said he was trying to stay warm. I said, 'Charlie, you're a nurse. You know and I know what's going on here.'"

If only his employers had known. But privacy concerns kept his personal medical history out of sight.

A few months after the basement suicide attempt, Cullen landed his eighth nursing job, this one at St. Luke's Hospital in Bethlehem, Pennsylvania. He worked there two years but quit abruptly in June of 2002, after he was questioned about a stash of unopened heart medication found in a needle-disposal bin. Concerns over the number of deaths on his shift prompted a police investigation, but a forensic pathologist and an investigator from the state's nursing board could find no concrete evidence.

Next, Cullen moved on to a hospital in nearby Allentown, where he was considered so odd that he was "weeded out" after 18 days, according to a hospital representative. By now he had been fired from four institutions, often under a cloud of suspicion over medication errors and unusual patient deaths. Relatives of victims, like Helen Dean's niece Sharon Jones, can't understand why investigators failed to pin any crimes on Cullen. "We know who did it, when he did it, and how," says Jones, adding that catching Cullen back in 1993 would have saved many lives.

Instead, Cullen kept working—and killing. After the Liberty Nursing Center fired him, personnel there notified the state Department of Health about the medication error. But no one bothered to call the police. Nor was the nursing home required to pass along its concerns to other hospitals that called for job references. Hospitals today (like other businesses) risk being sued if they make negative comments about former employees. As a result, even when a hospital grew alarmed enough to notify authorities, Cullen's misdeeds were not passed along to subsequent employers. No one was getting the big picture.

That picture was becoming increasingly grim in September 2002 when Cullen started work at Somerset Medical Center in Somerville, New Jersey. It was his tenth and last job.

Health care technology had changed considerably since Cullen first donned a nurse's uniform. At Somerset, the hospital used a high-tech computerized care system called Cerner that allowed health workers to punch up a patient's medical and drug history at a terminal within seconds. Another computer system, Pyxis, tracked drug disbursements. Pyxis worked like a cash register: By typing in data that included a patient's name and a nurse's ID number, a drawer for a particular drug would slide open.

Working the night shift as usual, Cullen became adept at circumventing the system to withdraw unauthorized drugs. Sometime during the evening of June 15, 2003, he ordered digoxin for one of his patients who had not been prescribed it. After picking up the drug, he tried to cover his tracks by canceling the order on the Pyxis computer. Meanwhile, he went into the Cerner system and accessed the records of Jin Kyung Han, a cancer patient who was not under his care.

The next morning, Han went into cardiac malfunction and was found to have high levels of digoxin in her system. She recovered after an antidote was administered, but died three months later.

Then, during the night of June 27, Cullen played his deadly game again—withdrawing digoxin for one of his own patients, canceling the order, and accessing the medical records of a heart-disease patient who was not his own. That patient, a Roman Catholic priest named Florian Gall, died the next morning. His body contained lethal amounts of digoxin.

At that point hospital officials could hardly ignore the situation. They alerted the New Jersey poison control center, but allowed Cullen to keep working while investigating other possibilities, including whether Han's condition could have been caused by an herbal tea she drank. Before long, Dr. Steven Marcus of poison control became convinced that someone was deliberately poisoning patients and notified the state health department.

Health officials began an investigation, but still Cullen kept working. On August 27, a patient in his ward received a nonfatal overdose of insulin, yet the hospital never reported the incident. (Somerset was later fined for that failure.) When another patient died after a suspicious drop in blood-sugar levels that could only have been caused by an insulin overdose, the hospital finally called the county prosecutor's office.

Belatedly, the hospital fired Cullen—on October 31, after discovering he had falsified employment history on his job application. The prosecutor's office, meanwhile, kept up its investigation. "The hospital's computer system made it pretty easy to track him," says Somerset County prosecutor Wayne J. Forrest. "We caught him red-handed by his ID number." On December 12 they arrested Cullen as he drove away from a Somerville restaurant.

When the police pulled him over, Cullen went quietly. As he had 10 years earlier when accused of the Pennsylvania break-in, he readily admitted to his crimes. Although initially charged on just two counts—murdering Reverend Gall and attempting to kill Han—Cullen said he had killed as many as 40 patients during the course of his career. If true, that would make him one of the worst serial killers in U.S. history.

And one of the most enigmatic. According to Forrest, Cullen claimed that the overdoses were mercy killings. But many of his victims were not mortally ill—or even in pain. Beatrice Yorker, director of the School of Nursing at San Francisco State University and an expert on killer nurses, says such a motivation is rarely an honest one. "These people are sociopaths mostly interested in getting their own needs met," she says. "I liken them to firefighters who set fires. Often what they need is power and control or excitement and attention." Unfortunately for Cullen's victims, it took years for the people around him to pay that attention. "I ask myself, What was I missing?" says Jeanne Hackett, Cullen's former colleague. "I can't imagine where that evil could be inside someone I knew and cared about."

Killer on Call

We may never know what made Cullen a killer. As investigators in seven counties huddled to sort through the Cullen case, relatives of possible victims wondered what to do next. Several lawsuits against hospitals have been filed, and bodies long buried are being exhumed. In April 2004, New Jersey Governor James McGreevey signed a law that requires health care facilities to report all serious medical errors to the state. But Cullen's mobility across state lines suggests the need for stronger federal monitoring as well.

*   *   *

In April 2004, Cullen pleaded guilty to killing 13 patients and attempting to kill two others in Somerset County. He also confessed to the murder of Ottomar Schramm, and charges for his crimes are still pending in other counties. In return for his plea and for agreeing to cooperate with authorities, Cullen will be spared the death penalty and will instead spend the rest of his life in prison.

Among Cullen's confessions was the 1993 murder of Helen Dean. Sharon Jones attended the plea hearing and sat less than four feet from the man who murdered her aunt. "He remembered right down to the time of day and the dosage he used," she says. One thing Cullen didn't do was make eye contact. "As he passed by in front of us, he had his head hanging down, cocked a little bit to one side," Jones remembers. "He took a quick look and then turned his head back again. He looked completely blank of emotion."

Jones says that while getting justice brings some satisfaction, it does little to take away the pain she still feels. "My aunt was like a second mother to me, and someone other than God made the decision that she should no longer be on this earth. Why did he pick her? That's the thing you always wonder." For Helen Dean and perhaps as many as 39 others, their loved ones can only hope that someday Charles Cullen will tell them why.

Originally published in the November 2004 issue of *Reader's Digest* magazine.

Charles Cullen is currently serving a life sentence and is incarcerated at New Jersey State Prison in Trenton.

Humor Hall of Fame

Cartoon by P.C. Vey

"In my day, Virginia was for people who were just friends."

My mother and father were driving when she was pulled over by the police. Mom was in a hurry and told the officer so. "I understand, ma'am," he said. "But I have to ticket anyone over 55." Mom was beside herself. "That's discrimination!" she shouted. The officer explained calmly, "I meant the speed limit."

—**TAMARA ENCKE** HOLLADAY, UTAH

After my mother suffered a bout of serious headaches, we persuaded her to visit her doctor. While we were in his office, the doctor asked, "Have you been seeing any flashes of lights or auras?" "I don't know," Mom said. "I didn't have my glasses on."

—**JUDY KELLEY**
CONWAY, ARKANSAS

I'm at the age where I can't take anything with a grain of salt.

—**MATT WOHLFARTH,**
COMEDIAN

Grizzly Attack!

by Peter Michelmore

A romantic hike turned into a fight for their lives.

Dale Johnson and his girlfriend, Rhonda Anderson, were hiking along a narrow trail leading to Trout Lake in Montana's Glacier National Park. It was early afternoon last October, with shafts of sunlight streaming through the trees, and Dale, 31, led at an unhurried pace.

"Not far now," he encouraged Rhonda, 27, who was a step behind. A trim, pretty woman in T-shirt and shorts, she wore a pink bandanna over her light-brown hair. Her beaded earrings were a gift from her lean, dark-bearded companion.

The couple had been chatting back and forth, their voices ringing through the silent woods, but now, in tune with the hushed tranquility around them, they had grown silent. As they approached a bend in the trail, Dale stiffened. He caught a movement in the brush ahead, and in the same instant he heard a guttural growl. To his horror, two bears, cinnamon brown, came snorting straight at him. His heart pounded. *Grizzlies!*

From the corner of his eye, Dale saw Rhonda jump behind a tree. But he stood rooted, frozen with fright. The bears were in full charge, their fur rippling in fury.

Don't run! was Dale's one thought. To the grizzly, a runner is prey, and the bear will give chase at speeds no man can match. Dale's mind seized upon a desperate ploy. *Make yourself bigger. Bluff them.* Leaping, yelling, waving his arms, he confronted the charging bears. Immediately, one veered off into the woods, but the other—400 pounds of unrestrainable savagery—bore down upon him.

Snatching a stick as long as a broom handle and as thick as his wrist, Dale brought it down on the bear's skull. At the same time he let out an unearthly scream. When the club shattered, Dale rolled to the ground and curled into a ball. Park rangers always advise people to assume a cannonball position if attacked. It is supposed to indicate to the bear it is not under threat.

Face in the dirt, Dale wiggled his backpack higher. You've got to protect your neck. He felt the sharp rake of claws across his back. Suddenly all sensation was lost in the sound of his screams. Only Rhonda, watching from behind the tree, would remember the terrible moments that followed.

* * *

"It's a seven-mile round trip to the lake," Dale had said when they parked their station wagon and set off about an hour earlier.

A sign at the trail head warned that they were entering bear country. But being from the nearby town of Whitefish, Rhonda and Dale were well aware that the park was home to black and grizzly bears, and they were ever watchful.

Park rangers always advise people to assume a cannonball position if attacked.

Noise was the best protection against a surprise meeting with a dangerous grizzly. Usually Dale wore a small bell on his pack for added security, but he had forgotten it this day.

Rhonda noted the time, 1 p.m., and remembered that bears were mostly spotted in the early morning or late afternoon. They'll all be sleeping at this hour, she thought. At any rate Dale and Rhonda knew that bears preferred to keep their distance. It was rare for a grizzly to make an unprovoked attack.

* * *

Grizzly Attack!

When Rhonda saw the grizzlies, her instinct was to climb a tree. In panic, she grabbed for a branch, but there wasn't one within reach. Paralyzed with terror, she saw the bear claw Dale's shoulders, then close its great jaws over his left arm, wrenching it from side to side, biting through muscle and bone. In anguish, she thought, *He's being killed! Do something!*

An image crossed her mind: her neighbor's fierce Labrador. Once he had come snarling at her when she was taking out garbage. She grabbed the metal can and held it in front of her, fending off the animal. "Don't, Buster, don't." At the command of her voice, the dog backed away.

Shucking her backpack, she held it out as a shield. Advancing on the hulking grizzly, she cried, "Bear! Go away!"

Startled, the giant dropped Dale's arm and looked around. With lightning speed, it charged Rhonda. She reeled back. In a blur, she saw the grizzly's lips pulled back over huge teeth and four-inch claws the color of amber. The teeth sank into her pack, and claws slashed her right wrist. Blood spurted from the wound as she fell to her knees and screamed.

Hearing Rhonda's cries, Dale came out of his daze just in time to see woman and bear, face to face, inches apart. "Bear! Bear!" he shouted, determined to lure the grizzly away from Rhonda. The attacker's head snapped around. With a rush, it turned once again on Dale.

"Get down!" he yelled at Rhonda. *We have no defense*, he thought, *We have to play dead!*

An instant later Dale was in the air, being shaken violently, the bear's jaws locked on his buttocks. Claws swiped at his shoulders. Flooding adrenaline had numbed him to pain, but Dale knew his body was being savaged. *If he doesn't stop, it's all over for me.*

Rhonda had heard Dale's cry to get down, but she could not abandon him. Grabbing her tattered pack, she advanced once more, yelling for the grizzly's attention.

This time the bear attacked on its hind legs. Towering over her, its claws ripped into her neck. Mouth open, the bear clamped its jaws on her upper left arm, teeth crunching hard to the bone.

Somehow Rhonda kept her feet, toe to toe with the bear, not conscious of pain, but of rising fury. Setting her jaw, she pounded a fist into the animal's stomach. In an instant, she was flung to the ground. Rhonda expected jaws to close on her, but the grizzly dropped to all fours and loped off into the trees.

* * *

Dale struggled up from the ground. His left arm was crushed at the elbow, the forearm laid open to the bone. From the feel of his buttocks, he knew the bear had bitten out a chunk of flesh.

Rhonda managed to remove the sweatshirt tied about her waist and bandage her wrist. Her neck and shoulder wounds oozed blood.

"I'm sorry I dragged you into this nightmare," Dale said. He vowed to himself that her life would not end in misery on a trail in the woods.

"We have to make it back to the car," he said. "No one will come for us."

Hooking her pack over her undamaged right shoulder, Rhonda led off down the trail. She didn't lack for confidence. From motel maid and fast-food waitress, she had moved on to a good job as an examiner in a real-estate-title office. Now her concern was for Dale. His wounds were deep, and they had to walk three miles. But she didn't question his determination.

In ten years, Dale had parlayed a degree in electronics from a small college in his native Oregon into a position as co-owner of a company that specialized in computerized aerial photography. Seeking out a spot where they could couple business with the sporting lifestyle, he and his partners moved the firm to Montana's Flathead Valley.

Walking behind Rhonda, Dale kept shouting to spook any bears that might still be nearby. The pain in his arm intensified. He felt lightheaded and realized that surrender to shock would be the end. As a veteran hiker and climber, he knew that he was at the edge of his limits.

Then Rhonda saw the creek she remembered was near the trail head. Her watch read 2:32 p.m.—32 minutes since the attack—when they reached their station wagon.

"We made it this far," said Dale, his voice labored. "The next part can't be as hard."

But his face was creased with pain, and Rhonda knew she had to take over. Tugging the keys from her pack, she unlocked the door and eased behind the wheel. "I think I can drive," she said.

Rhonda had no strength in her left arm to hold the wheel while shifting with her right, so Dale changed gears as Rhonda worked the clutch. Crouched dizzily at the wheel, she tried not to run off the road.

After several miles, they came to Lake McDonald Lodge. It was closed for the season, but Dale spotted a pay phone and shouted for Rhonda to swing into the driveway.

Mercifully, there was a dial tone, then a 911 operator on the line. "We need help," he said hoarsely. "We've been mauled by a bear." The operator took down the location and notified Glacier Park headquarters.

Ranger Charlie Logan reached the lodge within minutes, and a highway patrol car soon delivered a nurse, who set up intravenous lines. By 3:30 p.m., the battered hikers were beginning their ambulance ride to Kalispell Regional Hospital.

*　　*　　*

Dale and Rhonda spent eight days in the hospital, and each had three operations. In addition to wounds on his back and buttocks, the elbow of Dale's left arm was fractured, and the bear had broken off an inch-long knob of bone. Doctors performed a fourth operation later to repair the elbow damage. Rhonda's left biceps muscle was completely severed—and bear-tooth fragments were lodged in the bone of the upper arm. The claw that cut into her neck missed the jugular by a quarter-inch.

On their third night in the hospital, Rhonda sat at Dale's bedside and told him how she had attempted to drive off the grizzly with her backpack. "I thought you were being killed, and I had to do something."

"I didn't know that's why the bear left me," Dale said, his voice growing husky. "You saved my life."

As part of the healing, Rhonda went home to her two-room cabin. She put on a video documentary about life in the north country that she loved so much and let her cat curl up on her lap.

Before the grizzly attack, Rhonda had not really comprehended how dangerous such an attack could be. But the event had confronted her with her own vulnerability, and impressed upon her how much we need the closeness of family and friends—and to be there for them when they need us.

With her left arm in a cast, Rhonda found even the easiest chores difficult. One day she was trying to braid her long hair with fumbling fingers when the telephone rang. It was Dale. There was a new dimension to their relationship now. If love was built on respect, they knew they had a solid foundation.

"I can't even braid my own hair," she said brusquely. "I think I'll cut it all off."

There was a pause, then he said, "Come on over. I'll make you dinner."

When Rhonda arrived, Dale sat her down gently and began braiding her hair. It was, she thought, the sweetest gesture she had ever known.

Originally published in the June 1992 issue of *Reader's Digest* magazine.

Dale Johnson and Rhonda Anderson remained friends for many years but have since lost touch. Dale still lives in Whitefish, Montana, where he enjoys foraging for wild mushrooms, hiking, hunting and river-rafting in the area's vast outdoors. He tends to avoid the area of Glacier National Park where he and Rhonda were attacked and he always carries bear repellent.

A Five-Year-Old Teaches a Lesson in Grace

by Leslie Kendall Dye, from the *New York Times*

On the night the author loses patience with her mother and her dementia, a granddaughter's love unites them all.

It's eight o'clock on a cold spring night. Our apartment has been hit by a cyclone—the handiwork of a young, energetic child. Every bit of furniture is draped with paper chains, scissors and Scotch tape, modeling clay, piles of acorns, and party favors.

I'm so tired tonight. I've been on crutches for seven weeks, recovering from hip surgery, and I'm trying fruitlessly to clean up.

The phone rings—for the sixth time in less than an hour. We know who it is.

When my mother was 68, a hemorrhagic stroke claimed her brain, but not her life. She awoke from a coma severely damaged; the bleed instantly razed the landscape of her mind. Dementia soon built a Gothic fun house of distortions where coherent architecture had once stood. She has been manacled inside for a decade, with little to do but experience psychic distress.

She is dogged by paranoia—she thinks she has been kicked out of her assisted living facility (not true), she thinks her daughters have not visited in months (it has been a few days), she thinks that her friend Jimmy never wants to see her again (he calls and visits weekly).

Each time she calls, I play a game with myself called "How Good a Person Can I Be?" I've won five rounds of the game tonight; I am due for a fall.

She has no idea that she has repeated the things she is about to say a million times today and a million times yesterday. She has no idea that I had surgery, nor can she recall her own granddaughter's name. She is unaware of most of the past, and she drifts in the present. She is lonely.

I hurl my anger at the easiest target: my mother, the very victim of this chance horror.

"MOM!" I yell. "YOU ARE NOT BEING REMOVED FROM YOUR HOME! AND WE VISITED TWO DAYS AGO!" (Maybe it was four days, but she won't remember anyway.) "Mom, you have to believe me, and if you don't, I cannot talk anymore! Everything is fine!"

Silence. Then:

"I was only calling to say hi."

I feel the dagger of passive aggression, which is the only working weapon in her mental arsenal. My mother continues, having already forgotten that I yelled. (Sometimes she does remember; tonight I luck out.)

"But I'm also frantic about something; do you have a minute?"

"No, Mom, I don't. I can't again with this!"

"Why are you yelling?"

I'm yelling because you aren't my mother; you are a poorly rendered stand-in who cannot help me care for my child, or be a grandmother, or even remember to ask me about my day. I'm yelling because I have talked you off this ledge five times tonight, and I'm yelling because you remind me of everything I fear: aging, sickness, fragility, bad luck, loss, impermanence . . . You name it—if it's scary, you remind me of it!

I flop on the couch, aware of all my daughter is witnessing. She hears me reprimand my mother, lose my patience, announce that someone I love is an imposition. I have not only failed at being a Good Person; I have failed at being a Good Example to My Daughter.

I stew on the couch, defeated.

"Can I talk to Grandma Ellie?"

My five-year-old reaches for the phone.

Wordlessly, I hand it over.

"Hi, Grandma!"

I hear my mother exclaim through the receiver.

"Sweetheart! How are you? Did you go to school today?"

What witchcraft is this? All she said was "Hi, Grandma," and my mother sounds like a person fully alert to the heartbeat of a normal day.

"Yes, Grandma, and today was share day, and I brought my Wonder Woman bracelets."

"Can you put it on speaker?" I whisper to my daughter.

She obliges, and out of the phone comes a waterfall of good cheer.

My mother tells her how much she loves her and how lovely her voice sounds.

Then: "I hope I'll see you soon?" My mother makes her plea for a promise of companionship. I hear her voice differently now. I am not tired or angry; I am soft inside, watching my kindergartner handle her fragile grandmother with such deftness.

"Grandma, we are taking you to the carousel this weekend. I'm going on the frog, and you can go on the horse next to me."

"Oh, that's wonderful, darling!"

I'm mesmerized by their exchange.

"Tell me, did you go to school today?" She already asked that.

"Yes, Grandma, I went to school, and we had share day. I brought my Wonder Woman bracelets."

"You did? How wonderful!"

"Do you want me to sing you a song? I know three songs from *Annie*."

And then my daughter sings.

The sharp evening breeze sails through the window, and the mess in our apartment settles around me like an old soft quilt. I listen to my daughter crooning to her grandmother, caring for her with exquisite patience.

I spend so much time wishing she had a "real" grandmother, wishing she knew my "real" mother. In this moment, I see that she does have a real grandmother, and she does have a real relationship with her. It isn't the one I had hoped for, but to her, this is normal—to care for a loved one is a part of life.

When they hang up, after many kissing noises, I tell my daughter it is bath time. She wildly protests, but I draw the bath anyway. I am still Mommy, after all, and she is still five.

And yet tonight, she taught me how to answer the phone like a grown-up.

Originally published in the March 2019 issue of *Reader's Digest* magazine.

CAN YOU LOVE ONE CHILD MORE THAN ANOTHER?

As a mother of three grown and wonderful children, I am spending a lot of time looking back over my life. I wondered one day if it is possible for a parent to love one of their children more than another? I decided that it is indeed possible and so I let each one of my children in on my secret. To my oldest child Lisa, I told her, "I love you the very best because you were my very firstborn child and my only daughter." To my oldest son Rick, I said, "I love you the very best because you were my firstborn male child and the bearer of your late father's name." To my youngest son Mike, I said, "I love you the very best because you are my baby."

—Katherine Doe Johnson *Watertown, New York*

PETE LOVES SUE

When my husband and I were dating, we visited the home of our friend's parents and I noticed a note on their refrigerator that read, "Pete Loves Sue" (the parents' names). I told my then-boyfriend, Bruce, that I'd like to see a note like that on my refrigerator. A few days later I approached my refrigerator and what did I see on the door—a note that read, "Pete Loves Sue!" My husband and I have been married for 25 years and that joke has continued to show up, most recently on the screen of my phone.

—Laura Payne *High Point, North Carolina*

PHOTO OF LASTING INTEREST

Kingo of the Jungle

Q: What does a 300-pound silverback gorilla eat? A: Anything he wants. Kingo prefers the finest of jungle delicacies—that's kangwasika, an herb found in the swamps of the Congo basin of Central Africa, that he's getting ready to munch in this 2006 photograph. Researchers have been studying how his search for food affects his social behavior since 1995. One fascinating finding: When provisions run low, Kingo will sometimes steal from his own family. No wonder he keeps up to four "wives" at a time.

Photograph by Ian Nichols/National Geographic

LOVING MIDDLE SCHOOL

People think I'm crazy for teaching middle schoolers. The truth is that I enjoy learning about life from my students. Here's what they've taught me. You can be angry at someone one day, and be best friends by the next, if you're just willing to communicate. Asking for help can be scary, but usually works. Snacks should always be shared—they taste better that way. You can start believing in yourself if you make time to study for a test and then pass it. Once in a while, you just need to put your head on your desk and rest. But most importantly, it's never a bad day to giggle and smile.

—Guida Detamore *Boca Raton, Florida*

LUCKY COIN TOSS

My husband lost his wedding ring while working in the yard. We looked everywhere and decided it was no use. I was determined to find it, so I bought a metal detector. It didn't seem like it was working, so I tossed a nickel into the grass. My husband started moving toward it with the detector, but nothing happened. I bent down to pick up the nickel and saw his ring about a foot away. I couldn't believe my luck. Amazing. What a feeling of joy. I'll never forget that moment, and I'm going to keep that nickel.

—Joann Nelson *Tacoma, Washington*

Emergency Whistle on Block Island

by Floyd Miller

As they studied the forbidding rocks and the sullen seas, islanders were certain of just one thing: the children would be found alive—or not at all.

The single long blast of the whistle could be heard from one end of Block Island to the other—seven miles north to south, three and one-half miles at its widest. The summer people—swimming, surf casting, pleasure boating—were hardly aware of the sound. But the island people knew the whistle was a cry for help, a summons to the Block Island Volunteer Rescue Squad.

It was the afternoon of last August 4 and the sun was shining for the first time in a week. After the long days of fog and wind and rain, the drenched but refreshed island began to sparkle—a small green jewel set in the sea off the shore of Rhode Island at the eastern entrance of Long Island Sound. Several hundred visitors had poured out of Victorian hotels, cottages and rooming houses, eager to enjoy at last the sand and the sea.

The Kramek family, of Parsippany, New Jersey, had left their rented cottage at about 2:15 and, at the urging of their 18-year-old daughter,

Diane, headed north to Cow Cove, a rocky inlet at the northern tip of the island. On this forbidding shore stands a concrete-and-stone lighthouse, which looks not unlike a small, stern church with an automated light in its belfry. Just north of the light, the island narrows to a 50-foot-wide spit of sand called Sandy Point, which runs beneath the water to become the treacherous Block Island North Reef.

Diane's diary entry for August 3 reads, "Tomorrow I'll go and spend all day at Sandy Point. I've fallen in love with the view. Plan to build a house there; it is such a perfect place to go on a honeymoon."

*　*　*

Near the lighthouse, Stanley Kramek, a retired Marine Corps major, began to surf cast. His wife, Gudrun, set up an easel and began to sketch. Their 13-year-old son, Stephen, and his friend and house guest, Matthew Hikel, 12, went exploring to the west. Diane walked north and settled herself on top of a dune next to the lighthouse, there to dream her young, iridescent dreams. The time was 2:30.

After an hour and a quarter, as Stanley was throwing back his first catch, a sand shark, his wife called to him in alarm: "I hear Stephen shouting!"

He listened and heard only the surf, but Gudrun's ears heard something more. "It's Stephen and something is terribly wrong!" she cried.

Then Stanley saw his son. Stephen had run through the dunes all the way from the lighthouse, staggering from exhaustion and hysteria.

Gudrun saw her husband reach Stephen as he dropped to his knees, tears streaming down his face. Then Stanley came racing back, his face set and white. A couple were parked in a car nearby, enjoying the view. Stanley shouted to them, "Two children have been swept into the sea out there at the point! Send for help!"

> "Two children have been swept into the sea out there at the point! Send for help!"

The car sped away, and Kramek himself set off for the point. He floundered and scrambled his way along the "road" through the dunes, where the deep, dry sand sucked at his feet.

He made it past the lighthouse and finally came onto the wet hard sand of the point. The surf broke to his right and left; straight ahead was the reef. There was nothing else.

Ironically, the very emptiness of the place gave him a moment of hope, for there was no evidence that Diane and Matthew had ever been here. Then he saw a small pile of blue cotton fabric, the work shirt Diane had been wearing over her bathing suit. Beyond the shirt were prints of her bare feet leading directly into the sea.

When the emergency whistle blew, the 20 volunteer members of the Rescue Squad went into action. They were merchants, carpenters, fishermen, power linemen, highway maintenance men—all bound together by short-wave radios in their homes and cars. Weathered, 55-year-old Charles "Ed" Conley, captain of the Squad, was just arriving home from work when the dispatcher's voice crackled on his radio: "Possible drowning at Sandy Point." He yelled to his wife, "Call the Coast Guard." Then he turned his car and headed north.

Twelve minutes after the alarm, Conley and several other island men had joined the lonely figure of Stanley Kramek at Sandy Point. To a casual observer, the scene might not have seemed threatening. The sea appeared calm, the sky was clear. But Conley knew the place intimately, and at this moment he was scared. A strong ebb tide sweeps the vast waters of Long Island Sound over Sandy Point eastward into the Atlantic; no swimmer had ever made headway against it. As he began to search with his binoculars, he was certain of just one thing: they would find the children alive or not at all. The sea never returns bodies from the east.

Slowly, disjointedly, young Stephen Kramek told his story to his mother. "Matt and I were exploring," he said, "and we saw Diane sitting on a sand dune and asked her if she wanted to look for driftwood and she said okay. She wanted funny-looking pieces to arrange with flowers."

Eventually the three of them arrived on the point, where the sand was hard-packed and led into the water with a most gradual descent. "We decided to go wading," Stephen said. "Dad had told us not to go swimming, and we didn't plan to; we only wanted to wade. We got out to where the water was up to our knees, and it gave us a funny feeling. The waves came together from both sides and they would lift us straight up a few inches off the bottom, then drop us back down real gentle. It was real cool, kind of like walking on the moon. We went out a little farther, up to our waists, and we were lifted up and down quite high and Diane said we'd better go back to shore."

The next wave lifted them higher and when it dropped them down there was nothing beneath their feet, and they were swimming. Matthew Hikel was small, and the Kramek brother and sister put him between them, and tried for the shore in single file, Stephen leading. Shouting encouragement, Diane shepherded the boys forward a yard, two yards, three. Suddenly Stephen felt rocks beneath his feet. He scrambled forward and pulled himself up on the sand, then turned to give the others a hand. In that brief moment the tide caught Diane and Matthew and pulled them out to sea.

Stephen screamed, "Diane! You can make it! Matt! Swim!"

He started to wade back into the water but Diane yelled sharply, "Go back! Go tell Daddy. Hurry, Steve . . . get help!" He turned and ran.

✳   ✳   ✳

A small crowd had gathered, perhaps 50 people, islanders who had known what the whistle meant. There was no carnival atmosphere such as is often generated at disasters on the mainland. These plain-faced men and women, bred of sailors and fishermen, had stood here before, as had their ancestors.

Then there came a collective sigh as the crowd saw the low, gray silhouette of a Coast Guard utility boat appear beyond the swirling waters off the reef. She began a slow run down the west side of Sandy Point and disappeared from view. Ten minutes later she reappeared, her search obviously fruitless. Ed Conley waved her to the east, and she began to search off the mile-long shoreline of Cow Cove.

The children had now been in the water for nearly an hour and a half, and after a brief surge of hope upon seeing the Coast Guard boat, Gudrun felt the grip on her emotions slipping. She began to whisper her daughter's name. "Diane . . . Diane . . . oh, my golden girl." To Gudrun it seemed that Diane, at the threshold of so many wonders, had earned a chance at life. To be cheated of it now was an unbelievable injustice.

Stanley Kramek also began to feel despair. Diane was a strong swimmer, and he knew that if she had only herself to care for she might eventually get back to shore. But how could she save both herself and Matthew? He knew she would not abandon the boy.

After a brief surge of hope upon seeing the Coast Guard boat, Gudrun felt the grip on her emotions slipping.

Fog began to crowd northward over the island, heavy and fastmoving. Cow Cove was taking on a pale, pearly opaqueness. Conley exchanged significant glances with his men. If the Coast Guard did not find the children in the next ten minutes, the boat might as well just head back to its base.

*   *   *

Running southeast at half speed, the boat, under the command of Robert Widerman, came slowly about. From the shore, she seemed to pause for a minute, rocking slowly on the swells, then abruptly head northwest to a point about 600 yards offshore. There she cut her engines and put her bow into the wind.

Sure that something had been found in the water, the crowd on shore pressed around the Rescue Squad ambulance to hear the radio. A voice came through with a metallic boom that was broken by static. "Coast Guard . . . retrieved . . . person . . . headed Old Harbor."

As the voice ended, the boat could be seen heading south at full speed. The ambulance started off for Old Harbor, four miles away. Gudrun and Stanley Kramek followed, saying little, searching the dispatcher's words for a meaning. Does one "rescue" a living person but "retrieve" a dead one? And had the dispatcher said "person" or "persons"?

When they arrived at the harbor the Coast Guard boat was already there. Stanley ran to the dock, battling his way through the crowd. "Please," he called out, "let me through!" On the boat's deck he found two small figures wrapped in blankets. They were sitting up, they were alive! They smiled at him and laughed and wept all at once. And so did he.

The Rescue Squad nurse checked the children's blood pressure and pulse, gave them some oxygen and pronounced them fit to leave the boat. When the family stepped ashore, a burst of applause came from the crowd. There were tears in many eyes, and hands reached out to touch them as they passed. "We prayed for you," a few said.

Safely back at their cottage, the Krameks laughed, talked, touched each other, intoxicated with the knowledge that the family was whole. Diane, with her mother's candid gray eyes and self-possession, with her father's determination to face up to a job, with her own sweet gentleness—her parents looked on her with a new awareness.

> *"Each time a swell lifted us up I prayed I'd be able to see the lighthouse."*

"I knew Stephen had got help," Diane told them, "because I could see all the men at Sandy Point and I told Matt that pretty soon a boat would come for us. I kept Matt on my back while I swam the breast stroke most of the time, but when he'd get cold I had him swim by himself a while to get his circulation going. He was very good and did exactly what I told him to do and never once complained."

Matthew, his face flushed by the excitement of an adventure safely concluded, said "We talked and Diane told me jokes and asked me if I knew the song 'True Grit' but I didn't. She called me 'Matt, Matt, the water rat,' and I pretended to get angry. Sometimes she'd turn over and swim on her back while I rested on her stomach and held her around the waist. I'd kick my own feet real hard to help keep us afloat."

"The fog worried me," Diane admitted. "Each time a swell lifted us up I prayed I'd be able to see the lighthouse. I always could, but it got dimmer and dimmer. When we saw the Coast Guard boat, Matt and I waved our arms and screamed, but they went on by without seeing us. That was the worst moment of all. But then they saw us."

* * *

About dusk that evening Kramek left the cottage, announcing he was going to take a walk. A quarter of a mile away he came to the Town Hall, a small frame building where the regular meeting of the Town Council was being held. Kramek entered the crowded room and took a seat at the back. He felt like an intruder, but he had come to make a short speech and he asked for the floor. When it was given him, he could only express his thoughts in the bluntest words.

"My name is Stanley Kramek, and I've been bringing my family to your island for vacation for a couple of years. This afternoon my daughter and a young friend of my son were caught in the tide and taken out to sea. If it had not been for the prompt action of your Rescue Squad and the Coast Guard, I would have lost my daughter and the boy. What I want to say is . . . from the bottom of my heart . . ." His voice broke and his face flushed with the effort he made to continue. He cleared his throat and said, "From the bottom of my heart I thank you." Then he quickly walked out of the building.

The people of the island often talk of Diane Kramek. Coast Guardsman Robert Widerman says, "When my boat got to her, she had supported that boy on her back for an hour and a half, but there was no panic. She had a big smile for us. I've rescued a number of people at sea but none quite like her." Rescue Squad Captain Conley adds, "She is the gutsiest girl I've ever seen."

It will be a long time before Block Island forgets Diane Kramek. And a long time before the Kramek family forgets the people of Block Island.

Originally published in the June 1970 issue of *Reader's Digest* magazine.

Diane Kramek, 68, lives in Little Falls, New Jersey. Matthew Hikel, 62, owns M&M Color Studios, a photography studio, in Hopatcong, New Jersey.

The Baby and the Battalion

by Kenneth Miller

Navy medic Chris Walsh heard a woman's cry for help—then took on a risky new mission.

It started with a bomb.

The convoy was patrolling a rubble-strewn neighborhood of Fallujah, in Anbar Province, when the homemade mine detonated. The IED made a thunderous noise but succeeded only in cracking the windshield of one of the platoon's Humvees. The Marines leaped from their vehicles and tore off after the suspected triggerman, who'd been watching through binocs from the roof of a mud-walled house.

The temperature that June 2006 morning hovered around 125 degrees, normal for late spring in central Iraq. The men pounded down the alleyways in their Kevlar body armor—70 pounds of gear apiece. One contingent spotted the suspect running south and gave chase. They were searching house to house, M-4 carbines ready, when a wizened woman emerged from a doorway, cradling an infant and repeating a plaintive phrase in Arabic.

A corporal translated: "Baby sick." The soldiers shifted nervously, fearing a trap; even if the child was really ill, this delay would make the group a perfect target for a sniper. That's when Chris Walsh appeared. He stowed his rifle and knelt to examine the patient. Her name was Mariam. She was nine months old, with curly black hair, brown eyes and a face twisted in misery. What Walsh saw when her grandmother removed the child's diaper made him gasp, then reach for his digital camera.

Walsh, 30, had arrived in Iraq three months earlier as a Navy medic assigned to Weapons Company, First Battalion, 25th Marines. Before that, he was an EMT for the St. Louis Fire Department. He'd seen all the horrors that keep an ambulance crew busy, and men blown apart on the battlefield in Iraq. But he'd never seen a little girl turned inside out.

He snapped some photos as the corporal marked the house's location on a GPS grid. Then everyone scrambled back to their Humvees, and the patrol moved on.

At base camp—a cluster of half-ruined buildings on the city's eastern outskirts—Walsh showed his photos to Navy Capt. Sean Donovan, the battalion's chief medical officer. Donovan recognized Mariam's affliction: a rare condition called bladder exstrophy, in which the organ develops outside the body. As a further complication, the end of Mariam's large intestine protruded through the same opening and was severely inflamed. Without an operation, Donovan predicted, the child would soon die— and there wasn't a surgeon in Iraq who could help her.

"Then we've got to get her out of here, sir," Walsh said.

*　　*　　*

Chris Walsh didn't want to be thought of as a softy. "He had a very gruff persona, even by Marine standards," says Donovan. Tall and bony, with a glowering expression, Walsh could seem downright misanthropic. Fellow soldiers nicknamed him Doc Grumps.

They also saw right through him. "He had a heart of gold," says John Garran, senior Navy medic for the weapons company. Older than many of his comrades by a decade, Walsh looked after their health like a stern big brother. And he tended to the locals when he could. "We'd go in a house, there'd be someone with a broken leg and he'd say, 'I'm on it,'" recalls

S.Sgt. Ed Ewing, the platoon's second in command. "He didn't care if you were American or Iraqi."

Growing up in eastern Kansas, the eldest of five siblings, Walsh was a popular boy with a habit of befriending outcasts. "He felt a need to protect them," recalls his mother, Maureen, a research lab coordinator. In first grade he declared that he intended to be an EMT when he grew up. After getting his paramedic's license at age 22, he set about ministering to the wounded in St. Louis's toughest neighborhoods.

Chris Walsh

Walsh's brother Patrick joined the Marines after 9/11 and wound up in Iraq. Their father, a Defense Department computer analyst who'd served as a Marine in Vietnam, died of leukemia soon after Patrick enlisted. Walsh grew convinced that he had no right to stay out of the line of fire. "He didn't have a wife or family," says his mother. "He thought he could help somebody over there." He enlisted in the Navy Reserves, allowing him to alternate stints as a medic with his civilian vocation.

Walsh was attached to the 25th Marines, and his unit landed in Fallujah in March 2006. Saving Mariam went beyond his job description, and that of his platoon mates. Nonetheless, when he asked one evening over chow for volunteers to join the effort, hands shot up around the mess hall.

* * *

It would be a two-pronged operation: one side geared toward arranging Mariam's treatment overseas, the other toward keeping her alive long enough to make it there.

Navy Capt. Sean Donovan (back row, third from left, with his team of medics) oversaw Mariam's care in Iraq as well as efforts to get her treated in the U.S.

But first, the Marine Corps brass would have to agree that the mission was worth undertaking. Donovan—a radiologist with a practice in Mequon, Wisconsin, and five kids of his own—argued that it could provide the battalion a "tactical advantage," by winning a few Iraqi hearts and minds. He also promised that all patrols to Mariam's home would be done on the soldiers' own time.

It didn't take much to convince the battalion commander, Lt. Col. Chris Landro, whose wife had just given birth to a son. "I kept thinking, *What would any of us do if this was our child?*" he says. But carrying out the rescue would be a complex and risky proposition.

The greatest danger was, in fact, to Mariam's family. Any Iraqi seen as collaborating with the Americans would be marked for murder by the insurgents. When the Marines came to fetch the baby for an examination at the base, her grandfather suggested they lead him out in handcuffs, as if taking him in for questioning. Mariam came along in an equipment bag.

All subsequent visits to the family's home took place between 11 p.m. and 3 a.m. A mile from Mariam's house, four or five Humvees parked in hidden locations, and 20 Marines equipped with night-vision goggles stole through the darkness. Several soldiers stood watch in posts outside the family compound, while a handful of men entered its courtyard. Chris Walsh was always among them.

Mariam's grandfather was always the one to open the inner door. Though he was just 39, he looked two decades older—worn down, like his wife, by privation and worry. Islamic custom dictated that Mariam's mother, in her early teens, remain in seclusion; the father, a day laborer, never made an appearance. In a tiny vestibule lit by a gas lamp, the medics examined the baby. They made sure her pelvic area was clean and free of infection. Through an interpreter, they advised her grandfather on the fine points of her care. They delivered medications, sterile gauze, bottles and formula. Then they disappeared into the night.

Only a few surgeons in the world specialize in bladder exstrophies. Donovan learned that one, Rafael Pieretti, MD, practiced at Massachusetts General Hospital. He readily agreed to help baby Mariam.

But that hardly solved the child's problems. The Iraqi Health Ministry was flooded with requests from citizens who needed medical treatment abroad. And though cultural taboos prevented Mariam's female relatives from traveling without a male family member, U.S. officials were hesitant to issue visas to Iraqi men. Then there was the question of payment—the hospital bills would exceed $250,000. Dr. Pieretti and his colleagues would work for free, but Massachusetts General needed help to defray other costs.

The battalion's chaplain, Rev. Marc Bishop, began e-mailing his Bay State connections for help. "When a child is in danger," he says, "we are required by our deepest selves to respond." He received a response from Sen. Ted Kennedy, who said he'd try to break the visa deadlock. One of Bishop's parishioners rallied 16 companies to cover the $16,000 needed for transport. A nonprofit medical-evacuation group called Project HOPE agreed to coordinate the flights.

Meanwhile, the fighting in Fallujah was growing more intense, forcing the Marines to cut back on their house calls. By the end of August, says Donovan, "the situation on the ground had become poisonous."

* * *

Then came the second bomb. On September 4, Chris Walsh was riding in his Humvee with three members of the Mariam task force. LCpl. Cody Hill was driving; the other passengers were LCpl. Eric Valdepeñas, 21, from Seekonk, Massachusetts, and Cpl. Jared Shoemaker, 29, a former cop from Tulsa, Oklahoma. The convoy paused at an intersection where boys were playing soccer—normally a sign the insurgents were elsewhere.

The explosion caught the Humvee in its belly, lifting it off the ground and engulfing it in a massive fireball. Only Hill escaped, surviving with burns over half his body. Walsh and the other two servicemen died instantly.

The disaster came just a month before the battalion was to return home, and it was followed that night by an IED blast that cost two other members of Weapons Company their legs. "We were beat up pretty bad," says Ewing. His platoon was ordered to take a few days off—to recover from the shock and discourage retaliation against civilians.

The group spent much of that time talking about the buddies they'd lost and how they would carry on. One thing was certain: They would not abandon the mission Walsh had started. "You don't get too many positives out of Iraq," Ewing says. "We were gonna freakin' get it done."

The visits to Mariam resumed, with Navy corpsman Edgar Gallego, a 26-year-old EMT from New York City, tending to the baby.

* * *

By the last week in September, Donovan was in despair. The battalion was packing to leave Fallujah, but Mariam was still stuck in her hovel, in pain. "I don't think this is going to work," he told Bishop.

"We're so close, but we're a million miles away."

Bishop responded with a question: "Have you prayed?"

"No," Donovan admitted. Bishop sent him to the chapel with instructions to recite the Memorare—a prayer to Mary, which reads, in part, "Never was it known that anyone who fled to your protection . . . was left unaided." Donovan, a Sunday churchgoer, knelt and did as he was told.

The next day, he received an e-mail: Mariam was cleared for departure.

Maureen, mother of Chris Walsh, meets Mariam in November 2006.

The team made their last nighttime trip to the compound. They snuck the baby and her grandparents into a Humvee, which took them to Camp Fallujah. A helicopter ferried them to Baghdad International Airport. They caught a plane to Jordan and another to Boston. On October 13, Mariam was wheeled into an operating room at Massachusetts General.

The surgery took nearly five hours. A normal bladder is shaped like a ball, but Mariam's had never properly closed. Dr. Pieretti stitched the two hemispheres together, then tucked the organ inside her body. Other nearby organs were repositioned as well.

When it was over, Dr. Pieretti called Donovan at Camp Pendleton in Southern California, where the battalion had been demobilized, and declared the operation a success. Donovan relayed the glad tidings to the men in the cavernous barracks. "The word went around like electricity," he recalls. "There were waves of cheers. It was joy. Just joy."

Maureen Walsh learned of her son's death on Labor Day, when a pair of Naval officers drove to her house in Shawnee, Kansas, to deliver the news. (Patrick, who'd been stationed at a different base in Anbar Province, accompanied Chris's body home.) The loss hit her like an asteroid.

> *"There were waves of cheers. It was joy. Just joy."*

In his letters from Iraq, Chris described the weather and landscape yet was mum on what he actually did there. But on October 4, the day before he would have turned 31, Maureen received a letter that clarified everything. It came from Donovan and told the story of Chris's most important mission. "The hope for Mariam's very tiny life," Donovan wrote, "[arose] from the charity and gallantry of your son."

Six weeks later, Maureen flew to Boston, where she found herself in a crowded common room at Massachusetts General. Donovan and Ewing were present, along with the girl's grandparents. And there was Mariam herself, wearing a pink party dress and healing beautifully.

Maureen cradled the little girl in her arms, wondering at how healthy and alert she seemed. "She was like a brand-new child," Maureen recalls. "She had great big brown eyes, and she'd just look at you and smile."

The grandfather asked for pictures of Chris for a scrapbook. "God sent him to Mariam," he said in Arabic. "Thank you for your son."

Mariam and her family returned to Iraq a few days later, settling into their dangerous circumstances with a new sense of hope. Mariam is well enough now to be looked after by ordinary doctors, though she will need another surgery in two years—at Massachusetts General, if possible—to make her fully continent.

Maureen looks forward to meeting her again and getting another chance to touch the bit of Chris that still lives on. "It's hard not to have him around anymore," she says. "But I don't think he's in any way gone."

Originally published in the May 2007 issue of *Reader's Digest* magazine.

An Evening Drive

by Joe Posnanski, from joeposnanski.com

*If you could catch fatherhood in a bottle,
it would be filled with moments like these.*

She's 14 now, a turbulent age. Everyone warned us. There will be times when she's still your little girl, they said. And there will be other times when she lashes out with such fury, you will wonder where everything went wrong. Everyone warned us, and we believed them. We had planning sessions about the future, talks about patience and openness and firmness when needed.

We were ready.

We weren't ready.

Elite athletes will tell you that in their first professional game, everything moves so impossibly fast that there is no possible way to prepare for the speed and fury and violence of it all.

We were ready.

We weren't ready.

She gets into the car. It is nighttime, and I'm picking her up from an activity, and she is happy. She used to always be happy. Now it's a 50-50 proposition. She shows me a picture she wants to post on Instagram of her and a friend. She asks if it's OK. I tell her it's OK. I don't know if it's OK; I'm trying hard to keep up with the rules. She is happy.

We sit in the car, and we are stuck at a red light because of the indecision of the car in front of us. I growl at this car. She laughs and growls too. I remember when she was a baby and would make these funny growling sounds. We once took her to a spring-training baseball game in Florida. It was unseasonably cold, and we had her bundled up in this baby blanket. Every now and again from the blanket there would be a loud "Rahhhhrrrrrrr," and people in the few rows in front of us would look back to see who or what was making that sound.

The light turns green. We talk about nothing. It is pleasing for a moment not to be asking her about school or homework or friends, and pleasing for her for a moment not to be talking about any of it. The air is cool and perfect, and the windows are cracked; "Video Killed the Radio Star" plays on the radio. "I like this song," she says. I tell her that years ago, I made lists with my friends Tommy and Chuck of our favorite hundred songs, and this was on it.

"Would it be now?" she asks.

She's in a curious mood. She used to be curious all the time. "Tell me a story of when you were a little boy," she'd say. She does not say that much now. Curiosity for a teen is a sign of vulnerability, a too-eager admission that there are things she doesn't know. I remember that feeling. She yells sometimes, "I don't need your help!" I remember that. She yells, "Get away from me! You don't understand!" I remember that. She yells, "It doesn't matter. I'm going to fail anyway." I remember that most of all.

"Tell me a story of when you were a little boy."

She has little interest in remembering. For her, the clock moves forward, and she wants to look forward—there's so much out there. In a year, she will be in high school. In two years, she will be able to drive.

In three years, she will start looking hard at colleges. In four years, she will be a senior in high school. Forward. Always forward.

And I look back.

Always back. I am carrying her, her tiny head on my shoulder, and I'm singing "Here Comes the Sun," trying to get her to fall asleep. I am walking with her through the gift shop at Harry Potter World as she goes back and forth between wanting a stuffed owl or a Gryffindor bag. I am helping her with her math homework when the problems were easy enough that I could figure the answers in my head. I am watching *The Princess Bride* with her for the first time, and I hear her say in her squeaky voice, "Have fun storming the castle!"

"Hey, Dad," she asks, "can I have your phone? Can I play some music?"

"Sure," I tell her. She punches a few buttons, the song begins, and immediately I know. It's her favorite song.

"I once knew a girl
In the years of my youth
With eyes like the summer
All beauty and truth
In the morning I fled
Left a note and it read
Someday. You will. Be loved."

I introduced her to it a while ago. "What kind of music would I like?" she had asked. "Why don't we try some Death Cab for Cutie?" I had said. She was smitten.

She is smitten now. She sings along to every word. I do too.

"You may feel alone when you're falling asleep
And every time tears roll down your cheeks
But I know your heart belongs to someone you've yet to meet.
Someday. You will. Be loved."

She looks up at me and smiles.

Her teeth are straight; the braces are gone. She leans closer and says, "Don't you love this song, Daddy?"

I hear her say "Daddy" and think back to a time when she raced over to me at the airport after I returned from a trip, hugged me, and wouldn't let go. She's 14, a turbulent age. Tomorrow, she may look right through me. But now, in the coolness of the evening, she smiles at me and holds my hand, and we sing along with Death Cab for Cutie. We are off-key. We are off-key together.

Originally published in the November 2016 issue of *Reader's Digest* magazine.

Humor Hall of Fame

Cartoon by Mick Stevens

"Dear Diary: Incredible news! Unfortunately, it's all classified."

I asked a scruffy-looking soldier if he'd shaved. He answered, "Yes, Top Sergeant." I got into his face and said, "OK, tomorrow I want you to stand closer to your razor."

—RALLYPOINT.COM

A military base commander called to complain that the weather-forecasting software our company created for them kept reporting unexplainable wind shifts. "Do you know where the sensor is located?" my coworker asked. "Of course," he responded. "It's where we park the helicopters."

—**ANGELO GIORDANO** BELLEVUE, NEBRASKA

My five-year-old brother's eyes grew large as our father opened the top drawer of his dresser. Seeing John's reaction, Dad took out his Purple Heart and explained how he'd earned it during the Korean War. John was so impressed, the only thing he managed to say was, "Dad, are all those socks really yours?"

—**TRICIA HARNEY** GRAND HAVEN, MICHIGAN

Cartoon by Terry Colon

GREAT WEAPONS THROUGH HISTORY: THE TROJAN COCKROACH
Unfortunately, it was easily repulsed by the Trojan Boot
in their first and only encounter.

My high school assignment was to ask a veteran about World War II. Since my father had served in the Philippines during the war, I chose him. After a few basic questions, I very gingerly asked, "Did you ever kill anyone?" Dad got quiet. Then, in a soft voice, he said, "Probably. I was the cook."

—**MARIAN BABULA** PENN RUN, PENNSYLVANIA

One Wing
and a Prayer

by Penny Porter

*The "dumb bird" was capable of more
than we'd ever imagined.*

Jouncing down a twisty trail on our Arizona cattle ranch one morning we suddenly came across thousands of mourning doves. They were lined up like clothespins along miles of telephone wires, their bead-bright eyes riveted on our pickup loaded with grain.

"Dumbest birds on earth," Bill grumbled as he pulled up beside a cattle-feed trough.

"Daddy, why do you always call them dumb?" asked Jaymee, our eight-year-old daughter.

"Because they're always out to kill themselves," Bill said. "They fly into windowpanes and break their necks. They lean over too far and drown in stock tanks. And they build nests with holes so big they wouldn't hold a Ping-Pong ball, let alone an egg."

"Then how come there are so many?" Jaymee asked as Bill ripped open a sack and began to pour. He never had time to answer.

Alerted by the clatter of grain, scores of doves swooped down in a frenzied quest. Some lit on the cows' horns, others blanketed their backs. But most settled around the stomping hooves of our cattle.

"Daddy!" Jaymee screamed. "That cow's standing on a dove's wing!"

Bill hurried toward the cow and twisted her tail until she shifted her weight. "Dumb bird," he muttered. The dove was free, but one wing lay on the ground, severed at the shoulder.

The pathetic creature flapped its remaining wing and spun in circles until it mercifully lay still. *Thank God,* I thought with relief. *It's dead.* After all, there was nothing we could do for a bird with one wing.

Then Bill nudged the dove with the toe of his boot, and it flipped onto its back, wild-eyed with pain. "It's alive, Daddy!" Jaymee cried. "Do something!"

Bill leaned down, wrapped the tiny, broken creature in his red handkerchief and handed it to Jaymee.

"What are we going to do, Mama?" she asked, her brow creased with worry. She was forever rescuing kittens, rabbits and squirrels. But this was different: this was a grotesquely wounded bird.

"We'll put it in a box and give it water and grain," I said. The rest would be up to God.

* * *

When we got home, Jaymee put the bird into a shoe box filled with dried grass, and set the box near the wood stove for warmth.

"What are you going to name it?" asked her ten-year-old sister, Becky.

"Olive," Jaymee answered.

"Why Olive?"

"Because Noah's dove flew all the way back to the ark with an olive branch—and that wasn't so dumb."

While the girls were in school that day, I lathered the hideous wound with antibiotic salve. *Poor thing,* I thought, looking at the small, ghostlike creature. Certain it would die, I closed the lid. We'd done everything we could.

The next morning we heard a stirring in the box. "Olive's eating!" Jaymee shouted. "And she's a girl. I can tell because she's just plain gray—and sometimes pink."

We put the bird in a wire-mesh cage filled with leaves and twigs. In the sudden shock of light and space, Olive sensed freedom and flapped her wing, repeatedly hurling herself against the mesh screen. Finally she stopped and wandered around off-balance, like half a bird, yet taking the time to rearrange her feathers as though trying to draw a cape over the gaping hole. When evening came, she curled her pink claws around a small manzanita branch we'd wedged in a corner. She perched there in a trancelike state—dreaming, I supposed, of life in the sky.

Early one morning a few days later, Jaymee squealed, "Olive laid an egg! Come look!"

Resembling an elliptical, oversized pearl, the egg rolled around between a few twigs in the dove's favorite corner. "But why didn't she build a nest?" Jaymee asked.

"Too lazy," Bill said. "They slap three twigs together and call it home."

He was right. Doves' nests are flimsy little platforms that appear to be tossed at random among the bushes. I'd often discovered at my feet the empty, broken shells of eggs that had fallen through. Yet these birds kept right on laying in the same miserable nests.

Now here was Olive, piteously wounded, soon laying an egg almost daily. Since she had no mate, the eggs would be infertile. But for Jaymee, it was magic. She began collecting the eggs in a teacup.

*　*　*

At first Bill didn't pay much attention to the dove. Then one day he noticed Jaymee's teacup was full, and he disappeared into his workshop. When he emerged he handed her a wooden egg-box he'd made. It had 40 two-inch compartments that were padded with black velvet. "It's a treasure chest," he told her, "with a special place for each egg."

"Oh, Daddy, thank you!" Jaymee said, hugging him. "Maybe I can show Olive and her eggs for a 4-H project." At the Cochise County Fair that year, there was a special 4-H competition built around Arizona's wildlife. Kids' projects would be judged for originality, effort and record-keeping. "Maybe I could even win a blue ribbon!" Jaymee said. It was her big dream.

By this point, Olive was becoming tame. At the sight of Jaymee, she cooed softly and pecked seeds and morsels of apple from her palm. When Jaymee took her out of the cage, the dove perched contentedly on her finger and shared an ice-cream cone. She especially enjoyed her shower, a gentle misting from a spray bottle.

We liked to think she was happy. But when we moved her cage to the glassed-in porch where she could see other birds sail by, Olive's wing would quiver and her little gray head would bob anxiously.

Incredibly, the egg-laying continued: 16, 17, 18. *How much longer can this go on?* I wondered.

Around that time a fierce storm pounded our ranch. Fearsome winds ripped nests from trees, dashing eggs and newly hatched birds to the ground. Jaymee gathered many different kinds of eggs, miraculously unbroken, and put them in her treasure chest. Then she ran into the kitchen cupping a pink, open-beaked baby bird in her hands. "Maybe Olive can be its mama!" she cried.

Well, why not? I thought. My broody hen had raised ducks, pheasants and quail. Besides, if it worked, Olive wouldn't be so lonesome.

"We'll fix up a nice nest first," I said, "a sturdy one like a dove should make, soft and deep so the baby won't fall out." The girls found a storm-damaged nest and lined it with horsehair and chicken feathers. We laid the newborn in the nest and placed it inside the cage. "Maybe Olive will think the baby is really hers," Jaymee said.

During the night I awoke to strange sounds, reminders that wild birds belong outdoors—not in my kitchen. Expecting the worst, I hurried to the scene. The nest was destroyed. But huddled in one corner on three small twigs, Olive nested, bright eyes aglow, with the newborn cradled under her wing.

The egg-laying ceased and Olive became a proud and protective mother. She chirped anxiously when we took the baby out for feeding, and examined him thoroughly when we put him back. It was clear she loved him.

The fledgling thrived, and silver-white and black feathers soon appeared on stubby wings and then everywhere. The short, hooked beak was soon topped by a tiny, black bandit mask. Our bird book dubbed him a loggerhead shrike; Jaymee named him Bandit.

Soon Bandit was perching on Jaymee's finger, gobbling down spaghetti, bologna and pepperoni strips. His passion was live flies, which Jaymee fed to him with tweezers.

The morning we'd been dreading came when Bandit discovered he had wings. We found him clinging upside-down to the top of the cage, fluttering his wings eagerly. Olive cringed in her corner, feathers frazzled. "You'll have to let him go," Bill told Jaymee. "He's scaring the dove."

His passion was live flies, which Jaymee fed to him with tweezers.

When Jaymee removed Bandit from the cage, the young shrike instantly shot up to the chandelier. "Take him outside," Bill said. "I don't want feathers in my coffee." By now Olive was chirping with alarm.

I placed Bandit in a cottonwood tree so he could practice flying. We watched him flit from branch to branch, and grabbed him when he landed on the ground. But the moment we tried to step inside, he zipped through the doorway and landed on the chandelier again. Hearing Olive, he dived back to the cage.

Bandit grew increasingly adept at flying and darting in and out of the door at will. Soon he was flitting between barn roofs, trees and barbed-wire fences. Our little shrike had grown up, and gradually he flew farther away. One day we watched him head for the river. That was the last we saw of him.

* * *

Shortly after Bandit's departure, Olive began sleeping most of the day, perched unnaturally fluffed on her manzanita limb. In the early dawn she uttered a plaintive "Oooh-ah-hoo-hoo-hoo," like the sorrowful cry of a lost soul seeking comfort. Then she started molting.

We added sugar to her water and a night light to her cage. I played happy songs on the radio. Nothing seemed to work.

Then Bill returned from the feed store with a small box of "special diet for indisposed canaries." Looking sheepish, he said, "I thought maybe a couple of vitamins might help Olive." To our surprise, she seemed to perk up.

In her 4-H journal, Jaymee entered a paragraph about Olive's baby, listed miscellaneous dove-project expenses and wrote facts about doves. Meanwhile, Becky counted the eggs. "You have only 31," she said. "That leaves nine empty holes." Unless Jaymee filled the box with 40 eggs, Becky feared the judges might consider the project incomplete.

Despite the vitamins, Olive had never fully recovered from her sadness. She'd become frail, almost spectral. Yet the following morning, she laid another egg. Hope lit Jaymee's eyes. "Only eight more to go," she murmured, dashing off to catch every live fly she could find.

Olive rallied with six more eggs. Then, three days before the fair and two more eggs to go, our weary little dove huddled on her manzanita limb for the last time. We found her in the morning, motionless, like a tiny piece of driftwood washed up on the sand.

"Do you think Olive was happy in a cage?" Jaymee asked Bill as he wrapped the dove in his old red handkerchief.

"Why, of course she was," he answered awkwardly, trying to make sense out of the bird's life. Then, in a blur of words that a man could only say to a child, he stumbled ahead. "You took care of her, fed her and gave her showers and a baby. And you told her how smart she was." He paused. "And she *was* smart because she knew you loved her."

"And she gave me her eggs because she loved me too?"

"Her treasures," he said. "All that she had."

He watched Jaymee gather two handfuls of pale pink and gray feathers and fill the two empty velvet nests. "Even though Olive died," she murmured, "I'm going to show my egg collection anyway."

He smiled and hugged her. "I'll bet you win the blue ribbon."

And she did.

Originally published in the September 1997 issue of *Reader's Digest* magazine.

Summer's Magical Music

by Allan Sherman

We each have a special soundtrack that conjures that particular feeling of a glorious summer day.

My son and daughter were competing to see who could play which louder: he, a baseball game on TV; she, a Led Zeppelin record. I sat there in the living room with them, my eyes closed, a peaceful smile on my face.

Nancy yelled, "Too loud for you, Dad?"

"Nope," I said, without opening my eyes.

The enigmatic smile got to her.

"Dad, would you mind telling me what you're doing?" she shouted.

"I'm listening!" I hollered, still smiling.

This interested Robbie. "To the record or to the ball game?" he screamed.

"Neither!" I shrieked, smiling.

Both of them were fascinated. They turned off their noisemakers. "I was hearing it again," I explained. "I can close my eyes and hear it again any time I want."

"Hear *what*?" Nancy persisted.

"The old Summer Music. The sweet song of Summer As It Was." And I began to tell them about it.

*　　*　　*

Remember? The lazy chimes of ice cream trucks; the yells of boys playing ball in the streets; the drumbeat of moth wings flirting with porch lights. I can still hear the crooner moaning "Say It Isn't So" on a scratched 78-r.p.m. record, repeated endlessly by the neighbors' lovesick teenage daughter. I can still hear the baroque toccata of hand-operated lawn mowers, the crackle of backyard wood barbecue fires, the yelps of tiny kids allowed to toast marshmallows for the first time.

In summertime, the Midnight Special sang the blues as it fled through town on its moonlit journey: first, a long, lonesome howl on its steam whistle, then a short one, then another long one as it pierced the distance, the last plaintive howl modulating down to a minor key, kind of sad, like Gershwin. Airplanes were few, but the ones that came over roared and spluttered for attention, and you ran out on the lawn to see the miracle in the sky.

Summer was also the time of stillness, precisely measured by a meticulous cricket.

Summer played a patter song of rain on windowpanes, a xylophone solo on tin roofed garages, and now and then a cymbal crash of lightning that started you counting the seconds to see how far away the timpani roll of thunder was. Summer was also the time of stillness, precisely measured by a meticulous cricket. It was the click-clacking of a stick rattling along a picket fence. It was the excited words, "*Got* 'im!" from a boy who had caught a firefly in a Mason jar. It was the click of croquet balls colliding, the slap-slap of jump rope against sidewalk.

Summer was the soft rustling of leaves as you walked home on a dark street punctuated by yellow lights, after taking the keenest girl in town to a Fred Astaire movie. It was listening to her hum—"A Foggy Day in London Town"—and then hearing beautiful lyrics forming and bouncing around inside you, but knowing you would never have the courage or the Fred Astaire *suave* to utter them to her.

In summertime, at twilight, your mother somehow found a moment in the middle of doing everything for everyone, and sat down alone at the piano and played "Clair de Lune"—the one piece she still remembered. Summer was the sound of your father snoring on the couch, each snore fluttering the edge of the sports section he had been reading.

In summertime you could hear the boy who was "It," his eyes tightly shut as he leaned against a tree, counting to 500 by fives. The good ones did it so fast that the syllables all jumbled together. But they gave an honest count and yelled, "Here I come, ready or not!" Then the scuffling and scampering behind bushes as It ran after his quarry. Then a hush and another boy yelling, "Olee, olee! In free!" And a chorus of galumphing sneakers as boys ran in, *safe.*

There were kerplunks in the lake in the park as fathers lobbed stones so that sons and daughters could count the ripples. There was the magic flute some talented kids could make with a blade of grass stretched between their thumbs. There was the swoosh-slap, swoosh-slap of the new lawn-sprinkling gadget. The whirr and hum of electric fans. The jangling of marbles in a boy's pocket—and, from his other pocket, the untimely croak of the faithless frog who was supposed to keep quiet so that Mother wouldn't know he was in the house. And remember the crackle of cards being shuffled on the screen porch, the tinkling of ice in glasses of pink lemonade?

You thought, as you listened: *this is summer; this is the season for which all other seasons exist.* And you took a moment to memorize all of its melodies and harmonies forever.

* * *

The smile must have left my face. Nancy asked, "What's wrong, Dad?"

"I don't know," I said. "I guess it made me sad to think that you kids missed all that."

"But we have Summer Music of our own," Nancy said. Robbie agreed. I looked at them for a long moment, and then suddenly realized that of course they do. And of course it's different from ours.

Ours was the sound of a neighborhood; theirs is the music of a planet. The melody is motion: jet engines screaming, the crescendo of sports-car gears shifting, the roar of surfing, the petulant whining of dune buggies, the thunder of motorcycles.

I tried to hear summer through their ears, brave and new and honest, minus the candy coating of "moon" and "June" and "spoon."

Yet they also have a thirst for serenity. And so they steal away in summertime and sit alone on some hilltop, enjoying the aloneness, drinking in the stillness, waiting to hear the stretching of a sunflower. In my ancient summertimes, I simply heard a birdsong. The new ears can hear *what kind* of bird it is; the new eyes can see how few are left; the new hearts can feel how important it is that this bird and his summer song be cherished.

And so, my dear children, your Summer Music belongs to you alone. It is your own record of those warm and tender seasons of your ripening, when you were growing and stretching and reaching for the sun; it is the rhapsody of being alive, the mad waltz of energy and joy, the bittersweet ballad of first love, the song of all living things singing in unison: *I am! I am! And I'm glad I am!*

And in that glad cry—for you as for me—is the magical Music of Summer.

Originally published in the July 1971 issue of *Reader's Digest* magazine.

When Your Best Fish Story Is about Catching a Goat

by Rick Bragg, from *Garden & Gun*

Sometimes the fish are biting, and sometimes it's the goats.

I **should have** given up fishing, I suppose, after the goat. He was not a regular goat. He was more part goat, part rhinoceros, about the size of a small horse but with devil horns. He looked out on the world through spooky yellow eyes and smelled like . . . well, I do not have the words to say. My little brother, Mark, bought him at the sprawling trade day in Collinsville, Alabama, for $75; I would have given him $100 not to.

The first thing the creature did after coming into our possession was butt the side of a truck. You have to be one terror of a goat to assault a Ford. His name, my little brother said, was Ramrod.

"Why would you buy such a thing?" I asked my brother. He told me he planned to purchase a bunch of nanny goats to "get with" Ramrod, after whatever courtship it was that goats required. Ramrod would beget little

Ramrods, who would beget more, till the whole world was covered in ill-tempered mutant goats. I think, sometimes, we did not love that boy enough.

Ramrod moved into his new home in a beautiful mountain pasture in northeastern Alabama and, first thing, butted heads with my mother's ill-tempered donkey, Buckaroo. Buck staggered a few steps, and his head wobbled drunkenly from side to side, but he did not fall unconscious. This, in Buck's mind, constituted a victory, and he trotted off, snorting and blowing, like he was somebody.

My point is, Ramrod was a goat not to be messed with.

Later that year, I was fishing with my brothers in the pond in that same pasture. The water was mostly clear, and you could see the bream in the shallows and the dark shapes of bass in the deeper end. For a change, even I was catching fish and had pulled in a few nice little bass. My cast, to me, was immaculate, my aim perfect, my mechanics sound, especially for the clunky crankbait I was throwing.

"But I'm not gettin' much distance," I complained to my big brother, Sam.

"It's fine," he said, and with an easy flick of his wrist, sent a black rubber worm sailing beyond my best cast of the day.

I decided to put a little more mustard on it. I let my lure dangle about a foot and a half from the tip of the rod, reared back, torqued, and started forward with a powerful heave . . . and hooked Ramrod, who had crept up behind me to do me some kind of grievous harm, right between his horns.

Ramrod, who for perhaps the first time in his long life seemed unsure of what to do, took off running. Sam, who has never been too surprised by anything in his whole laconic, irritating life, gazed at the retreating goat as if this were a thing he witnessed every single day.

"Can't remember if that was a ten-pound test I put on that bait-caster," he said, as if it made a difference. "You can't catch no fish with heavy line. They can see it," and he made another cast.

The goat ran on. I considered, briefly, just standing my ground and trying to reel him in, to play him like a great tarpon or a marlin. Instead, I began to run parallel with him, reeling in the slack as I did, as I have seen great anglers do with giant fish on the TV. I guess I thought I could eventually get close enough to reach out and snatch the hook out of his head. I truly did not want to hurt him, but that was foolish, of course; you could not hurt Ramrod with hammer or hand grenade.

As it turned out, the point of the hook, not even to the barb, had snagged in the bony base of one horn, and the crankbait jangled atop his head. He was not wounded; he was just mad. He quit running about the time I ran out of line, and my little brother, who had a sort of telepathic bond with this creature, calmly walked over

I was done fishing that day and seriously considered being done for good.

and pulled the hook free while the goat stood there like a pet. Then he and the goat both gave me a dirty look, as if hooking him were something I woke up that morning intending to do.

I went back to the pond, frazzled, and—I am not kidding—immediately hooked a water oak, a blackberry bush, and a low-slung power line. I shuffled off with a rubber worm dangling high above me; it was Cherokee Electric's problem now. I was done fishing that day and seriously considered being done for good. I walked to the house defeated but not ashamed, at least as far as Ramrod was concerned. That goat never liked me anyhow.

Great anglers, the kind who tie their own flies and read the tides and have fished the deep blue for leviathans, will most likely shake their sun-bronzed heads in pity and sad wonder over this. But the bad fishermen out there—you know who you are—will merely nod in understanding and sympathy and, I hope, some degree of solidarity. The only reason they have not caught a goat is that, so far, one has not made their acquaintance or wandered into the proximity of their backswing.

But perhaps the worst thing about it is that the best fisherman I know, my brother Sam, did not even think that, in the long, sad epic of my fishing life, this episode was remarkable at all. He did not even tell it to anyone, not in the decade since. To him, it was just the kind of thing a poor fisherman like me was likely to do, was somehow fated or destined to do, assuming of course that he did not first fall out of a boat and drown.

"What is it, truly," I asked, "that I do wrong?"

He was too kind to give voice to it.

He just spread his hands, palms up, as if to say: Everything.

Sadly, as a fisherman, I am just missing something, something that is both mechanical and mystical and, I am sorry to say, apparently permanent. Still, fishing is the one thing I will get out of bed for in early morning . . . well, that and biscuits and gravy.

And, honestly, I'd rather be a bad fisherman than no fisherman at all.

Originally published in the November 2017 issue of *Reader's Digest* magazine.

CHRISTMAS IN A VENDING MACHINE

In 1997, I was long-distance friends with a girl. After visiting in early December, we were in love. On Christmas Eve, I found an airline running a last-minute special from Memphis to Boston. When it came time for Christmas dinner, I learned that everything in Boston is closed on Christmas night. We gathered our change and raided the hotel vending machine. Our Christmas dinner was Funyuns, Hot Fries, Fritos, Snickers and Cokes while watching TV. It was perfect. Parting was heartbreaking, but temporary. We were married by August. We look back on our "vending machine" Christmas and recognize how special it was. Some people live their whole lives hoping for a special moment like that. Christmas is not about where you are. It's not about extravagant meals. It's all about whom you are with, grasping that moment and appreciating how special it is.

—James Jennings *New Hartford, Iowa*

A LONG TIME COMING

After confirming her pregnancy, my friend told her 4-year-old daughter about the new addition that would be coming, but she made it clear it would be quite a long time yet. Her husband came home and they had dinner and discussed the good news. Finally it was time for bed and her daughter, very distressed, said to her mother, "I know you said it would be a long time until we got our baby, but this is ridiculous."

—Janet Simmonds *Mancelona, Michigan*

A Perfect Storm Shot

These clouds crawling over northwest Oklahoma in 2017 look plenty angry, but Canadian photographer Vanessa Neufeld wouldn't have minded if they had been nastier. Neufeld, who died of cancer in 2019, was a storm chaser. It wasn't all about the chase, however. "A big storm brings a mixed bag of emotions," she said. "You're in awe of it, and you're worried about who could be affected." In fact, after a bad storm, Neufeld often pitched in with the cleanup. "If anything gets hit, I'm there to help as much as I can." *Photograph by Vanessa Neufeld*

Horror in the Heartland

by Henry Hurt

One April morning in 1995, the morning routines of thousands of men, women, and children in Oklahoma City were shattered by one terrifying act.

Each in his or her own way was playing a part in the small daily pageants of life. All were striving for their own version of the American Dream: the Pursuit of Happiness. But on that 19th day of April, dreams were about to be smashed and hopes destroyed by what was then the worst terrorist attack ever to take place on U.S. soil. And yet, after the smoke and the dust lifted, Americans learned of the amazing stories of survival amidst the heartbreak, and the incredible spirit that created them.

The nine-story Alfred P. Murrah Federal Building in the heart of Oklahoma City had a cheerful face. Across the front, just above the entrance and behind a floor-to-ceiling tinted-glass façade, was the America's Kids child-care center. Some of the children belonged to the more than 500 men and women who worked in the 18-year-old glass-and-granite-clad building.

At around six on the morning of April 19, 1995, the area around the building began to come alive as hundreds of people from central Oklahoma—either workers or those with government business—converged on the downtown area. Among those heading toward the building that day was a man driving a large yellow truck, its sides emblazoned with the black-lettered logo Ryder.

Shortly before 9 a.m. the man pulled the yellow truck up to a parking spot on the street in front of the Murrah Building. The truck was just east of the center of the north-facing building. Thirty feet away the children of the America's Kids child-care center were playing.

Shortly before 9 a.m. the man pulled the yellow truck up to a parking spot on the street in front of the Murrah Building.

Inside the 20-foot truck were 4,800 pounds of a ghoulish, volatile mixture of diesel fuel oil and gray ammonium nitrate fertilizer, which filled as many as two dozen 55-gallon blue plastic barrels. The entire truck was a lethal bomb.

Just a few minutes before 9 a.m., the man lit the fuse and walked away. In the daycare center, the smallest children had just been placed in their cribs to settle down for naps. The older children sang their favorite songs and had free time to play.

At 9:02 a.m., in the cargo area of the yellow truck, the fuse burned down to the detonator. The 4,800 pounds of explosive witch's brew packed in the blue plastic drums exploded. Searing gasses shot from the bomb at 6,500 feet per second—virtually vaporizing the truck and creating a wave of scorching heat that enveloped the building and spread destruction across a two-block radius.

The fireball that hit the Murrah Building seven-thousandths of a second after detonation put 1,000 pounds of pressure on every square inch of the building's surface. It lifted all nine floors upward, shearing off the connecting steel reinforcing bars (called "rebar") and demolishing three of the building's major support columns. In violent undulations, whole floors were ripped loose from their moorings. Then, yielding to gravity, the floors collapsed, sandwiching together and funneling thousands of tons of debris down toward a giant crater blasted out by the bomb.

A few minutes after the blast, a breeze lifted the smoke and dust, and sunlight flooded the groaning carcass that the Murrah Building had become. Within minutes, a rallying cry spread through the confusion: the child-care center. It was unspoken that those children were the highest priority for rescue. With sirens drowning out the crescendo of screams, rescuers by the hundreds began to arrive. They struggled into the jagged heaps of rubble, seeking America's Kids on the second floor.

But soon they realized there was no child-care center. There was no second floor.

One of the first into the building was Det. Sgt. Don Hull of the Oklahoma City Police Department. He and fellow officers crawled through mazes of twisted rebar and shifting concrete slabs. The air was so thick with dust that rescuers—many of them, like Hull, dressed in business suits with no special equipment—were forced to take breaths as shallow as possible.

Early on, Hull saw a baby in the rubble he thought to be dead. A massive gash marked the side of its face, but there was no blood—and no movement. The baby's arm was twisted around so grotesquely—nearly wrung off—that bone protruded from the bicep.

For some reason Hull stopped just a moment to pick up the dead baby and straighten out its arm. "I heard a huge gasp," Hull says. "And blood burst from the wounds as if jostling the body somehow started the heart going."

Hull pressed the infant against his chest, holding the mangled arm in place, and began crawling upward through the heavy rubble. He and his fellow officers had been handing off living victims in a sort of bucket-brigade to the outside. But Hull was afraid the baby's arm would fall off if he did that. So he struggled on.

When the baby stopped gasping, Hull began to administer rudimentary CPR, breathing into the child's mouth and nose. This happened twice on the way out. As Hull broke from the building and headed for the closest triage area, he found himself screaming over and over, "Breathe, baby, breathe!"

As he reached an ambulance, Hull saw a couple running toward him—the woman screaming that it was her baby in his arms. Hull swiveled away, not letting them see the child. "I couldn't let them look," he says. "It was too horrible. The baby probably wasn't going to make it, and I didn't want that to be the last sight they had."

"Hold the arm tight!" he yelled to a paramedic, finally handing the baby off.

It was 9:30 a.m. and Hull, like so many others, would be there for hours—until he quit from exhaustion.

The initial response of local medical teams was as impressive as that of the police, fire and rescue units. Melissa Webster, a manager at an ambulance service, was at the scene with an ambulance 90 seconds after the blast. Fearing that her own trembling building was about to collapse, she had fled from her desk to the street and had seen the black smoke rising six blocks to the south. She and a colleague leapt into an ambulance with six other paramedics.

Within an hour, her paramedics—only one team of dozens—had sent more than 200 injured people to hospitals and managed to treat hundreds of others. By then, all the company's ambulances had arrived, and they were loading as many as five injured people into each vehicle.

Eventually Melissa Webster came face to face with the worst dilemma to confront paramedics in triage. A young woman lay before her with terrible neck and head injuries. "She's not breathing," said one of Melissa's associates. "You'll have to call her," meaning that Melissa needed to tag her as too far gone to help so they could move on to assisting people with better chances for survival.

Melissa felt for the woman's pulse. She wasn't breathing at all, but her heartbeat was strong. Melissa knew at that moment she could not "call" her. "Her pulse is as strong as mine," she said. She would see that the woman was given a chance.

"Put her in the ambulance and get her on a ventilator," Melissa told a colleague. She turned to minister to others. Quietly, a few days later,

Melissa checked on the young woman she had refused to declare dead. The woman had horrendous injuries that would take months to heal. But she was alive and would get well.

*   *   *

Priscilla Salyers, an investigative assistant for the Customs Service located on the fifth floor, had been talking to her boss at 9:02 a.m. when a thunderous gale-force roar of wind whooshed past her head. Then silence. And blackness. Priscilla tried to move but could not. She sensed a tremendous pressure. Something seemed to be crushing her head.

I'm having a seizure, she thought. *Is it a stroke? Am I paralyzed?*

But her mind was too clear, she thought, to have had a stroke or heart attack. *If I can just get my head up off my desk.*

Nothing. Priscilla realized there was little she could move except for her left wrist and hand. Her mouth was filled with earthy-tasting powder. There was a powerful pressure on her head from something that seemed to be slowly crushing her skull.

She was face down with her rump higher than her head, which was twisted to her right. Her right arm was pinned under her and her left arm splayed outward. With the fingers of her left hand, Priscilla began trying to dig into the dirtlike substance of the powdered concrete. She also began to pray for God to give her the strength to survive.

Oddly, her most immediate annoyance was a piece of chewing gum in her mouth that had become an irritant. The gum was infused with a foul grit, and Priscilla desperately wanted to get rid of it. But her mouth and jaw were so tightly constricted that it was impossible for her to spit it out. It was all she could do to breathe.

About 30 minutes into her entombment, Priscilla heard the far-off voices of men. Then, suddenly, close by, she heard a man speak sharply: "Okay, this is the day-care center. We have a lot of children in here."

Priscilla tried to speak, to scream, to let the man know she was there. But she couldn't make her mouth work. Priscilla's greatest terror was that the crushing pressure on her head was becoming greater and greater. She prayed for calm and wisdom, realizing that if the men began working on top of her it could push the pressure on her head to a breaking point. She also wondered why the men thought they were at the day-care center, three stories below her office.

But then the voices were gone. Eerie silence returned. Her breath was coming much faster now, and she began to feel sleepy: *But I've got to pick up Josh at school, so I need to stay awake to do that.* She fought the urge to sleep.

Priscilla had continued to rotate her left arm and hand. She prayed that her hand was visible and that she would be able to wave it if she again heard voices.

Suddenly, she heard a shout off to her left: "Hey! Here's a live one!"

Then Priscilla felt someone take her left hand and hold it and rub it. Her muscles first went limp with joy and relief—then she squeezed the hand as hard as she could. When the man asked her name, she summoned all of her strength to say: "Priscilla!"

The man realized how hard it was for her to talk, so he did most of the talking—the sound of his voice flowing into her brain like a glorious symphony.

Priscilla indicated to the man she didn't know what had happened. "The building blew up," he said. "We don't know why, but we're checking it out." By this time, others had crawled into the cramped, cave-like area to remove the rubble piece by piece. At every moment, someone held Priscilla's hand.

Then, as her hope rose, the man holding her hand spoke gently: "Priscilla, we're going to have to leave now. We'll be back, but we have to go get a tool." What he did not say was that rescuers were being evacuated because of a bomb threat.

She gripped the man's hand with all her might and found new breath as she begged him not to leave, wondering why they all had to go. She wouldn't release the man's hand. She felt him gently pry her fingers loose. "I'm so sorry," he said, his voice cracking. "We don't have any choice. We'll be back. I promise." Then they were gone, and Priscilla was alone in the terrible silence.

Her first reaction was a mixture of terror and anger. Because of the rubble that had been removed, her body was not as tightly constricted—though her head was still in a viselike grip.

As she writhed, she realized there was something poking her in the stomach. She worked her hand around so that she could feel the protrusion. It was a hand—a man's hand, judging by its size. Her heart leapt, thinking it was her colleague Paul Ice and that perhaps he was in the same situation. She squeezed the hand, but it was cold and unresponsive. For the first time, she began to weep.

Then, out of nowhere, a loud voice boomed: "Hey, over here!" The scene was just like the first time—though the voices were different. A man took her hand and she squeezed back.

"Get me out of here," she pleaded. Then she closed her eyes and waited and prayed. The men explained each step they took—the most dangerous one being to remove a massive metal and concrete column virtually resting on her head. It was a miracle that it had not slipped a single inch more. Above her were the awful sounds of circular saws and pneumatic tools. The rescuers worked fast, knowing that any instant the groaning building might shift at this location.

Priscilla's legs and body were freed first and then both arms. The rescuers told her the hardest part would be last—getting her tightly pinned head free by trying to lift the monstrous column crushing her and, at the same moment, whisking her out from under it.

What if something slips? Priscilla thought. For the first time she realized with horror what could happen.

But before another thought could pass through her mind, the column rose a fraction of an inch. At that instant, a man dragged her free and flipped her onto her back. Terrible pain exploded in her—she had broken ribs, a collapsed lung and countless nasty puncture wounds all over her body. Four hours and 15 minutes had passed since the bomb exploded.

Capt. Randy Norfleet, a 29-year-old Marine pilot who had flown 35 combat missions in Operation Desert Storm and was now in charge of recruiting Marine officers in Oklahoma and Kansas, had made a rare visit to the main office that morning. He needed to speak to some of his colleagues and to make a few business calls, so he had driven to the Murrah Building, parked in front of a big yellow Ryder truck and went up to the sixth floor.

As the fire in the fuse inched closer to the detonator, Norfleet walked toward a desk with a telephone to make his call, but Capt. Randolph Guzman was already on the phone. At the instant of the explosion, Norfleet was hurled against a wall with the force of a hurricane. With quickly fading eyesight he saw that he had landed about five feet from where the front of the building was sheared off. Then everything started to go black.

When Randy put his hand to his head, he could feel what he knew was a severed artery pulsing from his mangled right eye. The blood pouring from his face distracted him from noticing that flying glass had also severed arteries in his arm and wrist. He was quickly weakening.

He knew that he could not wait for rescuers but needed to risk everything to get out of the building and get medical help.

But as Randy's strength ebbed, a powerful instinct came over him. He knew that he could not wait for rescuers but needed to risk everything to get out of the building and get medical help. To wait, he sensed, would be fatal.

Someone clamped a T-shirt to his eye socket to staunch the flow. With others helping him, he dragged himself toward a rear stairwell, fighting through rubble clouded with thick dust, and staggered down six floors, where he collapsed into the hands of paramedics. When he reached the hospital, he learned he had lost 50 percent of his blood volume. After more than five hours of surgery and 280 stitches, Randy Norfleet survived—though he will never again be able to serve as a pilot.

Five days later, six floors down, rescuers found the body of Capt. Randolph Guzman. As rescuers gently removed the rubble from around him, they realized the officer was still seated in his chair at his desk—the very chair and desk Captain Norfleet had been waiting to use.

* * *

Hope for the others rose from the ghastly ruins of the Murrah Building that first day when hundreds of people were listed simply as missing. In the absence of solid information, people grasped at whatever they could find for sustenance.

One of those missing was Michael Loudenslager, 48, who was in his office at the General Services Administration on the first floor when the bomb exploded. For two days, his wife, Bettie, and their two children heard nothing. But their hopes brightened when one of Michael's friends, recuperating from terrible injuries, told a remarkable story.

Randy Ledger, 38, was also on the first floor at the time of the explosion. He was buried under the rubble, and blood poured from his slashed throat. As he lay there, bleeding to death, he heard the distinctively gruff, husky voice of his friend: "Don't worry, guy," Michael Loudenslager boomed. "I see you and I'm going to get help." When rescue workers found Randy, they clawed the rubble from his body. Paramedics rushed to stop the gushing blood and carried him away.

Only minutes from death, Randy reached the hospital and began a slow recovery from a severed artery and vein in his neck. Although he could not speak at first and communicated only by notes, he was able to let people know that it was Mike Loudenslager who had found him. He was certainly alive.

Days later, though, Loudenslager's body was recovered—crushed beneath a huge concrete block deep inside the building, far from the spot where he had last seen his friend. Apparently he had gone farther in to help get someone else. "That's the kind of guy he was," Randy Ledger says.

*　*　*

In the hospital, Priscilla Salyers's joy over being alive was muted as she wondered about the fates of co-workers—especially her friend Paul Ice. Several members of Ice's family brought good news to Priscilla's bedside. Paul's name was on the big board in the hospital lobby of patients who had been treated for minor injuries and released.

"Paul Ice is such an unusual name," they assured each other. "It has to be our Paul."

But Paul did not show up. Days later, Special Agent Paul Ice's crushed body was pulled from the building. Incredibly there was another Paul Ice injured in the explosion that day. It was he who had been treated and released.

Search-and-rescue crews attend a memorial service in front of the Alfred P. Murrah Federal Building in Oklahoma City.

Priscilla Salyers has now recovered. She says she sees her life as a clean slate, and small problems never bother her anymore. Why is she alive while Paul Ice, inches away at the moment of the explosion, is dead?

"There are no answers," Priscilla says. "And God doesn't owe us any. It is up to us to have faith that somehow everything is in his plan."

Even those not physically touched by the disaster will feel its effects for the rest of their lives. When Det. Don Hull went home to rest after spending seven hours at the Murrah Building, he felt he had to keep active. He dreaded what he would see if he let sleep take control of his mind. Images more awful than any nightmare he could imagine kept coming to mind. "As long as I kept my eyes open, I could control what I was seeing," he says.

Most of the people he had seen in the building had been dead or dying. But one of his most haunting images was of the child he had shielded from the distraught couple.

With their daughters, seven and three, in bed, Jill and Don collapsed in front of the television set to catch up on the larger story of the bombing. One late-night news report said most of the children in the child-care center were presumed to be dead; then it showed a very brief interview with one parent whose child had emerged alive from the blast.

Don Hull grabbed his wife's hand. "I know that guy. I pulled his baby out!" Hull had been told the baby had died, but the man on TV seemed to be hopeful about his child's chances, and then the interview was over.

At once, Don called the hospital, and an operator put him through to the waiting room where Dan and Dawn Webber were keeping vigil over their son Joseph. Don Hull wanted to know how the child was.

Dan Webber confirmed they were the parents he shielded from seeing the baby. Webber explained that the boy was in grave condition but that doctors thought he had a chance. "There's no way our son would be alive if you hadn't gotten him out," Webber told Hull.

*   *   *

Thirteen hours after the explosion, the last survivor was pulled from the building. Search-and-rescue operations continued for 16 days, before the building was turned over to investigators. On May 23 less than 200 pounds of dynamite were used to crumble the remains of the Murrah Building into a heap of rubble.

Originally published in the May 1996 issue of *Reader's Digest* magazine.

In all, 168 people died in the Oklahoma City bombing, which to this day is the biggest act of terrorism ever carried out on American soil by an American citizen. Exactly five years after the explosion, President Clinton dedicated the Oklahoma City National Memorial Museum on the site of the Murrah Building. Its centerpiece is the Survivor Tree, an American elm that stood 150 feet from the explosion yet survived—and continues to grow to this day. A Survivor Tree offspring is also growing on the lawn of the White House.

YOU JUST NEVER KNOW

After WWI, many of our soldiers returned home with war
brides. My Aunt Maggie's mother was one of them. She came
from France and taught French lessons privately to area
children. Sometimes my Aunt Maggie (Madeline by birth)
would play with one student while her mother was busy with
the sibling. One morning John was free to play while his
brother Joseph had his lesson. The game was hide and seek,
and my aunt was "it." John found a splendid hiding place in
a kitchen cupboard. My aunt, having home field advantage,
realized where he was and shut the door, trapping him. There
he stayed until Madeline's mother came looking for him and
heard tapping and a little voice calling "Madame? Madame?"
Years later my aunt watched John Fitzgerald Kennedy take the
oath of office. "Oh," she gasped. "I locked the President of
the United States under the kitchen sink!"

—Judy Paton *Cascade, Montana*

MUST HAVE TUNES

When I rescued a piano from an old house, I had not
considered I would need assistance moving it from the back
of my pickup truck and into my home. Consequently, I had to
drive with it there for several days until help arrived. Finally, a
CHP officer pulled me over. He had seen me before and asked
why I was driving around with a piano in my truck bed. I told
him that my car radio had broken and I couldn't afford a new
one. He laughed and let me go without a ticket.

—Pepper Rae *Crockett, California*

Thank You for Caring So Much

by Peter DeMarco, from the *New York Times*

After his wife suffered a devastating asthma attack at age 34, a grateful man wrote an open letter to her medical team.

As I begin to tell my friends and family about the seven days you treated my wife, Laura Levis, in what turned out to be the last days of her young life, they stop me at about the 15th name that I recall. The list includes the doctors, nurses, respiratory specialists, social workers, and even cleaning staff members who cared for her.

"How do you remember any of their names?" they ask.

"How could I not?" I respond.

Every single one of you treated Laura with such professionalism and kindness and dignity as she lay unconscious. When she needed shots, you apologized that it was going to hurt a little, whether or not she could hear. When you listened to her heart and lungs through your stethoscopes and her gown began to slip, you pulled it up to respectfully cover her. You spread a blanket not only when her body temperature needed regulating but also when the room was just a little cold and you thought she'd sleep more comfortably that way.

You cared so greatly for her parents, helping them climb into the room's awkward recliner, fetching them fresh water almost by the hour, and answering every one of their medical questions with incredible patience. My father-in-law, a doctor himself, as you learned, felt he was involved in her care. I can't tell you how important that was to him.

Then there was how you treated me. How would I have found the strength to make it through that week without you? How many times did you walk into the room to find me sobbing, my head down and resting on her hand, and quietly go about your task, as if willing yourselves invisible? How many times did you help me set up the recliner as close as possible to her bedside, crawling into the mess of wires and tubes in order to swing her forward just a few feet?

How many times did you check on me to see whether I needed anything, from food to drink, from fresh clothes to a hot shower, or to see whether I needed a better explanation of a medical procedure or just someone to talk to?

How many times did you hug me and console me when I fell to pieces, or ask about Laura's life and the person she was, taking the time to look at her photos or read the things I'd written about her? How many times did you deliver bad news with compassionate words and sadness in your eyes?

When I needed to use a computer for an emergency e-mail, you made it happen. When I smuggled in a very special visitor, our tuxedo cat, Cola, for one final lick of Laura's face, you "didn't see a thing."

And one special evening, you gave me full control to usher into the ICU more than 50 people in Laura's life, from friends to coworkers to college alums to family members. It was an outpouring of love that included guitar playing and opera singing and dancing and new revelations to me about just how deeply my wife touched people. It was the last great night of our marriage together, for both of us, and it wouldn't have happened without your support.

There is another moment—actually, a single hour—that I will never forget.

On the final day, as we waited for Laura's organ-donor surgery, all I wanted was to be alone with her. But family and friends kept coming to say their goodbyes, and the clock ticked away. By about 4 p.m., finally, everyone had gone, and I was emotionally and physically exhausted, in need of a nap. So I asked her nurses, Donna and Jen, if they could help me set up the recliner, which was so uncomfortable but all I had, next to Laura again. They had a better idea.

The author and his wife, hiking in Scotland

They asked me to leave the room for a moment, and when I returned, they had shifted Laura to the right side of her bed, leaving just enough room for me to crawl in with her one last time. I asked if they could give us one hour without a single interruption, and they nodded, closing the curtains and the doors and shutting off the lights.

I nestled my body against hers. She looked so beautiful, and I told her so, stroking her hair and face. Pulling her gown down slightly, I kissed her breasts and laid my head on her chest, feeling it rise and fall with each breath, her heartbeat in my ear. It was our last tender moment as a husband and a wife, and it was more natural and pure and comforting than anything I'd ever felt. And then I fell asleep.

I will remember that last hour together for the rest of my life. It was a gift beyond gifts, and I have Donna and Jen to thank for it.

Really, I have all of you to thank for it.

With my eternal gratitude and love,

Peter DeMarco

Originally published in the November 2017 issue of *Reader's Digest* magazine.

Humor Hall of Fame

"New system: Guess how many jelly beans."

My sister-in-law was teaching Sunday-school class. The topic for the day: Easter Sunday and the resurrection of Christ. "What did Jesus do on this day?" she asked. There was no response, so she gave her students a hint: "It starts with the letter R." One boy blurted, "Recycle!"

—MARI-LYNN FINLEYN,
RD READER

After a flood damaged their home, my aunt and uncle were forced to stay with friends. One Sunday, as everyone got ready for church, my uncle borrowed a suit from his host. The pants were too big, so my uncle said, "I'm going to also need a belt." His humorless hostess shot back, "We do not drink before church."

—BARBARA GAVLICK HARTNETT
SWOYERSVILLE, PENNSYLVANIA

Our two-year-old, Tess, was sitting quietly in church one Sunday when she became mesmerized by a balding man seated in front. Her curiosity got the better of her, and she shouted for all to hear, "Why is that man's head coming out of his hair?"

—JOAN ANASTASI, RD READER

During evening prayers, my five-year-old kept his uncle in his thoughts: "Please help Uncle Steve find a job that he's good at, like owning a cat."

—SANDI ROWE
NAMPA, IDAHO

Cartoon by Bill Thomas

"Three wise men radioed in to say the enemy can now see us."

At our weekly Bible study, the leader asked an elderly gentleman, Walt, to open the meeting with prayer. Walt did so in a soft voice. Another man, straining to hear, shouted, "I can't hear you!" Walt replied, "I wasn't talking to you."

—RICHARD STEUSSY
NOVATO, CALIFORNIA

We ran into our minister at the mall, but my son couldn't place him. It was only later that it hit him. "I know that man," he said. "He goes to our church."

—CHARLES STOCKHAUSEN ST. LOUIS, MISSOURI

At the Bottom of the Bay

by Anita Bartholomew

The car plunged off the bridge.
A little boy was trapped.

It was the kind of silky, warm November day that only happens in Florida. Pearly skies and clear vistas. The dark blue waters of Tampa Bay and the cleanly etched skyline of the city stood out as Amira Jakupovic and her family drove north across the Howard Frankland Bridge.

Now U.S. citizens, they had moved from Europe to St. Petersburg, Florida, six years earlier. Today they were on their way to lunch with relatives in Tampa.

Trim and fit, Amira could have passed for a teenager. Her husband, Mujo, an amateur soccer player, was in the front passenger's seat of their green Ford Explorer, and their two boys, Amar, 7, and Emrah, 13, were in the back. The younger boy had fallen asleep.

Traffic was light. As they approached the end of the bridge, there was a sound like a gunshot. The back left tire had blown out. The SUV, traveling at about 55 miles per hour, skated wildly across the reinforced concrete roadway. The car slammed into the left cement guardrail and careened across all four northbound lanes—spinning and rolling over several times, crushing the roof. It finally hit the highway barrier on the right, then, in a single vault, went over the rail and plummeted into the dark bay below.

*   *   *

Kerry Reardon knew the waters around Tampa and St. Petersburg as well as the snook and spotted sea trout. He was an engineer and an avid fisherman. Once, while crabbing with his wife and kids, he'd even hauled in a blacktip shark ("a little four-footer," he says, but big enough to take a kid's hand off).

This Saturday, Reardon had planned to compete in a fishing tournament, but he and his teammates hadn't caught enough bait and finally dropped out. That meant Reardon had the afternoon free to take his 15-year-old daughter, Kara, out for a driving lesson.

Out on the road, Reardon expected Kara to turn right, toward St. Petersburg's spectacular Sunshine Skyway Bridge. But on a whim, the young driver turned left instead, toward Tampa across the three-mile-long Frankland Bridge. When they were almost over, the traffic began to slow, then creep along.

"Dad, there's a backup," Kara said.

"Get used to it," Reardon joked.

Locals call the bridge the Frankenstein, due to its horrendous traffic snarls.

Then Reardon noticed a half-dozen or more people standing at the bridge's barrier, staring into the water. Glittering bits of glass covered the pavement, and there were skid marks across three lanes. This was not one of Frankenstein's usual jams, Reardon realized. Someone must have gone over the side.

*   *   *

Amira had blacked out. Chill salt water revived her. Frantically, she looked all about. Her long brown hair swirled in the water. In the murk, she saw a hint of blue and white—letters on the shirt her older boy, Emrah, was wearing. She reached out and grabbed the cloth. With her other hand, she searched for the door, a window, any way out. All the glass had blown away in the SUV's tumble across the bridge. Amira pulled Emrah to her and swam out the driver's-side window. The two struggled to the surface.

But her husband and their younger child were still below.

Taking a breath, Amira saw the blue prow of a fishing boat coming straight toward them. It slowed, and someone leaned over the side to take her son out of her arms.

Kerry Reardon and officer Luis Vasquez, on a police dive boat near the "Frankenstein" bridge.

Amira dived immediately, searching for the wreck. She found the car, but she couldn't get in and was forced to come up for a breath of air. She dived again. This time, she couldn't locate the SUV in the swirling, silt-laden water.

Surfacing a second time, she saw that her husband had made it out. Together they dived, hunting for their younger son—but it was as if the bay had swallowed the SUV and the child with it.

* * *

"Pull over, pull over," Reardon said to Kara. She did as her father told her. He bolted out of the car and looked over the edge. A charter fishing boat idled by the bridge. Reardon could see that the boat captain had already pulled three people out of the water: a man, a woman and a teenage boy. Soaked and frantic, the woman was screaming and crying.

Reardon yelled down to the boat, "Is there anyone left in the car?"

The answer chilled him—a child.

He hurried to his car, dropped his keys, wallet and shoes on the passenger's seat. Dressed in just his cutoff jeans and a T-shirt, he started back. "Lock the doors," he told his daughter. "I'll be back soon."

Reardon knew that the current around bridge supports is sharp and tricky, because it runs through narrow gaps. The swift water stirs up the silty bottom, so you often find yourself with only a foot of visibility. Even with a mask and fins, most people get lost in seconds.

Scanning the water, Reardon saw a stream of bubbles rising to the surface. There! That's where the car was. He climbed on top of the cement guardrail and dived off headfirst.

Kelli Earle liked to drive with all the windows open, letting the bay breeze play with her hair. The 25-year-old registered nurse had a baby shower to attend. She was on her way to pick up panini and other party sandwiches for the luncheon.

Suddenly, brake lights ahead of her glared red, and cars began shifting to the left lanes. Earle pulled to the right, stopped, got out of her car and walked over to the edge, where a group had gathered.

Glancing over the side, she saw a woman, a man and a kid being pulled out of the sea and into an idling boat. The woman was looking back into the water, screaming, "My son, my son."

A minute later, Earle noticed someone in cutoff jeans diving off the concrete barrier and into the bay. After the man hit the surface, 19 feet below, a lone soccer shoe popped up and bobbed along in the water.

The moment Reardon was underwater, he felt the current sweeping through the bridge's understructure, tugging him along. He plunged to the bay floor, where he knew the current would ease up. And if he'd estimated correctly, he'd be somewhere near the submerged vehicle.

He was almost on top of the SUV before detecting the hulking shape. He didn't want to leave without finding the boy, but his lungs were close to bursting. He had to surface.

Fearing he'd lose track of the car's position, he headed upstream, against the current. He hoped that when he descended again, the flow would carry him back to the car. He gulped air and quickly dived back down.

Reardon reached out to touch the car and skimmed along it, feeling for the door. He found the driver's-side window, already broken from the crash. Crawling through, he didn't see the boy at first. He shimmied into the backseat. Reardon was almost nose-to-nose with the child before he saw dark, unblinking eyes staring back.

The boy was still securely locked by his seat belt. Reardon groped for the buckle, touched the cold metal and snapped it open. He grabbed the front of the boy's shirt. The little, limp frame moved almost weightlessly with him. Reardon maneuvered him through the window, then kicked for the surface. Was he bringing up a dead boy?

When Kelli Earle saw the man in cutoff jeans resurface, carrying a small body, she kicked off her flip-flops, jumped in feetfirst and swam to the fishing boat. "I'm a nurse," she said. "Let me help." One of the men on the boat pulled her aboard.

She went to little Amar, tilted his head back to clear his airway, gave him two rescue breaths and then checked his pulse. His heart had stopped beating. His pupils were dilated. His skin was deathly pale, his lips blue.

The bay water was cool, but probably not cold enough to help preserve brain function as icy water sometimes does. The boy needed air—and fast. Earle began CPR. With each compression, fluid from the child's lungs and stomach spewed out onto her. The rocking boat didn't make the procedure any easier. And the boy's terrified mother grasped Earle, clawing at her. "Help him. Please, help him."

Earle ignored her and tried to stay focused. "Get us to land," she called to the boat captain.

A police officer met the boat and joined Earle in doing CPR. He compressed the boy's chest, while Earle blew air into his mouth. They kept up the rhythm, minute after minute—on a completely unresponsive body. Finally an ambulance arrived.

EMTs laid Amar on a stretcher and hooked him up to their equipment. They covered the child's nose and mouth with an oxygen mask that could be hand-pumped.

As the EMTs wheeled Amar into the ambulance, Earle checked his vital signs and turned to the distraught parents. "Do you pray?" she asked. The mother nodded.

"Now's the time," the nurse said.

* * *

Officer Luis Vasquez, the second policeman on the scene, accompanied Amar in the ambulance. A diver with the Tampa Police Department, Vasquez had pulled a number of children from the waters during his 17 years as a cop. None had survived.

It didn't look like this kid was going to either. Vasquez couldn't feel a pulse. It hurt like hell for the father of two to think he might lose another one. He kept up the compressions—he pressed, the EMT pumped air. Again and again. No response. Then he felt a faint movement against his hands. Was it the EMT pumping the oxygen out of sequence? He looked up and saw that wasn't so. "Did he just take a breath?" asked Vasquez.

"I don't think so," the EMT said.

But then, stunning them both, the child sucked in air a second time.

"He's breathing on his own," yelled the EMT. "Did you feel a heartbeat?"

"No," answered Vasquez, his hands still on Amar's chest. Then he did, the punch of the heart against his palm.

Vasquez knew Amar wasn't in the clear yet. He'd been underwater for five minutes, his heart had stopped, oxygen had stopped circulating through his body. If he survived, he would likely be brain-damaged.

* * *

At the hospital, doctors kept Amar on a ventilator and in an induced coma for ten days. Reardon, Earle and Vasquez came regularly to the intensive care unit to see the child and get progress reports. Would he live? And if he lived, would the little person who thought and played and had feelings survive? No one could say.

Amira stayed by her child night and day, rarely leaving his side. Doctors gradually lowered the oxygen to allow Amar to breathe on his own. Finally, on the tenth day, they decided to remove his breathing tube and rouse him from his coma. Hopefully, his youth would pull him through.

A raspy voice is the only residual effect Amar (No. 59 above, with family) has from his underwater ordeal.

It did. Two days later, he was sitting up in bed, playing Super Mario on a Game Boy, absorbed in digital adventures, oblivious of his own underwater odyssey.

A slightly raspy voice is the only residual effect Amar has. His father needed surgery on his leg, which he injured in the crash. He is recovering. Amira is fine, but Emrah suffers from lingering leg and back pain.

The Jakupovics are amazed and profoundly grateful that the right people, in the right order—diver, nurse, boat captain, police and EMTs—each one with the right skills, showed up in time to save their son.

Originally published in the January 2007 issue of *Reader's Digest* magazine.

The Jakupovic family still lives in St. Petersburg, Florida. Amar played football in high school. His older brother, Emrah, also made a complete recovery. He has a young daughter. The family stays in touch with rescuer Kerry Reardon.

Humor Hall of Fame

Tunisians, I've learned, are known for being generous with compliments. As I walked along the harbor with my husband one day, a Tunisian man shouted to him, "Hey, you a very lucky man! Your woman has big legs!" I could have done without such flattery.

—TRAVELMATCH.CO.UK

S.P.F. 1,000

WEYANT

Cartoon by Chris Weyant

Throughout our tour of an early American bathhouse in Hot Springs, Arkansas, I explained to my four-year-old grandson what people once did there. When we came upon a mannequin at a desk, I told him, "She was probably writing a letter home to her friends telling them about her vacation to Hot Springs." My grandson asked, "And then she died and they stuffed her?"

—CYNTHIA FRANKLIN
GRENADA, MISSISSIPPI

On our way to go spelunking, we got lost on a country road. We stopped to ask a farmer, "Is this the road to Waynesville?" "Yes, it is," he replied. As we started to drive off, we barely heard him add, "But you're going the wrong way."

—DOUG HISSONG
CYPRESS, TEXAS

Life on the Funny Farm

by Laura Cunningham,
condensed from the *New York Times Magazine*

Sometimes dreams are better left in bed.

My **husband and I** had always dreamed of raising our own food. Before purchasing our farm, I imagined I would pass platters of young vegetables across our table, along with the modest message "Our own." But today the two of us stagger, lugging 50-pound sacks of chow to a crowd of 45 fat animals who do little but exist in a digestive trance. How did I, a city person, get stuck running a salad bar for useless creatures?

We began with "our own" garden, a disaster from which we learned nothing. After a season of rototilling, fertilizing, fencing and back-dislocating labor, we produced "the $700 tomato." It was a good tomato—spared by the groundhogs who left their dental impressions on all the others.

The goats came next. We had always loved goat cheese and imagined a few dainty dairy goats would supply us with chèvre or feta whilst cavorting as adorable pets. Thus, I accepted delivery of two demented goat sisters, Lulu and Lulubelle.

While I knew goats didn't simply extrude neat white logs of Montrachet, I had not known that the "goat person" must become involved with milking platforms, teat problems and, most significantly, sexual liaisons. Goats won't give milk unless they have been mated, and in our town the only billy around was Bucky, a horned and whiskered creature with an odor that seemed visible. On his initial conjugal visit, he and "the girls" kicked up such a fuss that they did $2,000 worth of damage to the barn before eating the windowsills. The romance was canceled.

Lulu and Lulubelle now occasionally entertain us with a goat frolic on our front lawn, banging heads and performing a few choreographed moves that recall some Dionysian rite. But most of the time, the girls simply munch and relieve themselves.

Next came the dream of fresh eggs, gathered warm in the mornings—a dream that gave way to the reality of 38 irritable Rhode Island Red hens. After several hundred dollars' worth of chicken feed, there was, one morning, an egg—brown, silky and warm—under the hen who almost took my hand off when I reached for it.

Hens, I soon learned, are cranky creatures. Even the rooster has let us down. We expected him to wake us with his proud crow. But on the Phony Farm (as we call our spread), the rooster must be shaken awake at noon.

With the chickens came the geese, who make the least sense of all. We ordered them on impulse from the poultry catalogue when we read the listing: Toulouse goslings.

Goslings. The word had a nursery-rhyme appeal. But my five chartreuse-fuzzed baby geese soon quacked and snacked themselves into 20-pound fatties. For a time, I labored under the delusion they would fly south for the winter. I had seen a documentary, "The Incredible Flight of the Snow Geese," and thought of taping it on the VCR for my geese. But they fly about as well as I do—skidding a few feet down to their plastic kiddy swimming pool.

I became resigned to running a goose spa, but my husband had other ideas. "Christmas is coming and the goose is getting fat," he hissed with a Jack Nicholson glint in his eye. I was appalled. How could he consider roasting an animal that thought of me as Mother Goose?

The goslings had followed me to a nearby pond, where neighbors assured me I could relocate them ("Once they hit that water, they'll never leave"). But when I left, so did they—in single file. I turned around and saw them, their goony gray heads raised above the high grass, seeking only to walk in my footsteps.

The goslings had followed me to a nearby pond, where neighbors assured me I could relocate them.

I was touched. For life. Their fuzz gone, their voices raucous, the geese have become kind of repulsive pets. The only male, Arnold, has even goosed me when I turned my back on him. The bad news is, they can live to be over 30.

Today I buy my "farm-fresh fare." I pick up my goose from a prime meat market, and find "fresh laid" eggs and natural goat cheese at the fancy-food emporium. The eggs cost $2.50 a half-dozen, but they're still cheaper than my own eggs, which cost $300 each if you factor in things like henhouses.

But the best news is that I can roast a goose, baste it, enjoy the aroma and know: It's not Arnold. Arnold is out in the kiddy pool, having incestuous sex with his sisters.

Originally published in the September 1991 issue of *Reader's Digest* magazine.

Stopping a Kidnapper

by Alyssa Jung

A boy's bravery saves a little girl
from the unimaginable.

It **was a scene** Norman Rockwell might have painted: three kids laughing as they took turns riding a scooter on their quiet street. On a crisp December afternoon in Wichita Falls, Texas, 11-year-old TJ Smith had just jumped off the scooter as his neighbor Kim,* age 7, claimed her turn and her sister Julie,* 9, looked on. Kim straddled the scooter and paused to catch her breath. That was when the bearded man with a head of messy curls appeared. Without uttering a word, he picked Kim up off the scooter and calmly strode away.

"He cradled her like a baby and just walked down the street," says TJ. In fact, the composed way the man held Kim led TJ to believe he must have been a relative. But something wasn't right. "I could see her face," TJ said. "She was scared."

Kim began kicking and flailing, trying to get free of the man's grip. "What are you doing?" Julie shouted. But the man, unfazed, walked to an alley and disappeared.

TJ's first impulse was to chase after them. But what was a four-foot-tall, 70-pound kid going to do to stop a grown man? "I wanted to help, but I couldn't do it myself," he says. So he ran to his grown-up neighbors' home.

*Names have been changed to protect privacy.

Brad Ware and his wife were relaxing on the couch in their living room when their front door burst open.

"Brad!" yelled TJ. "A man just picked up a little girl and took her into the alley!"

And just like that, TJ was gone, back on the street sprinting after his abducted friend. "I ran back to see if they were still there," says TJ.

"Brad!" yelled TJ. "A man just picked up a little girl and took her into the alley!"

Ware and his wife jumped into their car and trailed close behind.

TJ ran to the end of the street and turned the corner. He had no idea what to expect or who might be waiting for him. But he needed to find Kim. If he lost her, TJ feared, she might never be found alive.

Once TJ hit the alley, he spotted the man a couple of blocks down, standing in front of an abandoned white house. He was shoving the panicked girl through a busted window.

Just then, Ware and his wife pulled up. "Stay here," Ware told TJ. With Ware now bearing down on him, the man let go of Kim in the window frame and walked away, almost nonchalantly, before breaking into a run. Ware caught up with him. They struggled. Ware kicked the man in the groin and wrapped him in his arms. The man squirmed free and fled across the street. When he stumbled, Ware lunged and tackled him.

Alerted by Julie, the police and the victim's mother arrived on the scene. Kim dashed into the safety of her mother's arms.

Meanwhile, officers cuffed and arrested Raeshawn Perez, 26. He was charged with aggravated kidnapping.

There were a few heroes that day, but Ware insists that the quick-thinking, dogged 11-year-old deserves most of the credit. "You know, he's the one who saved the girl," Ware told KFDX.

That news came as no surprise to TJ's mother. "This is exactly his character," says Angie Hess Smith. "His first thought is not of himself. It's always of others."

Originally published in the June 2017 issue of *Reader's Digest* magazine.

The Little Boat That Sailed Through Time

by Arnold Berwick

There is nothing for sale that can compete with what you make by hand with the guidance of your grandfather.

I spent the tenth summer of my childhood, the most memorable months of my life, in western Norway at the mountain farm where my mother was born. What remains most vivid to my mind are the times I shared with my Grandfather Jorgen.

The first thing I noticed about Grandfather was his thick, bushy mustache and broad shoulders. The second thing was how he could work. All summer I watched him. He mowed grass with wide sweeps of the scythe, raked it up and hung it on racks to dry. Later he gathered the hay in huge bundles tied with a rope, and carried them on his back, one after another, to the barn.

He sharpened the scythes on a grindstone, slaughtered a pig, caught and salted fish, ground barley in a water-driven gristmill and grew and stored potatoes. He had to produce enough in the short summer to carry the family and the animals through the long, snowbound winter. He stopped only long enough to eat and to sleep a few winks.

And yet he found time for just the two of us. One day after a trip to a faraway town, he handed me a knife and sheath, saying, "These are for you. Now watch."

With calloused hands, he showed me how to make a flute.

He slipped his own knife from its sheath, cut a thin, succulent branch from a tree and sat down beside me. With calloused hands, he showed me how to make a flute. Even today, 63 years later, whenever I hear the pure note of a flute I think of how he made music from nothing but a thin branch of a tree. Living on an isolated mountain farm, far from neighbors and stores, he had to make do with what he had.

As an American, I always thought people simply bought whatever they needed. Whether Grandfather knew this, I don't know. But it seems he wanted to teach me something, because one day he said, "Come. I have something for you."

I followed him into the basement, where he led me to a workbench by a window. "You should have a toy boat. You can sail it at Storvassdal," he said, referring to a small lake a few miles from the house.

Swell, I thought, looking around for the boat. But there was none.

Grandfather picked up a block of wood, about 18 inches long. "The boat is in there," he said. "You can bring it out." Then he handed me a razor-sharp ax.

I wasn't sure what to do, so Grandfather showed me how to handle the tool. I started to chop away to shape the bow. Later, after he taught me the proper use of hammer and chisel, I began to hollow out the hull.

Often Grandfather joined me in the basement, repairing homemade wooden rakes or sharpening tools. He answered my questions and made suggestions, but he saw to it I did all the work myself.

"It'll be a fine boat, and you'll be making it all with your own hands," he said. "No one can give you what you do for yourself." The words rang in my head as I worked.

Finally I finished the hull and made a mast and sail. The boat wasn't much to look at, but I was proud of what I had built.

Then, with my creation, I headed for Storvassdal. Climbing the mountain slope, I entered the woods and followed a steep path. I crossed tiny streams, trod on spongy moss and ascended slippery stone steps—higher, higher until I was above the timberline. After four or five miles, I came at last to a small lake that had been carved out by a glacier. Its sloping sides were covered with stones of all shapes and sizes.

I launched my boat and day-dreamed while a slight breeze carried the little craft to an opposite shore. The air was crisp and clean. There was no sound but the occasional warble of a bird.

I would return to the lake many times to sail my boat. One day dark clouds came in, burst open and poured sheets of rain. I pressed myself against a large boulder and felt its captured warmth. I thought of "Rock of Ages" (. . . let me hide myself in thee"). Through the rain, I saw my little boat pushing its way over the ripples. I imagined a ship bravely fighting a turbulent sea. Then the sun came out, and all was well again.

A crisis developed when we were ready to return to America. "You cannot bring that boat home with you," my mother said. We already had too much baggage.

I pleaded, but to no avail.

With saddened heart, I went to Storvassdal for the last time, found that large boulder, placed my boat in a hollow space under its base, piled stones to hide it and resolved to return one day to recover my treasure.

I said good-bye to my grandfather, not knowing I would never see him again. "Farewell," he said, as he clasped my hand tightly.

✳   ✳   ✳

In the summer of 1964, I went to Norway with my parents and my wife and children. One day I left the family farmhouse and hiked up to Storvassdal, looking for the large boulder. There were plenty around. My search seemed hopeless.

I was about to give up when I saw a pile of small stones jammed under a boulder. I slowly removed the stones and reached into the hollow space beneath the boulder. My hand touched something that moved. I pulled the boat out and held it in my hands. For 34 years it had been resting there, waiting for my return. The rough, bare-wood hull and mast were hardly touched by age; only the cloth sail had disintegrated.

I shall never forget that moment. As I cradled the boat, I felt my grandfather's presence. He had died 22 years before, and yet he was there. We three were together again—Grandfather and me and the little boat, the tangible link that bound us together.

I brought the boat back to the farm for the others to see and carved "1930" and "1964" on its side. Someone suggested I take it home to America. "No," I said. "Its home is under that boulder at Storvassdal." I took it back to its resting place.

I returned to the lake in 1968, 1971, 1977, and 1988. Each time as I held the little boat and carved the year on its side, my grandfather seemed near.

My last trip to Storvassdal was in 1991. This time I brought two of my granddaughters from America: Catherine, 13, and Claire, 12. As we climbed the mountain, I thought of my grandfather and compared his life with that of my granddaughters. Catherine and Claire are made of the same stuff as their ancestors. They are determined and independent—I see it in the way they carry themselves at work and play. And yet my grandfather seemed to have so little to work with, while my grand-daughters have so much.

Usually the things we dream of, then work and struggle for, are what we value the most. Have my granddaughters, blessed with abundance, been denied life's pleasures?

Working tirelessly on that isolated farm, my grandfather taught me that we should accept and be grateful for what we have—whether it be much or little. We must bear the burdens and relish the joys. There is so much we cannot control, but we must try to make things better when we are able. We must depend upon ourselves to make our own way as best we can.

Growing up in a comfortable suburban home, my granddaughters have been presented with a different situation. But I hope—I believe—they will in their own way be able to cope well as my grandfather coped, and learn the lesson my grandfather taught me all those years ago. On the day I took them to Storvassdal, I hoped they would somehow understand the importance of the little boat and its simple message of self-reliance.

High in the mountain, I hesitated to speak lest I disturb our tranquility. Then Claire looked up and broke my reverie as she said softly, "Grandpa, someday I'll come back." She paused. "And I'll bring my children."

Originally published in the May 1993 issue of *Reader's Digest* magazine.

A Jewel in the Pool

American Jessica Long (in the black suit, sitting next to her prostheses) gets a congratulatory hug from one of her teammates after winning the women's 200-meter individual medley at the 2016 Paralympics in Rio de Janeiro, Brazil. Long, 25, a double amputee who was born without bones in her lower legs and feet, competed in her first Paralympic Games at age 12 and came home with three gold medals. As the second-most-decorated U.S. Paralympian in history, she has become a world-champion hugger too.

Photograph by Buda Mendes/Getty Images

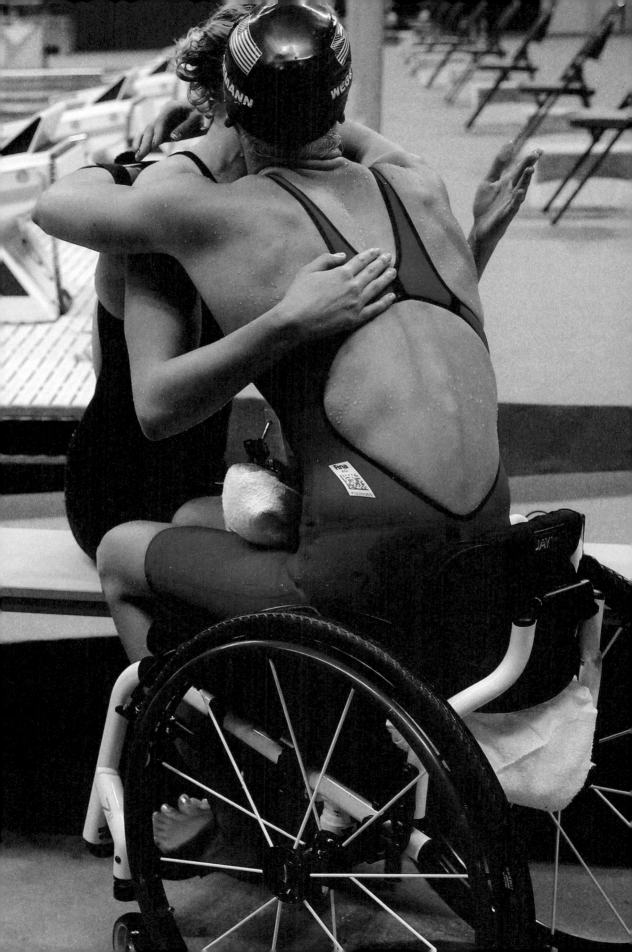

Buried in Mud

by Nick Heil

Michelle Grainger, husband Steve Le Goff, and their neighbors survived two days of raging floodwaters. It was what came next that almost killed them.

On a Wednesday evening, Michelle Grainger and her husband, Steve Le Goff, stood in a downpour in front of their two-story Victorian home, one of a handful of historic structures in the tiny hamlet of Salina, Colorado, a few miles west of Boulder. It had been raining for three days, and Gold Run Creek, the normally placid stream that flowed 40 feet from their home, had become a raging torrent.

"I think [the water] is going to reach the garage," said Steve, 51. Still, the couple believed they were well prepared for the rising stream. Ever since the Four Mile Canyon Fire in 2010, which had wiped out most of the trees and much of the vegetation in the foothills around Salina, authorities had warned of possible catastrophic flash flooding.

Steve and Michelle, 52, had listened and had stacked 2,000 sandbags around their property. They had strung safety line along the footpath switchbacking up the steep hill directly behind their house, in case they had to evacuate their home at night. Their backpacks were crammed with supplies. All they had to do was strap harnesses onto their two Rhodesian Ridgebacks, Lucy and Kayla, and put their two cats, Izzie and Sophie, into carriers, and they would be ready to bolt for high terrain.

Authorities were urging residents to do just that. Sections of the only road into and out of the narrow canyon were already underwater. If residents wanted to escape by car, this could be their last chance.

But Steve and Michelle hunkered down. They'd endured flooding before and expected to ride out this storm as well. It was one thing to prepare to leave and quite another to abandon your property and possessions.

They were worried, however, about their neighbors. Across the street, Russell Brockway, an 87-year-old fellow with a pacemaker, was staying put. Kay Cook and Doug Burger, retired English professors in their 70s who lived just up the road, were doing the same.

Eric Stevens, 48, and Michelle Wieber, 50, and their teenage sons, Colton and Caleb, lived next door. They had spent years restoring their 1875 log cabin and wouldn't leave it easily.

The creek continued to rise. By early afternoon, Steve and Michelle's sandbag barricade was underwater. The rising tide carried thick logs and refrigerator-size boulders that clogged the culverts and bridges. The crashing sounds from outside were so loud that the couple could hardly hear over them. They went outside once to try to trek up the hill to Cook and Burger's house but were cut off by dangerous waters.

Less than a half mile up the road, Brett Gibson, the Four Mile fire chief, sat in Salina's small fire station, talking on the phone with the emergency operations center in Boulder. During the day, Gibson, along with the other fire chiefs around the county, had realized that this was no ordinary storm. Flooding was not unheard of in the Colorado Front Range, but bad weather typically blew through in a few hours. This system was stubbornly parked overhead.

Around 10 p.m., Gibson took a call from the Emergency Operations Center (EOC). "This is the real s—," the dispatcher told him. "Tonight is going to be really, really bad."

"Most of my communication with EOC is quite formal," Gibson said later. "So I know when they start using profanity that we have a major situation on our hands."

Gibson immediately broadcast the fire department's most urgent warning to the locals, many of whom were equipped with weather radios: "Climb to higher ground immediately. Imminent threat to life and property. All residents should evacuate."

Still, Steve and Michelle stayed put. When they ventured outside the house early Thursday morning, the storm seemed to be easing. The raging creek had subsided slightly. They were relieved to find their garage intact, though nearby culverts and bridges that connected residents to the main road had been destroyed. The power was out, and the deafening noise from the creek still made communication difficult.

Steve and Michelle walked next door to the home of Eric and Michelle, and the families hatched a plan. Worst-case scenario, the six of them would take shelter in Eric and Michelle's guesthouse, which was nestled in the woods behind, 20 feet above the main house. Neither couple believed that the flood would swell to that height.

Up at the fire station, during a call with EOC at about 8:30 a.m., Gibson was informed that the weather lull was temporary. "All the data indicated that Thursday was going to be even worse," Gibson said. The National Weather Service, which rarely veered from drab, technical information in its statements, described the rainfall as "biblical."

Gibson worked diligently to orchestrate rescue efforts, but by now the full scope of the situation had been revealed: The flooding wasn't limited to a few canyons; it was spread across 14 counties. In Boulder County, the worst hit, Sheriff Joe Pelle declared a disaster, establishing an incident command center at the Boulder airport and queuing up resources, including two Black Hawk helicopters, several swift-water rescue teams, and dozens of search-and-rescue workers.

Steve and Michelle's neighbor Russell Brockway had ridden out the night in his tiny outhouse, perched 30 feet up the hill behind his cabin.

That morning, a few emergency personnel had arrived to evacuate some of the Salina residents, including the old-timer.

By late Thursday morning, the rain had begun to accelerate, and Gold Run Creek began to surge. What had moments earlier been heavy floodwaters now appeared to be a 20-foot-high wall of water, mud, and debris, sluicing through the canyon.

The surge plowed down the canyon, through the heart of Salina, ripping huge propane tanks from their foundations. The unhitched containers spun and hissed violently, filling the canyon with a pungent white haze. One-hundred-year-old trees snapped like toothpicks.

* * *

Farther down the canyon, Steve and Michelle, and Eric, Michelle, and the boys resorted to their last-ditch plan: take refuge in Eric and Michelle's guesthouse.

The two families piled into the small cottage that evening with another neighbor, Gurpreet Gil, and her cat. Steve, Michelle, Gurpreet, and the dogs and cats settled in the living room. Eric and Michelle climbed into the white wrought iron bed in the back of the cottage. The kids went upstairs to a small loft. The group planned to hike out in the morning to find help, tackling the long, steep trail that led to the ridge.

Steve and Michelle made themselves comfortable under blankets on the floor, their animals next to them. Michelle slept in her hiking boots and her parka, in case of an emergency.

Too nervous to sleep, Gurpreet stood in the doorway between the kitchen and the living room, monitoring the weather.

Around midnight, Steve heard "three loud crashes" and shot up. A massive mudslide had crushed the back wall of the cottage and was gushing into the bedroom where Eric and his wife slept. Steve heard screaming, but without power, during the howling storm, he didn't know from where.

The mud and water ripped through an interior wall. It picked Steve up and swept him toward the front of the house. As he approached a wall, he jammed his feet on either side of the entrance's doorframe and braced himself.

"I was 30 seconds from losing my wife," says Steve, with Michelle. "But I fought."

The mudslide then swept Michelle and Gurpreet and the five animals across the living room. The debris piled in the corner of the room before finally slamming out through the front wall of the house.

The animals were gone, buried, he assumed, in what was now four or five feet of mud inside the house. Apparently uninjured, Gurpreet stood in the kitchen. The boys had run halfway down the loft staircase and were shouting for their parents.

Water and mud continued to flow into the house, and Steve realized it had nowhere to go. He kicked at the front door until it burst open, providing some escape for the debris. Despite the chaos, a calm descended on him as he also felt an extraordinary physical strength. Free and seemingly uninjured, he began clawing at the dirt encasing his wife beneath him. She was buried up to her chest. "This is not how I want to die!" Michelle yelled.

"This is not how you're going to die," Steve shouted back. But the mud and debris might as well have been wet cement around the huge boulders. He sank his hands into the muck and tried to push away the debris. He had no sense of time. Finally, Steve was able to leverage the stones off his wife, freeing her upper torso.

Then he noticed a dog's leg sticking out of a pile of mud. He dug at the dirt and unearthed Kayla. Handing the dog over to his wife, Steve resumed digging around Michelle, who scooped mud out of Kayla's mouth. On impulse, she pressed her mouth against Kayla's and forced air into the animal's lungs. Again. Kayla's eyes flickered and opened. "She's alive!" Michelle screamed to Steve.

"OK. Help me dig," Steve said frantically. Michelle put Kayla down and started scraping at the mud that enclosed her legs. When she was free, she looked for Kayla, but the dog had disappeared.

In the bedroom, Eric had been buried up to his neck and entangled in the bedsheets. Muddy water flowed over him. As his wife held up his head to keep him from drowning, she yelled for the others.

She was buried up to her chest. "This is not how I want to die!" Michelle yelled.

Gurpreet had grabbed various kitchen utensils to dig with and passed them to Steve and Michelle. Many of the utensils merely broke in half. Meanwhile, the piles of debris had left just a few feet in which to move. Fearing that the structure could collapse entirely, Michelle Grainger took Colton and Caleb next door to Gurpreet's house, breaking a window to get in. Gurpreet managed to reach a 911 operator on her cell phone. The dispatcher told her that no one could reach them until daylight.

At the Gold Hill command post, Brett Gibson received word about the mudslide, but there was nothing he could do. "That was one of the worst nights I've ever had," he recalled. "These are my friends. But it would have been suicide to put a rescue team into those conditions."

Michelle ran up the trail behind her house and reached a neighbor's home where other Salina residents were taking shelter. Along the way, Kayla appeared, and then, amazingly, Lucy.

Buried in Mud

Michelle told her neighbors of the others' plight. One man followed Michelle back to the cottage to help dig Eric out of the mud. After three hours, the rescuers managed to free him. Finally, at 3 a.m., the ravaged survivors limped to the neighbor's safe house, where they drank soup, shivering in their soaked clothing. Later, Michelle would learn that she had suffered two broken ribs and a compression fracture in her back, the pain temporarily masked by the adrenaline coursing in her veins.

Between Wednesday night and Thursday night, nine inches of rain fell in and around Salina, twice the previous record. In all, the floods and mudslides resulted in billions of dollars' worth of damage and claimed eight lives—incredibly, none of them in Salina. On Friday morning, the storm at last abating, rescue efforts began in full force, including those of six helicopters operating continuously for four days.

Later on Friday, shaken and sore, Steve and Michelle hiked back to their house, which had survived the worst. Muck and silt covered their garage, but their preparations had paid off. As they inspected the guest-house where they'd almost lost their lives the night before, they found Sophie, her leg broken, under a pile of outdoor furniture. Only Izzie was still missing.

The next day, the remaining survivors were to fly from Salina to Boulder. Before leaving, Michelle and Steve made one last attempt to find Izzie. As they wandered into the woods behind the guesthouse, Michelle heard a faint meowing. As she called for Izzie, the meowing got louder. Finally, the cat burst from the woods and into Michelle's arms.

A few hours later, the couple hiked to a clearing where an Army Black Hawk awaited. Helicopters rarely evacuate animals, but that day the crew made an exception. With Michelle, Steve, the dogs, and the cats on board, the Black Hawk rose into the sky, torn clouds revealing the first peek of blue sky in more than a week. The helicopter flew over the ravaged canyons, carrying the survivors to Boulder, where their long recovery could begin.

Originally published in the April 2014 issue of *Reader's Digest* magazine.

I HAVE A SISTER

When I was six, as the younger sister of an autistic brother. I decided in a very child-like way that I would not be robbed of the "normal" sibling experience and therefore proclaimed to my mother, "I have a sister!" Her response? Crying. It turns out there actually was a sister who would have been exactly one year, one month and ten days older than me, had she not been stillborn. This rocked my previously death-free existence. I won't go into the years of survivor's guilt from being the "normal one," although to this day I still laugh when it comes up and say, "Me? Normal? So much for that one, Mom." When I was twelve, I met Marianne. My best friend and soul-sister. I will never forget the moment she told me her birth date. Exactly one year, one month and ten days before mine.

—Angela McGowan *Chattanooga, Tennessee*

25 FOR LIFE

My son-in-law Chuck snowblows and shovels driveways for several clients in the winter. Once while he was shoveling, a little old lady came by and asked if he could do her driveway too. Chuck agreed. When he finished, she asked him how much she owed him. Chuck told her "25." She went into the house, came back out, and gave him a quarter. She then asked if he was sure that was enough. Chuck just smiled and said, "Yeah, I guess that is good." He kept clearing the snow from her driveway for "25" until she passed away recently.

—Jean Litke *Pierz, Minnesota*

"I've Come to Clean Your Shoes"

by Madge Harrah, from the book *On Children and Death*

What does someone who has suffered a sudden trauma and grief need most?

Still in shock, I stumbled about the house trying to decide what to put into the suitcases. Earlier that evening, I'd received a call from my hometown in Missouri telling me that my brother, his wife, her sister, and both the sister's children had been killed in a car crash. "Come as soon as you can," begged my mother.

That's what I wanted to do—to leave at once, to hurry to my parents. But my husband, Larry, and I were in the midst of packing all our belongings to move from Ohio to New Mexico. Our house was in total confusion. Some of the clothes that Larry and I and our two young children, Eric and Meghan, would need were already taped up in cartons. Which ones? Stunned by grief, I couldn't remember. Other clothes lay unwashed in a pile on the laundry-room floor. Supper dishes still sat on the kitchen table. Toys were strewn everywhere.

While Larry made plane reservations for the following morning, I wandered about the house, aimlessly picking things up and putting them down. I couldn't focus. Again and again, the words I'd heard on the phone echoed through my head: "Bill is gone—Marilyn too. June—and both the children . . ."

It was as though the message had muffled my brain with cotton. Whenever Larry spoke, he sounded far away. As I moved through the house, I ran into doors and tripped over chairs.

Larry made arrangements for us to leave by seven o'clock the next morning. Then he phoned a few friends to tell them what had happened. Occasionally, someone asked to speak to me. "If there's anything I can do, let me know," that person would offer kindly.

"Thank you very much," I'd reply. But I didn't know what to ask for. I couldn't concentrate.

I sat in a chair, staring into space, while Larry called Donna King, the woman with whom I taught a nursery class at church each Sunday. Donna and I were casual friends, but we didn't see each other often. She and Emerson, her thin, quiet husband, were kept busy during the week by their own "nursery"—six children ranging in age from two to fifteen. I was glad Larry had thought to warn her that she'd have the nursery class alone the coming Sunday.

While I sat there, Meghan darted by, clutching a ball. Eric chased after her. They should be in bed, I thought. I followed them into the living room. My legs dragged. My hands felt gloved with lead. I sank down on the couch in a stupor.

When the doorbell rang, I rose slowly and crept across the room. I opened the door to see Emerson King standing on the porch.

"I've come to clean your shoes," he said.

Confused, I asked him to repeat.

"Donna had to stay with the baby," he said, "but we want to help you. I remember when my father died, it took me hours to get the children's shoes cleaned and shined for the funeral. So that's what I've come to do for you. Give me your shoes—not just your good shoes, but all your shoes."

I hadn't even thought about shoes until he mentioned them. Now I remembered that Eric had left the sidewalk to wade through the mud in his good shoes after church the previous Sunday. Not to be outdone by her brother, Meghan had kicked rocks, scuffing the toes of her shoes. When we'd returned, I'd tossed them into the laundry room to clean later.

While Emerson spread newspapers on the kitchen floor, I gathered Larry's dress and everyday shoes, my heels, my flats, the children's dirty dress shoes, and their sneakers with the food spots. Emerson found a pan and filled it with soapy water. He got an old knife out of a drawer and retrieved a sponge from under the sink. Larry had to rummage through several cartons, but at last he located the shoe polish.

Emerson settled himself on the floor and got to work. Watching him concentrate intently on one task helped me pull my own thoughts into order. Laundry first, I told myself. As the washer chugged, Larry and I bathed the children and put them to bed.

While we cleared the supper dishes, Emerson continued to work, saying nothing. I thought of Jesus washing the feet of his disciples. Our Lord had knelt, serving his friends, even as this man now knelt, serving us. The love in the act released my tears at last, healing rain to wash the fog from my mind. I could move. I could think. I could get on with the business of living.

One by one, the jobs fell into place. I went into the laundry room to put a load of wash into the dryer, returning to the kitchen to find that Emerson had left. In a line against one wall stood all our shoes, gleaming, spotless. Later, when I started to pack, I saw that Emerson had even scrubbed the soles. I could put the shoes directly into the suitcases.

We got to bed late and rose very early, but by the time we left for the airport, all the jobs had been done. Ahead lay grim, sad days, but the comfort of Christ's presence, symbolized by the image of a quiet man kneeling on my kitchen floor with a pan of water, would sustain me.

Now whenever I hear of an acquaintance who has lost a loved one, I no longer call with the vague offer, "If there's anything I can do . . ." Instead I try to think of one specific task that suits that person's need—such as washing the family car, taking the dog to the boarding kennel, or house-sitting during the funeral. And if the person says to me, "How did you know I needed that done?" I reply, "It's because a man once cleaned my shoes."

Originally published in the December 1983 issue of *Reader's Digest* magazine.

Gandalf and the Search for the Lost Boy

by Christopher W. Davis

Ignoring the odds, search-and-rescue teams set out to scour an impossibly vast woodland area to bring home a lost child.

T he moon was hanging low in the South Carolina sky as Misha Marshall finished loading her pickup. Then she led Gandalf to his cage in the back. It was 3 a.m. on Tuesday, March 20. Misha's husband, Chuck, came out to see her off. "Don't expect to go up there and find that lost Boy Scout in the woods, because it's just not going to happen," Chuck said. A retired paramedic and firefighter, he had seen more amazing things than a kid surviving three cold nights in the mountains, but he didn't want his wife to be disappointed in herself or her dog.

Three days earlier, 12-year-old Michael Auberry had vanished from his troop's campsite in Doughton Park, 7,000 rough acres in the Blue Ridge Mountains in North Carolina. A massive search had been launched, but there was barely a trace of the boy.

Misha, a corporate tax manager, and Gandalf, her two-year-old Shiloh Shepherd, had trained for a year with the South Carolina Search and Rescue Dog Association. But this was their first real job, and Misha worried that she'd miss Gandalf's subtle signs. A search dog doesn't learn specific signals. He doesn't act like a pointer spotting quarry. Animal and human work together intuitively.

A mountain girl from Asheville, North Carolina, Misha grew up with working dogs—German shepherds and collies. Even as a child, she could get these no-nonsense animals to do tricks no one in her family could, like make them line up and roll over. She could, she says, "feel like them."

When she was ten, her little collie, Laddie, ran away. Misha asked herself, *If I were a puppy, where would I go?* At the end of the block, across the main road, was a goldfish pond. She walked straight to the pond, looking nowhere else. Laddie was there—stuck fast in the mud.

Misha found Gandalf in a kennel in Tennessee when he was six weeks old. A little ball of black fur with oversize feet, he looked more like a bear cub than a puppy. A gentle, laid-back bear. Misha, a big fan of J. R. R. Tolkien, named him Gandalf, after the wizard in *The Lord of the Rings*, because she believed he was special.

* * *

After leaving home that March morning, Misha rendezvoused with her team of six other handlers, and they headed north. A sister squad in North Carolina had been searching through the night. Misha's team would take over later that morning.

Slippery moss and waterfall spray threaten footing, and thundering streams could drown out a child's cry for help.

Doughton Park is located in a bowl on the side of a mountain. It's traversed by heavily vegetated, treacherously steep ridges rising 2,400 feet. Rock overhangs look down into caverns snarled with wild rhododendron thickets and deadfall. Slippery moss and waterfall spray threaten footing, and thundering streams could drown out a child's cry for help.

Knowing how unforgiving the terrain was, park rangers had quickly called in search-and-rescue squads, some working with bloodhounds, from two neighboring counties to scour a 30-mile network of trails.

All they found the first day was some spilled potato chips. The chips were west of Michael's campsite along a fire road that ran deep into the park. Tactical trackers found footprints leading to another path and then to a stream about a quarter mile from the camp. It was a fairly good trail, but they lost the tracks at the creek.

As the sun began to set and the chill of an early-spring night set in, someone found the lid of a tin mess kit 100 yards upstream from where the footprints disappeared. A well-meaning but inexperienced volunteer brought the kit back to the base camp, ruining the trail for the bloodhounds.

After nightfall, a state highway patrol helicopter scanned the forest with infrared scopes. Rangers parked their biggest vehicle at the campsite, turned on the flashing lights and blasted Michael's name over a loudspeaker.

Michael had been wearing an insulated red coat and good boots, but even the searchers were falling into streams and getting wet. They continued through the night.

The next two days, results were much the same. High-angle rescue teams rappelled down cliffs to see if Michael had fallen. Divers dragged the dam at an abandoned fish hatchery with hooks and anchors. They checked logjams on creeks. They looked beneath every waterfall. On Sunday a Boy Scout sock was found in a creek. That was all. Through the night and into Monday, 566 trained rescuers searched the woods.

Misha and her teammates arrived at the staging area around 7 a.m. on Tuesday, day four. It was overrun by media trucks and satellite dishes. There was a huge mobile command center. Red Cross food tents and official vehicles were everywhere.

The team huddled with members of the North Carolina squad, who'd just returned after spending the night combing the ridges. They told Misha that the terrain was so rough, you had to go on your hands and knees much of the time. None of their dogs had found a trail of scent on the ground. Now a dog would have to pick up the missing boy's scent in the air after four days, a challenging task for even the keenest animal.

The North Carolinians did provide Misha's team with a bonus. They'd obtained an unwashed T-shirt from Michael's backpack that hadn't been touched by anyone else. They had handled it with gloves, carefully cutting it into smaller pieces and sealing them up in plastic bags.

At 8 a.m. the searchers were briefed on every detail about Michael. Misha studied his picture. She wanted to lock his image in her mind, the way Gandalf would lock in his scent.

The base camp command center sent out one dog team at a time to assigned territories. Misha and Gandalf—along with Erin Horn, a nursing student, and Danny Gambill, a volunteer firefighter—were directed to area 51, one of the steepest.

The three checked the map. Area 51 was an elongated north-to-south rectangle along a trail. The team decided to hike to the top of their zone, then let Gandalf zigzag his way back down. They estimated they had about 70 acres, 1 percent of the park area, to search. A sweep would take them at least eight hours.

It was a mild 50 degrees, but the night before, the mercury had dropped below freezing. Michael had basic Scouting skills, and searchers hoped he'd found shelter. He had read and loved the books *Hatchet* and *My Side of the Mountain*, about young boys surviving in the woods alone. But three days had passed now, and the cadaver dogs had been sent for.

Misha concentrated on the search ahead. She didn't want anything negative to cloud her focus. Michael is alive, she told Gandalf. We're going to find him.

She took out the bag containing the shred of Michael's shirt and let Gandalf sniff it. Head up and nose high, the dog started up the trail. Misha, Erin and Danny followed.

"Big dog, big heart" is how Michael described Gandalf, here with his handler Misha Marshall.

Gandalf fringed the trail, switching from side to side, funneled ever upward by the steep rock walls and sheer drop-offs. Erin was navigating with the map and a GPS device. After about an hour, they stopped and conferred. According to the GPS, they had gone up about 5,900 feet, putting them at the top of their assigned area. It was time to turn back and begin their descent. But the team agreed to go up a little higher, just to be sure.

Another 15 minutes or so of climbing couldn't hurt. It would be good to overlap another search area, they reasoned. They chose a spot about 200 yards away, crossing and recrossing Basin Creek, picking their way over stones and fallen logs.

While Erin was studying the GPS, Danny was scanning his side of the trail. The searchers headed up the right bank of the creek. All of a sudden, Misha saw Gandalf's head snap up, but she couldn't spot a thing in the underbrush.

The wind was coming toward them now, around the shoulder of a cliff. Gandalf was about 30 yards ahead, working the bank of the stream where it turned beneath a wall of rock. Misha saw him quickly lift his head again. Was that the sign she'd been waiting for?

Gandalf trotted to the left, out of sight behind the cliff face, and Misha scrambled up the trail behind him. She turned the bend, and there—50 yards up on the ledge, in a direct line ahead of Gandalf—was a boy in a red jacket. He was dazed from hunger and fatigue.

Misha and Danny began yelling, "Michael, is that you? Michael?"

The boy turned silently toward them. Danny clambered up the steep embankment to help Michael down. Working her way halfway across the creek, Misha passed the boy to Erin. The team carried him to the bank and set him down next to Gandalf. "Are you okay with dogs?" Misha asked. He nodded. "Well, this is Gandalf," she said as the dog nuzzled the boy.

While the rescuers contacted the base camp, Michael ate a few peanut butter crackers they'd given him. He set the rest of the crackers down, and Gandalf snatched them up. "Is a helicopter coming to get me?" Michael asked. "I'd like a chopper ride."

The terrain was too rough for a helicopter to land. Rangers came up to carry Michael out. After they arrived, Misha struggled to hold Gandalf back as he tugged at his leash. He wanted to follow the boy. Misha had never seen her gentle giant act this way. He was obviously proud of himself—"gloating" is what dog handlers call it. It was the equivalent of an NFL receiver dancing in the end zone.

Michael was dehydrated, hungry, exhausted and freezing. He had first-degree frostbite, and it would take a couple of weeks for the feeling to return to his toes. After a short stay in the hospital, he was discharged in good health.

As it turned out, Michael's experience was nothing like his novels. Unlike their protagonists, he had not been lucky enough to find a cave or a fishhook-shaped twig or any other tool that would have helped him. But he had remembered that it was important to stay warm and hydrated. He used leaves as insulation at night, and he sucked on icicles. Michael earned his Wilderness Survival Merit Badge last summer. He now knows the biggest mistakes he made: not staying in one place and not making enough noise to attract attention. He plans to never get lost again. He is grateful to everyone who looked for him, he says, but maybe no one more than Gandalf.

Back at the base camp, Misha finally got a strong enough cell signal to call her husband. "I can't tell you much right now," she told him. "But Gandalf has just found that Boy Scout."

"Yeah, right," Chuck said. Then he realized she was serious. "Well, I guess that's the last time I'll tell you what you and Gandalf can't do."

Originally published in the December 2007 issue of *Reader's Digest* magazine.

Humor Hall of Fame

At an art gallery, a woman and her ten-year-old son were having a tough time choosing between one of my paintings and another artist's work. They finally went with mine. "I guess you decided you prefer an autumn scene to a floral," I said. "No," said the boy. "Your painting's wider, so it'll cover three holes in our wall."

—**BETTY TENNEY** STERLING HEIGHTS, MICHIGAN

A new salesman saw the nameplate on my desk and said, "Sibyl Short. That's easy to remember, since you're short." The next time he visited our office, he approached me with a big smile and stated with great confidence, "Hello, Ms. Stout!"

—**SIBYL SHORT** LILBURN, GEORGIA

During a faculty meeting at our school, our principal grew frustrated with the lack of attention he felt was his due. Raising his voice, he shouted, "Listen, people. Communication is a two-way street. When I talk, you have to listen."

—**T.D.** RD.COM

SUGGESTIONS

RESIGNATIONS

Cartoon by Harley Schwadron

I was fired by my boss because of the way I laugh. Apparently, it reminds him too much of his ex-wife's laugh. I'm a guy.

—FMYLIFE.COM

Cartoon by Dave Carpenter

"I have to hang up now. I have an hour to get these reports done."

My boss likes to save pennies. How much? I caught him in the break room retrieving paper cups from the trash can and shoving them back into the dispenser next to the watercooler. He didn't even bother wiping off the lipstick.

—B.B., RD READER

After I worked through lunch to help my boss with a report, he offered to show his appreciation by taking me out for a bite. The place he had in mind had a wonderful buffet, he said, with foods from around the world. I was absolutely salivating with each detail. So what was his idea of an exotic dining establishment? Sam's Club. We spent the hour dining on the free samples they handed out.

—WENDY BROWN, RD READER

While interviewing a candidate for a receptionist position, I asked: "What do you see in yourself that you'd like to improve?" Her response: "My breasts."

—JIM BOEHM
DANA POINT, CALIFORNIA

MY FRIEND, AN INTERN, WAS GIVEN $50 TO GET THE CHAIRMAN OF THE BANK SOME LUNCH. TOLD TO GET HIMSELF SOMETHING, HE BOUGHT A SHIRT.

—STORIFY.COM

ARCTIC EXPLORERS

Ah, the magical words have been spoken over the radio.
SNOW DAY! There was instant electricity in the air. I knew
that as soon as I completed my shoveling obligations, I was
free! As excited as I was, there was another family member
who was even more excited than me. My beloved American
Eskimo dog, Sitka, knew that a new adventure with her best
friend was just an hour away. Once I finished my shoveling,
I stepped through the front door. There, Sitka sat at the
top of the stairs with her tail wagging frantically. She knew
exactly what came next. I strapped on her harness (which I
knew made her feel like a REAL sled dog) and out the door
we went. The neighborhood we both grew up in magically
transformed into a wonderland of snow and ice. We were no
longer boy and dog. We were arctic explorers.

—Michael Roberto *Danbury, Connecticut*

THE SAVIOR SOLDIER

Nearly 25 years ago, my father told me about his experiences
in the Vietnam War. One night, he was stranded in unfamiliar
territory with a flat tire and flat spare. Luckily, a fellow
soldier came along and gave my father his spare. Now I'm a
paramedic, and I recently worked with an older EMT I had
never met. At the end of our 12-hour shift, he said, "You
know, you look a lot like your father." He had recognized my
last name. I had been paired up with the hero who had saved
my father 50 years earlier.

—Albert Thweatt *Nashville, Tennessee*

The Curse of Sigurd the Fingerless

by Ruth Park

A woman reflects on her family's propensity for small accidents.

When I glued my fingers together the other day while repairing my gardening shoes in the laundry, I thought how extraordinary it is that some families are fated for big accidents, whereas members of my family are content with small, preposterous ones.

In a way, this lends one a devil-may-care confidence: you know you will be landed in all kinds of unbelievably mortifying situations, but they won't kill you. Recently, for example, my car brakes failed near my house on Norfolk Island, 930 miles from Sydney, Australia. Had I been traveling down one of our town's slippery-dip hills, I could have rocketed out into the Pacific. Instead, I was on flat ground and merely collided with the Commonwealth Bank, which resoundingly demonstrated the validity of its slogan: "The Strength."

Our family gets its propensity for being small-accident-prone from my mother's side. It was my Aunt Fedora whose dentures the dog ate. My cousin Helen got a strand of spaghetti stuck in her throat and almost choked. The young aunts of my childhood had a point system for burns—one for hot cocoa, two for porridge, and so on until you got an open-ended credit for boiling water, and no doubt a trophy while you lay in the hospital.

My father, before whom inanimate objects cowered, used to say, "You all go at things like bulls at a red blanket. Take it easy. Things are not just *there*. They're made to work. Think of how they work before you touch them."

"Okay, Dad," I would say, and take my fountain pen out of the ink bottle, press the wrong knob and squirt ink on his white shirt. He would never kill me or anything like that. He'd just say, "You never listen, do you?" and go and change his shirt.

Sometimes he would speculate mildly on what my mother's kinfolk must have been like before they emigrated from Sweden, conjuring up ancestors like Sigurd the Fingerless, Einar No-Nose and Burnt Njal.

Anyway, many Viking generations later, there I was with my fingers stuck together with powerful glue. I could scarcely believe my misfortune, having carefully perused the directions on the giant sheet of cardboard attached to the tiny tube of Magic Sticky. Despite my cautionary muttering of "Heat and Water Resistant, Sets Within Ten Seconds, One Drop Holds a Ton," the family curse had caught me out. I was, at least on one side, a finned creature.

I could just hear my father saying, "Are you daft? You read that acetone dissolves the stuff. Why didn't you get the acetone ready first?"

Anyway, many Viking generations later, there I was with my fingers stuck together with powerful glue.

Rummaging one-handedly in the bathroom cupboard, I found a bottle of acetone-based nail-polish remover. By this time all four fingers on my left hand were bent together like a mitten, so I was able to get the stopper out. As I rubbed away at the stretched skin between the fingers ("Do Not Use Force or Mechanical Means." Dear heavens, *what* mechanical means?), my whole life passed before me and I lived once more the high points as a descendant of Sigurd the Fingerless.

There was that day in Sydney when a stranger in foreign garb bowed low to me and extended a piece of paper on which was written, "This man wants the Immigration Department." Just as I turned to point it out to him, my jaw spontaneously dislocated and stayed that way. Judging from his hasty departure, the man headed straight back to Pakistan.

And then there was the definitive battle of my continuing war with zippers. Zippers hate me. They reach out and grab everything—necklaces, bits of underwear, lumps of lady—and then jam irrevocably.

This time I had been to a glamorous party and had worn a form-fitting dress with a zipper at the back. As I began to undress, the zipper got stuck. It was far too late to go next door and ask someone to rescue me, so up and down the room I raged, extending my arms to unbelievable lengths behind my back. I was like an advanced Yogi—but not advanced enough.

Finally I tried to get out of the dress without unzipping it. It had long sleeves. With dire and painful contortions, I got one arm out of the sleeve and down inside the dress. Now I had only one arm and the dress was more form-fitting than ever.

Exhausted, I fell on my bed and slept fitfully through the rest of the night. Imagine, then, the humiliation of having to go next door at eight o'clock in the morning with only one arm and smeared make-up, and beg to be released—especially when the zipper just purred open.

"What a party!" I could see the words written all over my neighbor's face.

During these recollections, my fingers had gradually been letting go of one another. But a fearful thought struck me. Had I, when I realized my fingers were glued together, dropped the tube of Magic Sticky and perhaps fastened the washing machine to the floor forever? Fortunately, in my delirium I had placed the Sticky on the hammer, and I now had a hammer with a tube on its head, as if it were convalescing from brain surgery. Once again, though, Sigurd had protected a descendant from *major* mishap.

The hammer brings me to the matter of the screwdriver in my lavatory. I have rewarded myself in my declining years with a singularly lush john full of books and potted plants and other comforts, including a screwdriver. Let guests think what they like when they see the screwdriver between the works of Paul Theroux and the gloxinia. Their amazement and even their sympathy leave me unmoved.

Recently the john door jammed immovably, with me on the wrong side. Not wishing my whitened bones to be found in such a place in six months' time, I spent an hour fighting strips of glass out of the louvered window. Then with terrible difficulty I climbed through, all hunched up like a dead fly, and fell out on the veranda.

The entire time I could hear my father nagging, "You never listen, do you? If you kept a screwdriver inside, you could have taken off the doorknob!"

So that's why the screwdriver is in my lavatory. I have at last listened and taken one small step toward neutralizing the curse of Sigurd the Fingerless.

Originally published in the September 1984 issue of *Reader's Digest* magazine.

The Day We Planted Hope

by Conrad Kiechel

I tucked five seeds into the dirt,
then sat down and . . .

We had just moved to France, and my wife Nancy and I were unpacking on a quiet August afternoon, busy making the rental apartment into a home for our uprooted family. At our feet our three-year-old, Claire, sat leafing through books. Far from friends and relatives, she was clearly tired of living with packing boxes.

"Please read me this," she said, thrusting a thin blue book in my direction. *It's Fun to Speak French* was stenciled on the spine of the faded cover. My grandfather, who had grown up speaking French, had given me the book when I was a child, and my parents had unearthed it from somewhere and sent it along with us.

Claire pointed to a page with line drawings below the bars of an old French children's song: "Do you know how to plant cabbages?" In blue ink, someone had crossed out cabbages and written "Watermelons!"

"Daddy! Did you do that?" Claire asked, looking up with an expression of shock. We had only recently convinced her not to write in books, and suddenly here was proof that her parents weren't practicing what they preached. I told her my grandfather had written in the book.

"Daddy!" Now she was really confused. "Why did your grandfather do that?" As I sat down to tell the story, my thoughts traveled a well-worn road back to Nebraska.

"Are we almost there?" my sister Vicky demanded from the back seat of our family's '54 Ford station wagon. It was the last, and toughest, day of our annual drive west to our grandparents' house perched above a creek bed in Tecumseh, Nebraska. For a few weeks each summer, Vicky and I had all the adventure we needed—working the old pump to see what kind of bugs came up in the water, choreographing fireworks displays in the back lot, escaping the midday sun under a canvas tarp thrown over two clotheslines.

When we pulled into their driveway, my grandmother burst from the back door to greet us. Behind her, Grandad hobbled over the lawn, then gathered us in his strong arms.

As a young man, Grandad had been a comer: a farmer, teacher, stockman and, at age 26, a Nebraska state senator. The trajectory of his life was straight up—until a massive stroke felled him at age 44 and crippled him for life. Sometime between his stroke and my boyhood, he had made peace with his life. His scrape with death had convinced him not how awful life is, but how precious. His zest for living made him a playmate Vicky and I fought over.

Each morning we pressed into Grandad's car for the drive to the post office, entertained along the way by the incessant patter of his nonsense rhymes: "Hello, Mrs. Brown. Why are you going to town?"

Best of all were trips to "the eighty," the only bit of farmland Grandad had managed to keep; the rest had been sold, or repossessed, to pay the bills in his years of recovery. Vicky and I would climb into the barn's hayloft and, from an old cow stall below, Grandad made mooing noises that sent us into convulsions of laughter.

"I'm going to be a farmer too," I announced proudly one afternoon as Grandad sat playing solitaire at his desk.

Laying card upon card, he asked, "What are you going to grow?"

Suddenly I thought of a favorite pastime—spitting watermelon seeds as far as possible. "How about watermelons?" I asked.

"Hmm, there's a crop I haven't tried!" Brown eyes sparkling, he put his cards aside. "Better get your seeds in the ground quick though."

It was mid-August, and the days were growing shorter. Soon we would pack up for the drive back to Virginia—and school. I shuddered, feeling the first chill of autumn separation.

"Let's do it now!" I said, leaping out of my seat. "What do we do?"

First, Grandad said, we needed seeds. Remembering the slice of watermelon I'd seen in Aunt Mary's refrigerator, I raced out the door and across the yard to her house. In a flash I was back, five black seeds in my hand.

Grandad suggested a sunny spot in back of the house to plant the seeds. But I wanted a place where I could easily watch my plants' progress skyward.

We walked outside into the shade of a huge oak. "Right here, Grandad," I said. I could sit with my back against the tree, reading comic books as the watermelons grew. It was perfect.

"Go to the garage and get the hoe," was Grandad's only reaction. Then he showed me how to prepare the ground and plant the seeds in a semicircle. "Don't crowd them," he said quietly. "Give them plenty of room to grow."

"Now what, Grandad?"

"Now comes the hard part," he said. "You wait." And for a whole afternoon, I did. Nearly every hour I checked on my watermelons, each time watering the seeds again. Incredibly, they had still not sprouted by suppertime, although my plot was a muddy mess. At the dinner table I asked Grandad how long it would take.

"Maybe next month," he said, laughing. "Maybe sooner."

The next morning I lay lazily in bed, reading a comic book. Suddenly, I remembered: the seeds! Dressing quickly, I ran outside.

What's that? I wondered, peering under the oak. Then I realized—it's a watermelon! A huge, perfectly shaped fruit lay nesting in the cool mud. I felt triumphant. Wow! I'm a farmer! It was the biggest melon I'd seen, and I'd grown it.

Just as I realized I hadn't, Grandad came out of the house. "You picked a great spot, Conrad," he chuckled.

"Oh Grandad!" I said. Then we quickly conspired to play the joke on others. After breakfast we loaded the melon into Grandad's trunk and took it to town, where he showed his cronies the "midnight miracle" his grandson had grown—and they let me believe they believed it.

Later that month Vicky and I got into the back seat of the station wagon for the glum ride back east. Grandad passed a book through the window. "For school," he said seriously. Hours later, I opened it to where he'd written "watermelons"—and laughed at another of Grandad's jokes.

Grandad showed his cronies the "midnight miracle" his grandson had grown—and they let me believe they believed it.

Holding the book Grandad had given me that day long ago, Claire listened quietly to the story. Then she asked, "Daddy, can I plant seeds too?"

Nancy looked at me; together we surveyed the mountain of boxes waiting to be unpacked. About to say, "We'll do it tomorrow," I realized I had never heard Grandad say that. We took off for the market. At a small shop with a metal rack filled with seed packs, Claire picked one that promised bright red flowers, and I added a sack of potting soil.

On the walk home, while Claire munched a buttery croissant, I thought about those seeds I'd planted. For the first time I realized that Grandad could have met my childish enthusiasm with a litany of disappointing facts: that watermelons don't grow well in Nebraska; that it was too late to plant them anyway; that it was pointless to try growing them in the deep shade. But instead of boring me with the how of growing things, which I would soon forget, he made sure I first experienced the "wow."

Claire charged up the three flights of stairs to our apartment, and in a few minutes she was standing on a chair at the kitchen sink, filling a white porcelain pot with soil. As I sprinkled seeds into her open palm, I felt for the first time the pains Grandad had taken. He had stolen back into town that August afternoon and bought the biggest melon in the market. That night, after I was asleep, he had awkwardly unloaded it and, with a painful bend, placed it exactly above my seeds.

"Done, Daddy," Claire broke into my reverie. I opened the window over the sink and she put her pot on the sill, moving it from side to side until she found the perfect spot. "Now grow!" she commanded.

A few days later, shouts of "They're growing!" woke us, and Claire led us to the kitchen to see a pot of small green shoots. "Mommy," she said proudly, "I'm a farmer!"

I had always thought the midnight miracle was just another of Grandad's pranks. Now I realized it was one of his many gifts to me. In his refusal to let his crippling hinder him, he had planted something that neither time nor distance could uproot: a full-throttle grasping at the happiness life offers—and a disdain for whatever bumps get in the way.

As Claire beamed with satisfaction, I watched my grandfather's joy take fresh root in her life. And that was the biggest miracle of all.

Originally published in the March 1994 issue of *Reader's Digest* magazine.

A Soldier's Best Friend

It's a bird, it's a plane, it's an . . . airborne dog? When military canine handlers drop into combat zones, their dogs jump with them. And while the two- and four-legged warriors often ride in a harness attached to each other, sometimes—especially when jumping into water—the dogs go it alone. This Special Forces soldier and his dog were practicing their solo jumps off the ramp of a CH-47 Chinook helicopter during a training exercise over the Gulf of Mexico in 2011. Don't worry—this was a low-altitude jump, so neither man nor dog needed a parachute. *Photograph by Manuel J. Martinez/U.S. Air Force/Alamy*

The Over-the-Hill Gang

by Mark Seal, from *Vanity Fair*

How a ragtag crew of aging criminals pulled off one of the most daring robberies in British history.

The audacious April 2015 ransacking of safe-deposit boxes in Hatton Garden, London's jewelry district, was epic. So much cash, jewelry, and other valuables had been taken that the loot had been hauled away in giant trash containers on wheels. London's newspapers were filled with artists' renderings of the heist, featuring hard-bodied burglars in black turtlenecks doing superhuman things. Experts insisted that the heist was the work of a foreign team of Navy-Seal-like professionals, likely from the infamous Pink Panthers, an international gang of master jewelry thieves.

British crime aficionados saw the operation as a throwback to the meticulously planned, supremely executed jewelry heists of yesteryear, which had inspired such classic crime movies as *To Catch a Thief* and *Topkapi*.

193

The vault was in the basement of this building at 88–90 Hatton Garden

But when arrests were made the following month, Great Britain collectively gasped.

The Hatton Garden heist, it turned out, had been the work of a ragtag group of superannuated criminals. "Run? They can barely walk," Danny Jones wrote to a reporter from jail. "One has cancer, he's 76, another heart condition, 68. Another, 75, can't remember his name. Sixty-year-old with two new hips and knees."

Yet they had defied age, physical infirmities, burglar alarms, and even Scotland Yard to power their way through walls of concrete and solid steel and haul away a prize estimated at more than £14 million, at least £10.3 million of which is still missing.

* * *

Retirement is a bitch. Your wife has passed away. Most of your mates are in exile, prison, or the grave. You skulk around your run-down mansion in the suburbs of London, infuriating your neighbors by running a used-car dealership out of your home, and "hobbling over to the news agent," as one neighbor put it, for the daily papers to read about younger men doing what you used to.

This was the life of Brian Reader at 76. "He ain't got no friends no more," a colleague would say of him. "Sitting down there in the café, talks about all their yesterdays," said another.

And yet for practically his whole life Reader had exasperated Scotland Yard. First arrested for breaking and entering at age 11, he was allegedly part of the "Millionaire Moles" gang, which burrowed underground to loot safe-deposit boxes in a Lloyds bank vault in London in 1971, a haul worth more than £41 million today.

Reader had generally managed to walk away until the Brinks-Mat Job in 1983, involving the theft of what today would be worth more than £83 million in gold bullion from the high-security warehouse at Heathrow Airport. Reader was a "soldier" on that job, moving the gold between a "fence" and dealers. He was found guilty of conspiracy for handling stolen goods and sentenced to nine years.

When he got out of prison, it seemed he had put the life of crime behind him. But two decades later, suffering from prostate cancer and other ailments, he decided to get back into the game with his biggest caper yet. Scotland Yard commander Peter Spindler, who oversaw the London police in investigating the Hatton Garden heist, told me that Reader was called "the Guvnor," the leader in British gangster parlance, who, possibly with associates, "set it up, enlisted the others, and called the job on, to the best of our understanding."

Number two on the heist was Terry Perkins, 67, suffering from diabetes and other health issues, living in a little house in Enfield. He was a ghost to the neighbors, who had no idea he had once been a ringleader in the largest cash robbery in British history at that time: the 1983 Security Express Job, in which a gang raided a cash depot in East London and stole cash equivalent to £19 million today. Perkins was sentenced to

22 years but escaped when he was close to release and went on the run, returning to jail in 2011 to serve out the rest of his sentence. He wasn't a known criminal before the Security Express robbery, said retired detective Peter Wilton. "Usually wore a suit and had a portfolio of houses."

Extraordinarily fit, Danny Jones, 58, was, according to a friend, a "Walter Mitty" type, who read palms and ran marathons when he wasn't in and out of prison serving sentences of 17 years. His passions were for the army and crime, and his rap sheet was filled with convictions. "Everyone who knew Danny would say he was mad," said Carl Wood, another member of the Hatton Garden team. "He would go to bed in his mother's dressing gown with a fez on."

Carl Wood, 58, was sentenced to four years in prison in 2002, after he and his accomplices were recorded planning to torture a money-launderer who owed them £600,000. Having no trade, Wood would testify he dabbled in "a bit of painting and decorating."

In debt at the time of the Hatton Garden heist, Wood claimed to have been living on disability payments after being diagnosed with Crohn's disease, an inflammation of the intestines. He may have been selected for the Hatton Garden job for his slim physique, which enabled him to crawl into tight spaces.

Driver and lookout man John "Kenny" Collins, 74, was a "dodgy" but elegant figure in the streets of London with his beloved Staffordshire bull terrier, Dempsey, nipping at his heels. He was a walking pawnshop. "He'd buy cars, expensive watches . . . and sell it back to you later," said a friend. His rap sheet, stretching back to the 1950s, included convictions for robbery and burglary. Diabetes had exiled him into semiretirement.

Two peripheral members of the team, Hugh Doyle, 48, and William Lincoln, 59, stored and helped move the stolen treasure.

One unidentified member of the team still at large is Basil, as he was called by the other thieves and the police. He is believed to be the inside man, who knew the building, disarmed the alarms, and let the others in. There is a £20,000 reward for a tip that leads to his arrest.

* * *

The vault, belonging to the Hatton Garden Safe Deposit Ltd. (HGSD), was located in the basement at 88–90 Hatton Garden. The building is seven stories tall and has around 60 tenants, most of them jewelers. The vault's two-foot-wide impenetrable bomb-and-burglar-proof door—operated by a combination that has to be worked by at least two men—opened up a labyrinth of safes.

The wooden main door to the building and a glass door behind it—both left unlocked during the day—lead to an unstaffed lobby. The elevator in the lobby is disabled so it can't descend lower than the ground floor. Beside the elevator is a door that leads to a flight of stairs to the basement. This door is also unlocked during business hours. At the bottom of the stairs is another wooden door, behind which is a sliding iron gate, which forms an air lock with a second sliding gate. To enter the first gate you need a four-digit security code; a security guard opens the second gate to let you out the other side. Inside the air lock are locked shutters, behind which are the doors, no longer used, to the elevator shaft.

The wooden main door to the building and a glass door behind it—both left unlocked during the day—lead to an unstaffed lobby.

There is a much easier way to get to the vault area: a street-level fire exit with an outside lock on Greville Street, from which iron stairs go down to a courtyard adjoining 88–90's basement. From the inside, the Greville Street door is locked merely with a hand-operated bolt—no key is required to open it. The Hatton Garden basement is accessed from the courtyard by a door with two sliding-bolt locks, and that door leads to the HGSD basement foyer. At the far side of the basement foyer is a white door, behind which is the HGSD air lock.

Strange things began happening in the days leading up to the heist. A local diamond company worker was visiting a firm in 88–90 and had to wait what seemed like forever for the elevator. When it arrived, she found an aging repairman inside, wearing blue coveralls and surrounded by tools and building gear. A pair of blue coveralls was later found at the home of Terry Perkins, who had apparently been casing the building.

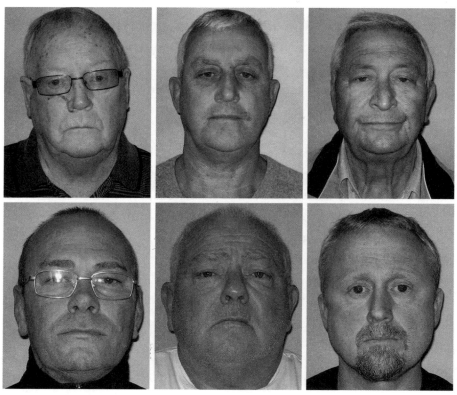

From top left to bottom right: John "Kenny" Collins, Daniel Jones, Terry Perkins, Carl Wood, William Lincoln, and Hugh Doyle after their May 2015 arrests in London

Then came the fire. On Wednesday, April 1, a gas main ruptured and slowly leaked gas into the tunnels that house London's electrical and telecommunications cable networks. A spark in an electrical-junction box ignited the gas, causing smoke to billow from manhole covers and flames to shoot up from the ground. Power failed. Gas supplies ceased. Thousands of people in the area were evacuated.

It would take firefighters and police officers nearly two days to bring the situation under control. This was a fortuitous break for the thieves, entangling the cops and setting off dozens of false alarms.

The next day, the Thursday before Easter and Passover weekend, there was practically a line of people to deposit their valuables at HGSD.

"Four carats, five carats, all shades, brilliant-cut, heart-shaped—a magnificent collection!" one jeweler told me, describing what he had stored in his box that weekend.

The jewelers believed the vault to be safe. The owners were apparently so confident of its construction that they gave their security guards weekends off.

At 9:19 p.m. that Thursday, April 2, the staff locked up the vault for the long weekend. Minutes later, a thin man dressed in a blue jacket with a red wig and a flat cap passed in front of a CCTV camera on Greville Street. A black bag on his shoulder hid his face. This was Basil. He evidently had keys with which he entered 88–90 through the front door and made his way to the basement fire door. He disabled the alarms and the cameras inside the building, but made one crucial mistake: he neglected to disable a CCTV camera in the fire-exit passage and another on the second floor.

Shortly after Basil appeared, a CCTV camera in the street showed a white van pulling up to the building's fire-escape entrance and several men unloading tools, bags, and two wheelie bins, in full view of the people strolling along the dark streets. These men—Brian Reader, Terry Perkins, and Danny Jones—were disguised as municipal workers, wearing reflective yellow vests, hard hats, and white surgical masks.

Basil opened the fire-escape door from within, and the men unloaded their gear. Kenny Collins entered an office building across the street, where he would serve as a lookout, but, according to one of his accomplices, he "sat up there and fell asleep."

It was to be a three-day job, during which they planned to loot all 996 safe-deposit boxes in the vault, as evidenced by diabetic Terry Perkins's bringing three days' worth of insulin. "If I don't take the insulin for three days you'd a had to carry me out in a wheelie bin," Perkins later said.

Once inside the 88–90 fire-door corridor, the men evidently could not breach the white door that led to the HGSD basement foyer. But they had planned a more ingenious way to get in—one that presupposed deep inside knowledge of the building's layout. They walked up to the second floor and called the elevator, which they disabled, then returned to the ground floor, and pried open the elevator doors to the open shaft. Then one or more of them dropped down the three to four yards to the basement, pried open the flimsy steel shutter covering the disused basement elevator door, and entered the air lock.

They cut the telephone cable and broke off the GPS aerial so that the alarm's signal range was compromised—but not quite compromised enough. A short time later a text alert was sent to the monitoring company, which contacted HGSD co-owner Alok Bavishi.

Kelvin Stockwell, chief custodian guard of the vault, arrived shortly after 1 a.m. to find no sign of forced entry on the front door to the building or the fire exit. Nothing seemed amiss. "It's all locked up," Stockwell told Bavishi.

The police also dismissed the incident, concluding that "no police response was deemed to be required," according to police reports.

Meanwhile, the team pulled the second air-lock iron gate open. They were in!

The safe-deposit boxes lay within a Chubb safe embedded in a 20-inch-thick concrete wall. Anchoring a 77-pound Hilti DD350 diamond-tipped coring drill to the floor and wall, and connecting it to a water hose for cooling and reducing the amount of dust, the team began boring through the concrete. The DD350 made only a quiet hum as it breached the wall.

Within two and a half hours, three overlapping circular holes had been cut through the concrete. The thieves stared through the holes not into the diamond-filled vault but at a wall of solid steel: the rear of a cabinet of safe-deposit boxes. Unmovable. Bolted to the ceiling and floor.

They had a Clarke pump and hose with a 10-ton hydraulic ram, strong enough to force the doors off of almost anything. But the pump broke. The steel cabinet stood firm.

Around 8 a.m. on Friday, April 3, they temporarily surrendered, leaving the vault—but in a move that shocked the others, the ringleader, Brian Reader, left for good. He was convinced that to return would mean certain capture.

Jones and Collins didn't walk away, though. Instead they went shopping. At Machine Mart in the London suburb of Twickenham, Jones paid £96 for another fire-red Clarke pump ram and hose, using the name "V. Jones" and his street address on the receipt.

They returned around 10 p.m. on April 4. Finding the fire-escape door locked, Carl Wood followed Reader's lead and quit. After Basil finally let them in again, Collins returned to his post as lookout. Back at the vault, Perkins, Basil, and Jones anchored the new pump and hose to the wall opposite the vault, and 10 tons of pressure went to work.

Then Perkins exclaimed, "We're in! We're in!" They could see the bounty beckoning. Now at least one of them had to slither through the overlapping concrete holes, a tiny opening measuring 10 by 18 inches across.

Inside the vault, fitness enthusiast Danny Jones and the slim Basil were busting open the old but still-sturdy metal deposit boxes with sledgehammers, crowbars, and angle grinders. Since they were now two burglars short, they were able to ransack only 73 of the 996 boxes, but it was enough, a vast array of loose diamonds and other stones, jewelry, and cash. There was also gold and platinum bullion.

The burglars felt they were stealing from the rich, including the Hatton Garden jewelers who, Perkins later said, had ripped off his daughter by using a fake stone in her engagement ring. "They deserve all they get, Dad," his daughter reportedly told him.

"I'll tell you what he lost, shall I?" said Jones, counting the proceeds from one box alone. "£1.6 million worth of gold he lost, plus £70,000 in notes."

Around 5:45 a.m. on Easter Sunday, April 5, the job was done: empty metal boxes were strewn across the floor, along with the drill and broken jack, but no DNA evidence, thanks to the thieves' careful study of *Forensics for Dummies*. Jones and Perkins hauled up a wheelie bin so heavy Perkins had to stop at the top of the stairs, visibly gasping.

Collins drove the burglars away in the white van. Within 36 hours, the loot was divided up among them.

* * *

"I think we've been burgled," Kelvin Stockwell recalled being told by his associate guard on Tuesday morning, when he arrived at work.

"I went downstairs, and I saw the top lock of the door was missing," Stockwell told me. "I called the police. Fifteen, 20 minutes later they turned up. We went inside. It was like a bomb had hit the place."

By 10 a.m. the street in front of the vault was filled with emotional boxholders, who were barred from entering the building. The media soon arrived, along with insurance adjusters. Then came the excruciating wait as the police sorted through the rubble. The calls from police to the victims began on Thursday.

Some couldn't say with certainty what was in their box, and others wouldn't say. Did their boxes contain stolen goods and cash that hadn't been declared to the tax authorities? "That is why we will never know how much was actually stolen—because safety-deposit boxes are used for a number of reasons, and one of them is anonymity," said former senior detective Barry Phillips.

As the heist dominated the British media, the public seemed to be rooting for the daring, still-at-large thieves, while blaming the victims and the police, who had failed to respond to the burglar alarm.

For six weeks after the heist, the burglars reveled in their rewards and relived their crime. Old age and infirmities be damned—they were full-on thieves again, back in the cafés and the Castle pub, where they had spent three years researching and planning the heist.

* * *

The Flying Squad, the elite investigative unit within London's Metropolitan Police department, was formed in 1919 and named for its ability to "fly" across London without regard to districts. They have solved some of the biggest and most famous cases in Britain.

I met the two lead detectives in the Hatton Garden case at New Scotland Yard, in central London: Paul Johnson, 54, a tall, chiseled Clint Eastwood type, and his bright and intense deputy, Jamie Day, 43. Both wore business suits and ties bearing the squad's descending-eagle logo. Day, 20 years a London cop, seven on the Flying Squad, was the first detective through the vault's door on the morning that the burglary was discovered.

Detective Chief Inspector Paul Johnson addresses the press, April 9, 2015.

The team on the Hatton Garden heist consisted of most of the 50 or so officers in the Flying Squad's western unit. "The Hatton Garden case is not usually what the Flying Squad would take, per se," said Johnson, because no one was injured and none of the perpetrators appeared to have carried guns. "But obviously there was the magnitude of it and the detail that the gang had gone to to get themselves in. Clearly, we'd have to take it."

The Hatton Garden investigative teams were overseen by Peter Spindler, who, like the thieves, was approaching retirement. Working around the clock, officers and detectives deciphered more than 350 pieces of evidence. Most important, Spindler said, they "trawled" through days of CCTV footage collected from the 120-plus cameras in and around Hatton Garden.

Early on in the investigation, a young member of the CCTV team spotted the Flying Squad's first big break: a white Mercedes E200 with a black roof and alloy rims had passed through Hatton Garden multiple times prior to the Easter/Passover weekend.

The [car] belonged to an ex-con: Kenny Collins.

Using the easily traceable Mercedes was a major screwup. Through automatic license-plate recognition the police tracked the car's movements from Collins's home to the store where Danny Jones bought the replacement hydraulic pump.

Just as foolhardy, the burglars, while using walkie-talkies during the actual heist, used their own cell phones before and after the burglary. "Researching cell phones and call-data analysis, we started building a picture," recalled Spindler. It was more than enough to get special approval to plant listening devices in Kenny Collins's Mercedes and in Terry Perkins's Citroën Saxo.

The thieves were trailed by detectives, observed by lip-readers, bugged in their cars, and videotaped in their favorite bars. The Flying Squad was astounded by what they heard. "The biggest robbery in the world . . . we was on," said Terry Perkins in just one of many endlessly incriminating statements.

One evening in May, a month after the heist, the Flying Squad dispatched an operative with a hidden video camera to the Castle pub, where Reader sat drinking with Perkins and Collins. In the middle of the pub, Perkins pantomimed for Reader the moment that Danny Jones and his 10-ton hydraulic pump knocked over the massive wall of safe-deposit boxes. "Boom!" Perkins exclaimed, according to a lipreader, who deciphered the conversation.

Damning as the recordings were, it wasn't enough to arrest.

"You've still got to work your way through everything else and make sure you've got enough to corroborate what they're saying," said Paul Johnson. "If you don't, they would have an option of saying that 'we're just a bunch of elderly fantasists who were talking a lot of old nonsense.'"

They had to catch them with the goods.

Once the heat died down, the thieves planned to sell their haul for cash, provide for family members, and fund their pensions. But by this time people were talking and other villains seemed to know about the heist. It was imperative that they consolidate everything and sell it off fast.

Their mistake was letting the increasingly careless Kenny Collins handle the logistics. The day after the burglary, Collins gave most of his loot for safekeeping to "Billy the Fish" Lincoln, the brother of Collins's longtime girlfriend.

At 60, Lincoln suffered from incontinence, sleep apnea, and a recent double hip replacement. He had convictions for attempted theft, burglary, and battery. He duped his nephew Jon Harbinson, 42, a London taxi driver (who was eventually acquitted of having any part in the crimes), into storing three bags of the stolen goods at his house and transporting them to a handover point. Even more reckless was Collins's choice of the handover point: a pub car park in the borough of Enfield, under CCTV surveillance.

At 9:44 a.m. on Tuesday, May 19, in full view of the CCTV camera and with the Flying Squad monitoring their every move, the burglars transferred three canvas holdalls filled with jewels from the taxi to Collins's Mercedes. The police already knew the location because Perkins and Jones had previously revealed the address in conversations recorded in their car.

Almost six weeks after the heist, the Flying Squad was ready to descend. Just after 10 a.m., they stormed 12 addresses simultaneously. From Enfield to Bethnal Green to the suburb of Dartford, more than 200 officers, some in riot gear, battered through doors and dragged out the suspected burglars and their accomplices. Lincoln was stopped in his car. Reader was escorted from his old mansion "a little unsteady on his legs and clutching his heart," said a neighbor.

More than 200 officers, some in riot gear, battered through doors and dragged out the suspected burglars and their accomplices.

On Sterling Road, Terry Perkins, Danny Jones, and Kenny Collins were at the dining room table, on which a smelter had been set up to melt multi-million British pounds-worth of precious metals, when officers burst through the front door wearing riot helmets and flame-proof overalls.

"Jones tried to run out the back door, but only made it a few yards into the garden," recalled Jamie Day.

*   *   *

Presented with the recordings, the CCTV footage, and other digital evidence, Reader, Perkins, Jones, and Collins felt they had no choice but to plead guilty. The others charged in the heist—Carl Wood, Hugh Doyle, and William Lincoln—were found guilty at trial in January.

The seven were sentenced in March 2016 to a total of 34 years' imprisonment, most receiving sentences of between six and seven years (with the exception of Doyle, who received a suspended sentence).

Hatton Garden Safe Deposit Ltd. went into liquidation in September 2015, unable to recover from its damaged reputation.

The mysterious Basil is still at large, as is more than two-thirds of the haul, worth over £10 million.

The thieves had disabled the CCTV cameras and stolen their hard drives inside the actual building and its basement vault. "What they forgot, or didn't know," said the prosecutor, "was that one little camera in that walkway outside the back of one jeweler was still working and recording what they were doing."

Said Spindler, "They were analog criminals operating in a digital world, and no match for digital detectives."

Originally published in the 2017 *Reader's Digest* international editions.

Basil's real name is Michael Seed. The 58-year-old electronics expert was arrested in March 2018 after London police found 143,000 pounds worth of gold ingots, gems, and jewelry in his apartment. He was convicted a year later and sentenced to 10 years in prison.

The rest of the gang served their jail sentences and were released, except for Terry Perkins, Hugh Doyle, John "Kenny" Collins, and Danny Jones. Perkins died in prison in 2018. Doyle received a suspended sentence. Collins was released, then sent back to jail when he failed to repay a share of the haul. Jones is still serving his sentence.

My Mamma's Letters

by Octavia Capuzzi Locke,
from *Johns Hopkins Magazine*

One woman's letters help families pulled apart by the call to war feel a little closer together.

I still remember to this day my Mamma's letter-writing. It began in the winter of 1941. Every night she would sit at the big kitchen table and compose a letter to my brother Johnny, who had been drafted the preceding summer and hadn't been heard from since Pearl Harbor.

I couldn't understand why Mamma kept writing when Johnny never answered.

"You'll see—we'll get a letter from him," she insisted. Mamma said there was a direct line from the brain to the written word that was as powerful as any God-given light. She was counting on that light to find Johnny.

Whether she said this to reassure herself or Papa or all of us, I don't know. I do know it helped hold us together, and one day a letter did arrive. Johnny was alive in the South Pacific.

It always amused me that Mamma signed her letters "Cecilia Capuzzi," and I teased her about it. "Why not just write 'Mamma'?" What I had not known was that she always thought of herself as Cecilia

Capuzzi. Not Mamma. I began to see her in a new light, this petite woman who in heels scarcely measured five feet.

She wore no makeup, and no jewelry except for a yellow-gold wedding band. Her hair was fine, straight and black, tied in a bun that she refused to cut or "Americanize" with a permanent. Her tiny spectacles with the silver frames pinched her nose.

After she finished a letter, Mamma gave it to Papa to mail. Then she would put on the coffeepot, and we would sit around the table, talking about the good times when there were ten of us sitting there—Papa, Mamma and eight children. Five boys and three girls. It didn't seem possible that everyone had gone away to work or to war or to get married. Everyone except me.

By springtime, Mamma had added two more sons to her letter-writing list. Every night she would compose three different letters, then pass them to Papa and me to add our greetings.

Bit by bit, news of Mamma's letters traveled. One morning a little woman with gun-metal gray hair knocked on our door. Her voice trembled when she asked, "Is it true that you write letters?"

"I write to my sons."

"And you read too?" the woman whispered.

"Si, si."

The woman opened her shopping bag and pulled out a stack of airmail letters. "Read . . . read to me, please."

The letters were from the woman's son fighting in Europe, a boy with red hair who, Mamma remembered, used to sit on our front steps with my brothers. One by one, Mamma read the letters, translating them from English to Italian. The woman's eyes misted and sparked. "Now I must answer," she said. But what words to use?

"Make some coffee, Tavi," Mamma called to me, as she led the woman to the kitchen and a chair at the table. She took out her pen and ink and airmail paper and began to write. When she had finished, she read the letter to the woman.

"How did you know I wanted to say that?"

"I often stare at my boys' letters, the same as you, and I wonder what to write."

Soon the woman returned with a friend, and another and another—all with sons at war, all in need of letters. Mamma had become the neighborhood letter-writer. Sometimes she would spend a whole day writing.

Mamma placed great importance on people signing their names, and the little woman with the gray hair asked Mamma to teach her. "I want to learn to write my name for my boy to see." So Mamma took the woman's hand in hers, and led it up and down and around on paper, over and over, until she could do it without help. After that, whenever Mamma wrote a letter for her, the woman signed her name and smiled.

One day she came to our house, and with one look Mamma knew what had happened. All hope had gone from her eyes. They sat together for a long time, their hands touching and their hearts locked as one. Then Mamma said, "Maybe we'd better go to church. There are some things too big for people to understand." When Mamma came home, she couldn't think of anything except the boy with the red hair.

"There are some things too big for people to understand."

After the war Mamma put away pen and paper. *"Finito,"* she said. But she was wrong. The women who had come to her with their sons' mail now returned with letters from their relatives in Italy. They also came to her for help in becoming American citizens.

Mamma once confessed that she had always dreamed of writing a novel. Why didn't she? I asked.

"Everyone has a purpose in life," she said. "Mine seems to be letter-writing." She tried to explain her zeal for it.

"A letter pulls people together like nothing else. It can make you cry or shout with joy. There's no finer caress than a love letter, because it makes the world very small, and the writer and reader, the only rulers. Girl, a letter is life!"

Mamma's letters are all gone now. Yet the recipients still talk of her, carrying memories of her letters next to their hearts.

Originally published in the June 1992 issue of *Reader's Digest* magazine.

Humor Hall of Fame

theycantalk.com

i wonder if this will bounce

maybe that one will

Cartoon from the book *They Can Talk*, published by Ulysses Press

Uncle Bart was a city boy whose familiarity with wildlife began and ended with pigeons. One time he joined us at our cabin in the woods. In the evening, he opened the door to let our cats in. The first cat walked in; then the second. Bart stood there coaxing the third cat to come, which we found strange—we had only two cats. The third cat was a possum.

—**JONATHAN HAKULIN** BALTIMORE, MARYLAND

My cat just walked up to the paper shredder and said, "Teach me everything you know."

—**TWITTER** @NICCAGEMATCH

The Stranger Who Taught Magic

by Arthur Gordon

Perhaps you stand to learn the most from the most unlikely friendships.

That **July morning,** I remember, was like any other, calm and opalescent before the heat of the fierce Georgia sun. I was 13: sunburned, shaggy-haired, a little aloof, and solitary. In winter I had to put on shoes and go to school like everyone else. But summers I lived by the sea, and my mind was empty and wild and free.

On this particular morning, I had tied my rowboat to the pilings of an old dock upriver from our village. There, sometimes, the striped sheepshead lurked in the still, green water. I was crouched, motionless as a stone, when a voice spoke suddenly above my head: "Canst thou draw out leviathan with a hook, or his tongue with a cord which thou lettest down?"

I looked up, startled, into a lean, pale face and a pair of the most remarkable eyes I had ever seen. It wasn't a question of color; I'm not sure, now, what color they were. It was a combination of things: warmth, humor, interest, alertness. Intensity—that's the word, I guess—and underlying it all, a curious kind of mocking sadness. I believe I thought him old.

He saw how taken aback I was. "Sorry," he said. "It's a bit early in the morning for the Book of Job, isn't it?" He nodded at the two or three fish in the boat. "Think you could teach me how to catch those?"

Ordinarily, I was wary of strangers, but anyone interested in fishing was hardly a stranger. I nodded, and he climbed down into the boat. "Perhaps we should introduce ourselves," he said. "But then again,

Ordinarily, I was wary of strangers, but anyone interested in fishing was hardly a stranger.

perhaps not. You're a boy willing to teach, I'm a teacher willing to learn. That's introduction enough. I'll call you 'Boy,' and you call me 'Sir.'"

Such talk sounded strange in my world of sun and salt water. But there was something so magnetic about the man, and so disarming about his smile, that I didn't care.

I handed him a hand line and showed him how to bait his hooks with fiddler crabs. He kept losing baits, because he could not recognize a sheepshead's stealthy tug, but he seemed content not to catch anything. He told me he had rented one of the weathered bungalows behind the dock. "I needed to hide for a while," he said. "Not from the police, or anything like that. Just from friends and relatives. So don't tell anyone you've found me, will you?"

I was tempted to ask where he was from; there was a crispness in the way he spoke that was very different from the soft accents I was accustomed to. But I didn't. He had said he was a teacher, though, and so I asked what he taught.

"In the school catalogue they call it English," he said. "But I like to think of it as a course in magic—in the mystery and magic of words. Are you fond of words?"

I said that I had never thought much about them. I also pointed out that the tide was ebbing, that the current was too strong for more fishing, and that in any case it was time for breakfast.

"Of course," he said, pulling in his line. "I'm a little forgetful about such things these days." He eased himself back onto the dock with a little grimace, as if the effort cost him something. "Will you be back on the river later?"

I said that I would probably go casting for shrimp at low tide.

"Stop by," he said. "We'll talk about words for a while, and then perhaps you can show me how to catch shrimp."

So began a most unlikely friendship, because I did go back. To this day, I'm not sure why. Perhaps it was because, for the first time, I had met an adult on terms that were in balance. In the realm of words and ideas, he might be the teacher. But in my own small universe of winds and tides and sea creatures, the wisdom belonged to me.

Almost every day after that, we'd go wherever the sea gods or my whim decreed. Sometimes up the silver creeks, where the terrapin skittered down the banks and the great blue herons stood like statues. Sometimes along the ocean dunes, fringed with graceful sea oats, where by night the great sea turtles crawled and by day the wild goats browsed. I showed him where the mullet swirled and where the flounder lay in cunning camouflage. I learned that he was incapable of much exertion; even pulling up the anchor seemed to exhaust him. But he never complained. And, all the time, talk flowed from him like a river.

Much of it I have forgotten now, but some comes back as clear and distinct as if it all happened yesterday, not decades ago. We might be sitting in a hollow of the dunes, watching the sun go down in a smear of crimson. "Words," he'd say. "Just little black marks on paper. Just sounds in the empty air. But think of the power they have! They can make you laugh or cry, love or hate, fight or run away. They can heal or hurt. They even come to look and sound like what they mean. Angry *looks* angry on the page. Ugly *sounds* ugly when you say it. Here!" He would hand me a piece of shell. "Write a word that looks or sounds like what it means."

I would stare helplessly at the sand.

"Oh," he'd cry, "you're being dense. There are so many! Like whisper . . . leaden . . . twilight . . . chime. Tell you what: when you go to bed tonight, think of five words that look like what they mean and five that sound like what they mean. Don't go to sleep until you do!"

And I would try—but always fall asleep.

Or we might be anchored just offshore, casting into the surf for sea bass, our little bateau nosing over the rollers like a restless hound.

"Rhythm," he would say. "Life is full of it; words should have it, too. But you have to train your ear. Listen to the waves on a quiet night; you'll pick up the cadence. Look at the patterns the wind makes in dry sand and you'll see how syllables in a sentence should fall. Do you know what I mean?"

My conscious self didn't know; but perhaps something deep inside me did. In any case, I listened.

I listened, too, when he read from the books he sometimes brought: Kipling, Conan Doyle, Tennyson's *Idylls of the King*. Often he would stop and repeat a phrase or a line that pleased him. One day, in Malory's *Le Morte d'Arthur*, he found one: "And the great horse grimly neighed." "Close your eyes," he said to me, "and say that slowly, out loud." I did. "How did it make you feel?" "It gives me the shivers," I said truthfully. He was delighted.

But the magic that he taught was not confined to words; he had a way of generating in me an excitement about things I had always taken for granted. He might point to a bank of clouds. "What do you see there? Colors? That's not enough. Look for towers and drawbridges. Look for dragons and griffins and strange and wonderful beasts."

Or he might pick up an angry, claw-brandishing blue crab, holding it cautiously by the back flippers as I had taught him. "Pretend you're this crab," he'd say. "What do you see through those stalk-like eyes? What do you feel with those complicated legs? What goes on in your tiny brain? Try it for just five seconds. Stop being a boy. Be a crab!" And I would stare in amazement at the furious creature, feeling my comfortable identity lurch and sway under the impact of the idea.

So the days went by. Our excursions became less frequent, because he tired so easily. He brought two chairs down to the dock and some books, but he didn't read much. He seemed content to watch me as I fished, or the circling gulls, or the slow river coiling past.

A sudden shadow fell across my life when my parents told me I was going to camp for two weeks. On the dock that afternoon I asked my friend if he would be there when I got back. "I hope so," he said gently.

But he wasn't. I remember standing on the sun-warmed planking of the old dock, staring at the shuttered bungalow and feeling a hollow sense of finality and loss. I ran to Jackson's grocery store—where everyone knew everything—and asked where the schoolteacher had gone.

"He was sick, real sick," Mrs. Jackson replied. "Doc phoned his relatives up north to come get him. He left something for you—he figured you'd be asking after him."

She handed me a book. It was a slender volume of verse, *Flame and Shadow*, by someone I had never heard of: Sara Teasdale. The corner of one page was turned down, and there was a penciled star by one of the poems. I still have the book, with that poem, "On the Dunes."

If there is any life when death is over,
These tawny beaches will know much of me,
I shall come back, as constant and as changeful
As the unchanging, many-colored sea.
If life was small, if it had made me scornful,
Forgive me; I shall straighten like a flame
In the great calm of death, and if you want me
Stand on the sea-ward dunes and call my name.

* * *

Well, I have never stood on the dunes and called his name. For one thing, I never knew it; for another, I'd be too self-conscious. And there are long stretches when I forget all about him. But sometimes—when the music or the magic in a phrase makes my skin tingle, or when I pick up an angry blue crab, or when I see a dragon in the flaming sky—sometimes I remember.

Originally published in the June 1970 issue of *Reader's Digest* magazine.

Runaway Train

by William M. Hendry

Tons of poisonous phenol were barreling toward Kenton, Ohio. They had ten minutes to stop the runaway train.

Looking out the weather-streaked window of the control tower 40 feet above the Toledo rail yard, Jon Hosfeld anxiously scanned the maze of tracks and belching locomotives. Just then a light on the electronic map of the yard's main tracks flashed white—confirming his fear. A freight train had run a switch and was rolling onto the main line into high-speed traffic. In 31 years with the railroad, Hosfeld had never seen that happen.

A bizarre sequence of events had set the train loose. There are three braking systems on a train. Leaving the cab, the engineer had set two— but when he reached for the third, he grabbed the throttle instead. After he stepped out, the locomotive hauling 47 cars pulled away. Two of the cars in the CSX Transportation freight contained molten phenol, a poisonous chemical used in making adhesives, dyes and paints. A wreck could release a lavalike flood of the toxin.

Hosfeld and another supervisor dashed down the tower and leapt into a truck. Believing the train was just coasting, they planned to race to the first crossing, jump aboard and stop it. Just 12 minutes later, calculating that they were well ahead of a slow-moving train, they pulled up to a

"Catch it!"—The dispatcher's order sent Hosfeld, Knowlton and Forson on the ride of their lives.

crossing in the tiny village of Dunbridge and surveyed the tracks. There was no train in sight—it had already gone through.

Hosfeld almost choked at the realization: "It's not coasting—it's under power!"

It was about 12:40 p.m., May 15, 2001, and hundreds of unprotected crossings and dozens of towns lay in the train's path. A loaded freight under power was a weapon weighing thousands of tons. It could blast through a village like a Tomahawk missile. The town in greatest danger was Kenton, about 70 miles south. There was a steep downhill grade and 25-m.p.h. curves as the track weaved into town, passing fuel storage tanks, gas stations and homes. If the runaway crashed into those tanks, there could be an inferno.

Instantly railway officials warned police in towns all along the line.

At that moment a gleaming blue and yellow locomotive was leaving Kenton headed north, directly into the path of the runaway. Engineer Jess Knowlton, 48, and conductor Terry Forson, 30, were piloting the big engine labeled Q636. They had heard reports about a driverless train on their radio, but had no idea where it was. Just then a dispatcher's voice jarred them: "Q636, you need to get into a siding ASAP!"

The nearest siding was ten miles straight ahead. Knowlton stiffened. He glanced at his young, sandy-haired conductor. Both men wore jeans and short-sleeve shirts, safety glasses and steel-toed work boots. "Hey, kid, you know what we're doing?" asked the wiry, 28-year veteran.

Forson, tall and strongly built, had only 14 months with the railroad and just two riding with Knowlton—but he knew. "Yeah," he said, swallowing hard, "we're racing against something head-on."

The radio squawked again. "636, get into the siding now!"

Fighting their way through traffic in Bowling Green, Jon Hosfeld and his co-worker Mike Smith made it back to the interstate. They darted around cars at speeds up to 95 m.p.h. Finally they spotted the runaway off to their left—vapor streaming from its exhaust stacks, its brakes squealing. It was under full power. "Look at that S.O.B. go!" Hosfeld said.

Jess Knowlton nervously nudged the throttle on Q636 to the eighth notch—full out. The engine was howling. If they popped over a hill and hit the runaway, it was all over. But minutes later, steel squealing against steel, he ran his train onto the siding—15 m.p.h. over the speed limit. As they ground to a stop, Knowlton took a deep breath and blew it out slowly.

Moments later a call came from the dispatcher. He asked that they secure their cars, disconnect their locomotive and move it to the north end of the mile-and-a-half-long siding. Then came a final appeal: "Once the runaway goes by, you've got to go after it."

That's insane! Jess Knowlton thought. But he also saw the logic. His engine was the only thing that could stop the runaway before it barreled into Kenton.

Knowlton keyed his microphone. "We understand," he answered simply—but his body was surging with adrenaline.

Waiting for the runaway, Knowlton used his cell phone to call his wife, Hollie. He didn't have time to explain, he said. Just turn on the news. "This may be the last time we talk." And he told her goodbye.

Forson overheard the conversation and wondered if he should call home. Then it was too late. The earth began to shake, and the two trainmen heard the bellowing roar of a 3000-horse, diesel-powered locomotive. Knowlton and Forson turned to one another. "Good God!" they said in unison. They, too, had been expecting a string of coasting cars, not a train running at full throttle. Stopping a coasting train would have been challenge enough. This monster was racing south at almost 50 m.p.h. Stopping that was unimaginable.

Alerted by railroad officials, law enforcement agencies established roadblocks at dozens of crossings in four counties. Evacuations in Kenton were already underway, and Jon Hosfeld and Mike Smith abandoned their chase to speed directly there.

Along the line, the runaway had been routed through slow-speed sidings in the hope that it would derail in an unpopulated area. Three times it had overrun the switch and plowed back onto the main line. At one point railway workers rushed out and set a portable derailing device onto the track. The 50-pound wedge-shaped chunk of steel worked on trains traveling at slow speeds. But the racing locomotive hit the derailer, kicked the device aside like a roller skate and sped on toward Kenton.

As the runaway shook past them, Knowlton and Forson jumped into action. Knowlton stood at the throttle facing a network of gauges and levers. Forson was at his side, coordinating switch alignments with the radio dispatcher. When they were back on the main line, the dispatcher gave them the order: "Go catch it!"

They had about ten minutes before the runaway hit the downhill curve into Kenton. Knowlton turned around to look backward out a narrow window—the engine housing blocked half his view. Yet the entire chase would have to be done in reverse. On right-hand curves, he'd be blinded completely. Forson would have to guide him.

Of course, he'd operated in reverse thousands of times in rail yards, on straight track, inching along. Never at speeds approaching 70 m.p.h. No one had ever done that. But now he shoved the throttle forward to the eighth notch.

As the 190-ton locomotive gathered speed, Forson darted outside down the narrow gangway that ran the length of the engine and took a position on the rear platform. From there, he'd give Knowlton arm signals about turns and the approach to the runaway. The train was shaking so badly he had to grab the waist-high railing with both hands and spread his feet wide just to keep his balance.

For safety, the rule book said that without cars attached, a locomotive the size of Knowlton's wasn't to exceed 30 m.p.h. It was too prone to derailment. But rules were useless now. The runaway was about two miles ahead. They would have to catch it before it went another six.

In less than two minutes, Jess Knowlton pushed Q636 to over 65 m.p.h. He had about four minutes until they hit the downhill. The massive locomotive heaved from rail to rail. If it came off the tracks, there was little chance of survival.

Three minutes left. Knowlton leaned on the whistle as they blew through one road crossing after another. At this speed, he would never be able to stop if a car pulled into his path. He pressed so hard the metal whistle handle broke off in his hand. "Damn!" he said, tossing it aside.

They had maybe two minutes left.

On the rear deck, the wind blasted Terry Forson. He held on with all he had, swaying 18 inches side to side as the wheel flanges caught one rail and bounced to the next. He fought to keep his focus, signaling speed changes to Knowlton, scanning the horizon.

Just then, Forson spotted the runaway, a hopper car at its tail. The car was loaded with grain, and the rush of wind pelted his face with corn.

They were 90 seconds from the downhill. Forson prepared for impact. He pulled himself along the railing toward Knowlton; then he sat on the steel gangway, pressed his back to the cab door and wrapped both arms around a steel pipe.

Knowlton deftly inched Q636 closer. *Here we go*, he thought. The gap between the two trains narrowed quickly. Too quickly! They were moving at ten times the normal coupling speed. If they hit too hard, they would knock the hopper car from the track, derail the train and plow straight into it.

They had less than a minute. Knowlton eased off the throttle and tapped the brakes, slowing to 50. Then 40. Two car lengths away now. "Easy. Easy . . ."

Thirty seconds.

He eased off the throttle and tapped the brakes . . . Wham!

Wham! The impact was jarring, but not catastrophic. But had they coupled?

Forson jumped to his feet and hurried back to his post on the rear deck. He signaled thumbs-up to Knowlton. The coupling was good.

Now what? Knowlton wondered. The two engines were in a tug of war, with 47 cars between them. If just one coupling in the string snapped, they'd all fly off the rails.

Knowlton let the trains settle, easing the slack between cars as Forson returned to the cab. He then applied full dynamic braking, a process akin to reverse thrust on a jet engine. The effect was almost immediate. The runaway slowed to 30 m.p.h., 20 . . . 10.

Then just as suddenly, the speed began to climb again. The great mass of the runaway was pulling them over the crest onto the downhill track. The speed jumped to 15, then 20 m.p.h.

Knowlton leaned on the brake levers. At 22 m.p.h., he felt them grab again. He had no hope of stopping the runaway completely—not with its throttle wide open. But if he could slow it enough to get safely through Kenton, perhaps someone could scramble aboard and shut it down.

Seconds later they rounded the first bend into Kenton—and there below was the fuel depot. Knowlton checked his speed. It was just under the maximum for the curve.

* * *

Waiting at the other end of town, Jon Hosfeld stood in the middle of a blocked-off road crossing. He knew he'd get only one chance at this. As a much younger man, he'd often leapt aboard slow-moving trains in rail yards. But at 12 m.p.h., this train wasn't creeping and he was 52 years old.

The train was bearing directly down on him now, its engine still howling. As it swept past, Hosfeld took two quick side steps, reached for the railing with both hands and kicked up his left foot.

In that instant, he was jerked from the pavement. His foot caught a step, and he hoisted himself onto the platform. Then he scrambled inside the locomotive and jammed the throttle off.

* * *

At the opposite end of the train, Jess Knowlton felt the power come down immediately. "It's over," he said to Forson, ". . . nobody's hurt."

They powered down Q636, set all three braking systems and, totally exhausted, exited their cab. They had done the unimaginable—caught, coupled and stopped a runaway train. And saved the town of Kenton.

Originally published in the March 2002 issue of *Reader's Digest* magazine.

Jon Hosfeld, Terry Forson and Jess Knowlton all served as advisors for the 2010 movie "Unstoppable," which was based on the CSX incident. Hosfeld and Knowlton are retired from the railroad. Forson still works for CSX and advocates for train safety.

FOLLOWING DIRECTIONS

I looked away settling in a lounge chair, and it happened.
Stephen, my four-year-old son, disappeared. He was playing
in a swimming pool one moment, then he was missing. I
scanned the water more carefully. No Stephen. I asked the
lifeguard, who shook her head. Only a mother could react
with the intense panic that flooded me. For 25 minutes,
I searched frantically for a boy in a red swimsuit. Then I
noticed an announcement being repeated. "If you are looking
for a lost child, come to the courtesy booth." I reached the
booth breathless, and noticed Stephen seated, leafing through
a brochure. He looked up. "Mom! Where have you been?" he
demanded. "Don't you remember telling me to come here if
I couldn't find you? Well? Here I am!!!" I shook my head. If
only I could follow directions as well as Stephen.

—JoAnn Cohen *Havertown, Pennsylvania*

AN EVEN SWAP

When I got engaged in my early 20s, my wife-to-be was a
soft-spoken young lady who rarely raised her voice or spouted
off a retort regardless of the often snarky remarks I made
about one thing or another. One day, I asked her why WE got
engaged but SHE got a diamond ring. She said, "Well, you're
getting me." I said, "But you're getting me!" "Right," she
replied, just as calm as you please, "and you had to put up a
diamond ring to make it an even swap."

—CA Hamilton *Aurora, Illinois*

A Miracle of Mermaids

by Margo Pfeiff

A balloon, mermaids and kind hearts conspire to help a grieving girl.

Rhonda Gill froze as she heard her four-year-old daughter, Desiree, sobbing quietly in the family room that morning in October 1993. Rhonda tiptoed through the doorway. The tiny dark-haired child was hugging a photograph of her father, who had died nine months earlier. Rhonda, 24, watched as Desiree gently ran her fingers around her father's face. "Daddy," she said softly, "why won't you come back?"

The petite brunette college student felt a surge of despair. It had been hard enough coping with her husband Ken's death, but her daughter's grief was more than she could bear. If only I could tear the pain out of her, Rhonda thought.

Ken Gill and Rhonda Hill of Yuba City, California, had met when Rhonda was 18, and had married after a whirlwind courtship. Their daughter, Desiree, was born on January 9, 1989.

Although a muscular six feet, three inches tall, Ken was a gentle man whom everyone loved. His big passion was his daughter. "She's a real daddy's girl," Rhonda would often say as Ken's eyes twinkled with pride.

Father and daughter went everywhere together: hiking, dune-buggy riding and fishing for bass and salmon on the Feather River.

Instead of gradually adjusting to her father's death, Desiree had refused to accept it. "Daddy will be home soon," she would tell her mother. "He's at work." When she played with her toy telephone, she pretended she was chatting with him. "I miss you, Daddy," she'd say. "When will you come back?"

After Ken's death, Rhonda moved from her apartment in Yuba City to her mother's home in nearby Live Oak. Seven weeks after the funeral, Desiree was still inconsolable. "I just don't know what to do," Rhonda told her mother, Trish Moore, a 47-year-old medical assistant.

One evening the three of them sat outside, gazing at the stars over the Sacramento Valley. "See that one, Desiree?" Her grandmother pointed at a bright speck near the horizon. "That's your daddy shining down from heaven." Several nights later Rhonda woke to find Desiree on the doorstep in her pajamas, weeping as she sought her daddy's star. Twice they took her to a child therapist, but nothing seemed to help.

"How about if we tie a letter to a balloon and send it up to heaven?"

As a last resort, Trish took Desiree to Ken's grave. The child laid her head against his gravestone and said, "Maybe if I listen hard enough I can hear Daddy talk to me."

Then one evening, as Rhonda tucked her child in, Desiree announced, "I want to die, Mommy, so I can be with Daddy." *God help me*, Rhonda prayed. *What more can I possibly do?*

* * *

November 8, 1993, would have been Ken's 29th birthday. "How will I send him a card?" Desiree asked her grandmother.

"How about if we tie a letter to a balloon," Trish said, "and send it up to heaven?" Desiree's eyes immediately lit up.

On their way to the cemetery, the back seat of the car full of flowers for their planned gravesite visit, the three stopped at a store. "Help Mom pick out a balloon," Trish instructed. At a rack where dozens of helium-filled silver Mylar balloons bobbed, Desiree made an instant decision: "That one!" Happy Birthday was emblazoned above a drawing of the Little Mermaid from the Disney film. Desiree and her father had often watched the video together.

The child's eyes shone as they arranged flowers on Ken's grave. It was a beautiful day, with a slight breeze rippling the eucalyptus trees. Then Desiree dictated a letter to her dad. "Tell him 'Happy Birthday. I love you and miss you,'" she rattled off. "'I hope you get this and can write me on my birthday in January.'"

Trish wrote the message and their address on a small piece of paper, which was then wrapped in plastic and tied to the end of the string on the balloon. Finally Desiree released the balloon.

For almost an hour they watched the shining spot of silver grow ever smaller. "Okay," Trish said at last. "Time to go home." Rhonda and Trish were beginning to walk slowly from the grave when they heard Desiree shout excitedly, "Did you see that? I saw Daddy reach down and take it!" The balloon, visible just moments earlier, had disappeared. "Now Dad's going to write me back," Desiree declared.

* * *

On a cold, rainy November morning on Prince Edward Island in eastern Canada, 32-year-old Wade MacKinnon pulled on his waterproof duck-hunting gear. MacKinnon, a forest ranger, lived with his wife and three children in Mermaid, a rural community a few miles east of Charlottetown.

But instead of driving to the estuary where he usually hunted, he suddenly decided to go to Mermaid Lake, two miles away. Leaving his pickup, he hiked past dripping spruce and pine and soon entered a cranberry bog surrounding the 23-acre lake. In the bushes on the shoreline, something fluttered and caught his eye. Curious, he approached to find a silver balloon snagged in the branches of a thigh-high bayberry bush. Printed on one side was a picture of a mermaid. When he untangled the string, he found a soggy piece of paper at the end of it, wrapped in plastic.

At home, MacKinnon carefully removed the wet note, allowing it to dry. When his wife, Donna, came home later, he said, "Look at this," and showed her the balloon and note. Intrigued, she read: "November 8, 1993. Happy Birthday, Daddy. . . ." It finished with a mailing address in Live Oak, California.

"It's only November 12," Wade exclaimed. "This balloon traveled 3,000 miles in four days!"

"And look," said Donna, turning the balloon over. "This is a Little Mermaid balloon, and it landed at Mermaid Lake."

"We have to write to Desiree," Wade said. "Maybe we were chosen to help this little girl." But he could see that his wife didn't feel the same way. With tears in her eyes, Donna stepped away from the balloon. "Such a young girl having to deal with death—it's awful," she said.

Wade let the matter rest. He placed the note in a drawer and tied the balloon, still buoyant, to the railing of the balcony overlooking their living room. But the sight of the balloon made Donna uncomfortable. A few days later, she stuffed it in a closet.

As the weeks went by, however, Donna found herself thinking more and more about the balloon. It had flown over the Rocky Mountains and the Great Lakes. Just a few more miles and it would have landed in the ocean. Instead it had stopped there, in Mermaid.

Our three children are so lucky, she thought. *They have two healthy parents.* She imagined how their daughter, Hailey, almost two years old, would feel if Wade were to die.

The next morning, Donna said to Wade: "You're right. We have this balloon for a reason. We have to try to help Desiree."

*　　*　　*

In a Charlottetown bookstore Donna MacKinnon bought an adaptation of *The Little Mermaid.* A few days later, just after Christmas, Wade brought home a birthday card that read "For a Dear Daughter, Loving Birthday Wishes."

Donna sat down one morning to write a letter to Desiree. When she finished, she tucked it into the birthday card, wrapped it up with the book and mailed the package on January 3, 1994.

*　　*　　*

Desiree's fifth birthday came and went quietly with a small party on January 9. Every day since they'd released the balloon, Desiree had asked Rhonda, "Do you think Daddy has my balloon yet?" After her party she stopped asking.

Late on the afternoon of January 19, the MacKinnons' package arrived. Busy cooking dinner, Trish looked at the unfamiliar return address and assumed it was a birthday gift for her granddaughter from someone in Ken's family. Rhonda and Desiree had moved back to Yuba City, so Trish decided to deliver it to Rhonda the next day.

As Trish watched television that evening, a thought nagged at her. Why would someone send a parcel for Desiree to this address? Tearing the package open, she found the card. "For a Dear Daughter . . ." Her heart raced. *Dear God!* she thought, and reached for the telephone. It was after midnight, but she had to call Rhonda.

✳   ✳   ✳

When Trish, eyes red from weeping, pulled into Rhonda's driveway the next morning at 6:45, her daughter and granddaughter were already up. Rhonda and Trish sat Desiree between them on the couch. Trish said, "Desiree, this is for you," and handed her the parcel. "It's from your daddy."

"I know," said Desiree matter-of-factly. "Grandma, read it to me."

"Happy birthday from your daddy," Trish began. "I guess you must be wondering who we are. Well, it all started in November when my husband, Wade, went duck hunting. Guess what he found? A mermaid balloon that you sent your daddy . . ." Trish paused. A single tear began to trickle down Desiree's cheek. "There are no stores in heaven, so your daddy wanted someone to do his shopping for him. I think he picked us because we live in a town called Mermaid."

Trish continued reading: "I know your daddy would want you to be happy and not sad. I know he loves you very much and will always be watching over you. Lots of love, the MacKinnons."

When Trish finished reading, she looked at Desiree. "I knew Daddy would find a way not to forget me," the child said.

Wiping the tears from her eyes, Trish put her arm around Desiree and began to read *The Little Mermaid* that the MacKinnons had sent. The story was different from the one Ken had so often read to the child. In that version, the Little Mermaid lives happily ever after with the handsome prince. But in the new one, she dies because a wicked witch has taken her tail. Three angels carry her away.

As Trish finished reading, she worried that the ending would upset her granddaughter. But Desiree put her hands on her cheeks with delight. "She goes to heaven!" she cried. "That's why Daddy sent me this book. Because the mermaid goes to heaven just like him!"

* * *

In mid-February the MacKinnons received a letter from Rhonda: "On January 19 my little girl's dream came true when your parcel arrived."

"On January 19 my little girl's dream came true when your parcel arrived."

During the next few weeks, the MacKinnons and the Gills often telephoned each other. Then, in March, Rhonda, Trish and Desiree flew to Prince Edward Island to meet the MacKinnons. As the two families walked through the forest to see the spot beside the lake where Wade had found the balloon, Rhonda and Desiree fell silent. It seemed as though Ken was there with them.

Today whenever Desiree wants to talk about her dad, she still calls the MacKinnons. A few minutes on the telephone soothes her as nothing else can.

"People tell me, 'What a coincidence that your mermaid balloon landed so far away at a place called Mermaid Lake,'" says Rhonda. "But we know Ken picked the MacKinnons as a way to send his love to Desiree. She understands now that her father is with her always."

Originally published in the September 1995 issue of *Reader's Digest* magazine.

Humor Hall of Fame

In a discussion about America in the '60s, I asked if anyone had heard of LBJ. One of my students asked, "Do you mean LeBron James?"
—**ERIC BELL** LEXINGTON, NEBRASKA

Former senator Alan Simpson does not blame politicians for a dearth of upstanding congressmen. "About 15 percent of Americans are screwballs, lightweights, and boobs," he says. "And you don't want people like that NOT represented in Congress."

Mothers all want their sons to grow up to be president, but they don't want them to become politicians in the process.
—JOHN F. KENNEDY

To me, political office should be like jury duty. You should just get a notice in the mail one day and be like, "I'm secretary of state next month!"
—**WANDA SYKES,** COMEDIAN

Cartoon by Teresa Parkhurst Burns

PREHISTORIC ELECTIONS

BURNS

"Congratulations. Looks like you are in office."

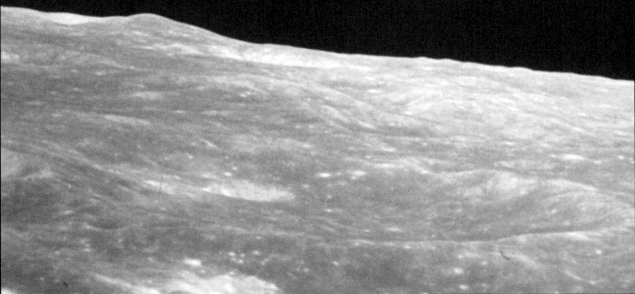

PHOTO OF LASTING INTEREST

Earthrise

Planet Earth rises above the moon's surface in this breathtaking photo, taken by Apollo 8 astronaut Bill Anders on Christmas Eve in 1968. Former Vice President Al Gore, chair of the Climate Reality Project, notes, "*Earthrise* showed for the first time the delicate balance between our planet's beauty and the dark void in which it resides. This photo had a profound effect on our global consciousness and, in turn, gave birth to the modern environmental movement." *Photograph by William Anders/NASA*

I Captured
Adolf Eichmann

by Peter Z. Malkin and Harry Stein,
condensed from *Eichmann in My Hands*

*The Mossad, Israel's secret service, had
spent months setting its trap, tracking its
target with painstaking care.*

Which route would he take back from work? How likely was he to
travel alone? Did he always arrive on time? Now, as night fell on Buenos
Aires, agent Peter Malkin stood in the shadows, waiting.

Soon he would face a man whose name was synonymous with
Nazism and evil. Under that name millions had been transported to the
gas chambers. And under that name Malkin's own sister had gone to her
death. Adolf Eichmann. For years the unrepentant killer had escaped
justice. But the moment had come, Malkin promised himself, for Eichmann's luck to run out. It was Judgment Day.

* * *

It had never been a secret that part of our mission at the Mossad was to
hunt for Nazi war criminals. A thick file of names—administrators, camp
guards, commanders of death squads—was kept constantly updated for

our operations. But in 1960, 15 years after the war, I, like so many of my colleagues, forced myself to view the matter realistically.

The trails of many of these killers had grown cold. And it was now the Arabs who threatened Israel's security. We could not allow ourselves to be obsessed with the search for Hitler's men; nor could we allocate too many resources to it.

Then in April 1960 came news that would turn my world upside down. Intelligence operatives had confirmed that Adolf Eichmann, the man whose crimes set the standards of Nazi barbarism, was alive and living in Argentina. And I would be joining the team that would actually make the capture.

I sat now in our Tel Aviv office with the three men I would work with most closely: Uzi, my pal; Meir, a mechanical genius; and Swiss-born Aharon, whose responsibility would be logistics and planning. Someone flipped out the lights, and on the screen before us appeared a slide. A head-and-shoulders shot of a man in his mid-30s in full SS regalia, with a sharp nose, thin lips and impassive eyes peering from beneath the shiny black visor. The face was the very image of a Nazi commander—cruel, decisive, utterly sure of himself.

Uzi motioned for the next slide—also taken during the war, but this time unposed and from a distance. The man, wearing a greatcoat and jackboots and holding a riding crop, was looking off to the left.

I knew these likenesses were hard to come by. Eichmann had refused to pose for any photos other than those essential for official purposes—seeing to it that the negatives were destroyed and keeping tabs on every print. Frustrated investigators found that even in group shots he had tried to obscure his face, positioning himself in the last row behind larger men. But he was unmistakable.

Uzi moved on to the next slide: a man of later middle age, balding and hollow cheeked, a pair of spectacles perched on his nose above a thick mustache. The man who called himself Ricardo Klement stood near his home on the outskirts of Buenos Aires, Argentina, wearing a neat but obviously cheap suit.

"These shots have been examined by our best photo-ID people," noted Aharon, "and they feel good about them."

"Obviously there's a risk," cut in Uzi. "We can't be sure it's Eichmann until we've got him."

There was a long silence. Except for Uzi, every one of us had lost immediate family in the concentration camps. "Once we're certain," Meir said, "why don't we kill the bastard on the spot?"

Uzi nodded. "We all share that feeling, I'm sure."

Meir shook his head bitterly. "What chance did he give those people?" he demanded. "I saw them, the ones that survived. What kind of consideration did he show them?"

For a long moment, no one made any response.

"Let's never forget," said Uzi finally, "that's part of the difference between him and us."

*　　*　　*

I studied the thick Eichmann file in the days that followed and found myself profoundly apprehensive. We would be attempting to kidnap a man on the soil of a friendly country and spirit him abroad without due process. While the morality of our mission was clear, the legality was not. One wrong move, one error in judgment, and there would be an international uproar. All that would be remembered by my colleagues, possibly by the entirety of the Jewish people, was that Adolf Eichmann had been in our grasp and we had let him get away. Never before in my career had I been frightened of an assignment. Now I was terrified.

I reassured myself that the men selected for the capture were as capable a crew as could be assembled. Then, too, there was a final member of the team: the head of our country's secret service, Isser Harel himself. In spite of the possibility of international repercussions, there was still no way Isser was going to miss this assignment.

Dubbing the operation "Attila," we put together a plan that was quite simple: we would seize Eichmann at night, in a deserted area, working with as small a crew as possible. He would then be driven to a safe house and kept in a camouflaged room until we could find some way to get him out of the country and back to Israel for trial.

This last element would be especially tricky, and it had yet to be resolved. A return trip from Buenos Aires to Israel by boat would take as long as two months, with several potentially dangerous stops at foreign ports. Getting out by plane was risky since our country had no direct service to Argentina. But Isser reassured us that he was working on a plan.

With so little time, every preparation was vital. I began a crash program in the gym, emphasizing strength and reaction time. I also started work on various disguises for members of the team. If an already wary Eichmann began spotting the same faces in his neighborhood, the operation would be fatally compromised.

And I made my emotional preparation. An effective agent has to work up a powerful dislike for the target. This is not a parlor game he is engaged in. The dislike must be intense, and ideally it should be personal. In this case, it would hardly have seemed to be a problem. Adolf Eichmann was a monster.

And yet, it proved to be not so simple. I'd learned to regard the Holocaust with dispassion, unspeakable horror though it was, refusing to acknowledge my own depth of loss and pain. For the first time I found myself asking, *Why hadn't I listened when my parents talked about my sister, her children, our village? Why hadn't I been strong enough to stay in the room?*

*   *   *

I arrived at my mother's apartment late one Friday afternoon and told her that I would be leaving on assignment soon. As we spoke, my eyes strayed to the near wall of the living room and a display of family photographs. Though they had been there for years, I'd always avoided looking at them closely. Now I asked if there was an extra of my sister, Fruma, and her two children—all killed in the Holocaust.

Where was I going that had me thinking about my sister, my mother asked. I said nothing. She knew I couldn't tell her. But later, along with the photo I'd asked for, she brought a stack of Fruma's letters, tied with a brown ribbon—"now that you're suddenly so sentimental."

As I read the letters that night, the memories came in a jumble.

Agent Peter Malkin

I was only 4½ years old in 1933 when my parents took me and my older brothers, Jacob and Yechiel, and fled Poland for Palestine. My sister, Fruma, was left behind. Permission to settle in Palestine was difficult to obtain, and at 23 Fruma had a husband and children of her own. Somehow she would join us later.

Our family settled with almost nothing in a small apartment in Haifa. None of us had anticipated how harsh this new world would be. My father and Yechiel put in backbreaking labor for 15 hours a day, under a brutal sun, hauling sand and breaking stones to make bricks. When I asked my father how we would survive, he said simply, "Don't worry, Peter. You're braver than you think."

I was vaguely aware that whenever my mother had a free hour, she spent it at some immigration office or refugee agency, but to a young boy that was just her routine. How could I know that Fruma's situation was increasingly desperate? How could I begin to grasp my parents' apprehension and crushing powerlessness? It was 1938. How could I have known the tragedy we were all about to live?

The next year, as the Germans moved into Poland, we began to hear reports that Jews were being rounded up and sent to mass gathering places. We knew that under these terrible circumstances some were probably dying. But how could we fathom anything more?

At war's end, there was an eerie silence. All of us waited to hear from loved ones.

Nothing.

Then reports began to come in, followed by the first newsreels from the camps. The enormity of what had occurred began to register. They had been murdered. Not by the thousands or even hundreds but by the millions.

In our house we avoided one another's eyes. And yet even then my mother did not stop hoping. With so much confusion, there always remained the possibility: maybe one of them had escaped.

Sometimes it happened. Miraculously, someone would appear. The daughter of a couple across the street turned out to have been hidden by Polish peasant neighbors. Letters came—a brother, a cousin, a friend had survived the camps.

But it never happened for us.

*　　*　　*

It was during that time—as we struggled to come to terms with the loss of so many loved ones—that we first started hearing the name Eichmann. He was the one the survivors talked about, more than Himmler or Goring, more even than Hitler. Newspaper articles appeared. Eyewitness accounts were recorded. In the public mind, he soon took on mythic proportions of evil; a contemporary Satan, the one who had organized it all.

Adolf Eichmann began his spectacular rise to power during the early, heady days of the Third Reich, when anything was possible for an ambitious young man unburdened by conscience.

In just three years' time, he rose from the modest rank of sergeant to become head of the SS department charged with deporting Jews from recently annexed Austria, rendering it *judenrein*—Jew-free.

After several months in Czechoslovakia, where he was responsible for Jewish "emigration," he was moved to Berlin as head of the Jewish section in the Gestapo. By 1941 the files in Eichmann's headquarters contained the order for the "Final Solution": the Jewish population was to be physically exterminated.

Shortly after the program began, Eichmann traveled east to witness the action. In Minsk, hundreds of Jews were marched from the city. As Eichmann watched, soldiers ordered them into a long trench, then began moving along the line, firing point-blank into the backs of their heads. "I can still see a woman with a child," Eichmann would recall later. "She was shot and then the baby in her arms. His brains splattered all around, also over my leather overcoat. My driver helped me remove them."

The Nazis began to chart the results of the program closely, tabulating numbers in Berlin as the totals ran into the hundreds of thousands, and finally into the millions. But like other Nazi leaders, Eichmann recognized that shooting was inefficient, a frightful waste of ammunition. The process also had a negative impact on the morale of some of the German soldiers. The need for them to be spared all these bloodbaths led to the search for new killing techniques.

In the fall of 1941, Eichmann visited the site chosen for the Belzec camp in Poland. The gas chambers that would be built there could annihilate up to 15,000 people a day. Such camps lent themselves to the merciless deception at which the Nazis had become adept. The newer camps were set up far from population centers, and in some the gas chambers were flanked by flowers or shrubs and disguised as showers.

Quite simply, Eichmann saw his mission—the elimination of Jews from the face of the earth—as a priority at least equal to that of winning the war. Nothing could be allowed to impede it. Even as the war began to go badly, Eichmann opposed deals with outsiders in which Jewish lives were to be ransomed. As the Reich collapsed, he pressed for the destruction of those Jews remaining in the camps.

In early May 1945, as the Allies closed in, Eichmann led a unit into the Austrian Alps to fight on as guerrillas. But almost immediately the men received orders to lay down their arms: Germany had surrendered. Heeding the entreaties of the others, who had no wish to be captured in the presence of so notorious a figure, Eichmann agreed to move off on his own.

They watched him leave, making his way down a mountain trail, carrying a couple of days' provisions. For years afterward, that was the last the world would know of him.

*   *   *

On the evening of May 3, 1960, Uzi, Meir and I departed for Argentina.

The address we'd been given turned out to be an elegant four-story apartment building in the wealthy quarter, rented by David, Operation Attila's front man. The kind of safe house we needed—large enough to accommodate our entire contingent and suitably laid out to hide a prisoner—had proved hard to come by. Few owners were willing to lease their properties for just a month or so, as we required.

Even worse, most residences of any size included on-site employees as part of the package. Indeed, a uniformed concierge manned the lobby of the apartment we were in now, making it impossible for us to use it as a permanent hiding place.

> *Indeed, a uniformed concierge manned the lobby of the apartment we were in now, making it impossible for us to use it as a permanent hiding place.*

The automobile situation was almost as desperate. On the trip from the airport, I had noted that most of the cars on the road were at least a decade old; many were bona-fide museum pieces. David would simply have to round up the best models he could, and then we'd rely on Meir's magic mechanic's hands.

Isser, who had already arrived, had left word he wanted to see Uzi and me as soon as possible at a café ten minutes away. As we drove over to meet him, I noted heavily armed soldiers and armored personnel carriers at several intersections. We were well aware that Perón sympathizers were attempting to disrupt preparations for Argentina's upcoming 150th anniversary. The presence of armed soldiers in the streets would not make our task any easier.

Isser wanted us to look over the operational area immediately. So in a few minutes Uzi and I were back in the car, heading northeast on Route 202 toward the suburb of San Fernando, where Eichmann—Ricardo Klement—lived.

As we approached the district, rain fell steadily. Aharon eased the car off the main road, then made a sharp turn onto a side street, weaving his way around the large puddles. It was a poor area, even worse than the photos had shown. The houses were small and ramshackle.

A few minutes later we turned onto a lane parallel to Garibaldi. Aharon killed the engine and we got out, slogging our way through the mud and rain. My suit was soon plastered to my body, and my shoes began to squeak. We made it to the base of a steep hill, then crawled to the top. We were on the railroad embankment. Directly beneath us lay another set of railroad tracks. The setting unnerved me. Eichmann had always considered "collection and transport" to be his field of greatest competence.

Before us was the view we had become so familiar with in photographs: off to the left, Route 202, heavy with traffic; and directly ahead, the Klement home. We knelt on the wooden ties and rested our elbows on the cold tracks. With field glasses, I felt I could touch the house.

I checked my watch. According to the reports, Klement usually appeared between 7:20 and 8 p.m. I turned my glasses toward the highway, nudging Uzi as a brightly lit bus detached itself from the traffic and squealed to a stop. My watch read 7:35.

The bus pulled away, leaving two figures at the curb. One was a woman, the other a man in a hat and trench coat.

"That's him!" hissed Aharon.

The two separated, the man turning onto Garibaldi Street. It was too dark to make out his features, only that he wore heavy-rimmed glasses.

But there was his walk—purposeful, measured, head erect. Instantly any doubt melted away.

Eichmann!

*　　*　　*

The following day my surveillance of the target area began in earnest and continued for nearly a week. I walked the street in front of Klement's house; I rode the dilapidated bus on which Klement traveled to and from his job at a Buenos Aires auto plant.

The point was not only to be familiar with his neighborhood and movements, but to place myself in his shoes. I wanted to know what he would be experiencing immediately before we met.

That evening I returned to San Fernando on my own. When I arrived shortly after 6 p.m., it was already dark. I lay prone atop the railroad embankment and waited. The interior of the house was well lit, and there, playing on the living-room floor, was Klement's little boy.

A little after 7 p.m. a motorcycle pulled up to the house, and a moment later those inside were joined by a blond man in his late teens. Probably Dieter, one of the older sons. We'd had reports that Dieter owned a motorcycle.

A little past 7:30 the No. 203 bus pulled up to the stop and Klement got off. He was dressed exactly as he'd been the evening before, and he moved toward the house with the same purposeful stride, his hands at his sides.

This last was vital. Even if he was armed, he would not have ready access to the weapon.

He could not have been better suited to our purposes; a man of absolutely rigid habits. On the crucial night, any spontaneity on his part could cause trouble.

I was further pleased to see the light in the house get brighter as soon as he stepped through the door. The same thing had happened the night before; as, I would learn, it did every night—another piece of Klement's routine.

Now, his hat and coat off, Klement was at the boy's side. He lifted him in the air and spun him around. Both of them were laughing. It was a universal scene and on any other occasion it would have had me smiling. They moved to the window next. The boy sat on the man's lap, both of them gazing out.

They stayed as they were, just staring out for a long time, seeming to daydream in unison. Then, off to my right, there came a rumbling noise. Slowly, it began to grow louder. Now the man stirred and pointed. A moment later a freight train appeared, roaring by on the tracks directly below me.

All at once I was hit by an almost indescribable sense of revulsion.

The father was smiling, and his lips were moving. Finger extended, he was helping the child count.

You bastard, I thought. Still the trains!

* * *

There was a general relief when David found a new villa in a resort district an hour north of the capital. It had no heat, but was reasonably isolated; the house was surrounded by an eight-foot wall and came free of staff. Meir proposed that a bedroom adjacent to the kitchen be set up for the prisoner. It had only one tiny window and offered easy access to a veranda through which, in the event of trouble, Klement could be hidden or even spirited away.

The villa had a courtyard inside the wall, which provided an ideal spot for Meir to work on the automobiles. With only a few days remaining until the capture, he was concentrating entirely on the two that would see action that night: a gray Chrysler and a black Mercedes. Especially the Mercedes. It was the vehicle in which Attila would travel to captivity.

As the day approached, a dispute arose over the method for the actual capture. The approved plan had been devised by Hans, the agent who had stalked Klement in preceding months.

His plan called for me to be out of sight on Garibaldi Street and to jump Attila on his way from the bus stop to his house, wrestling him to the ground. Meir, who was to hide nearby, would help me hold him. The rest of the team would be waiting around the corner on Route 202 in the two cars. As soon as they saw that we had secured him, they would swing around the corner, pick us up and take off. We would be exposed until then.

"But what," I asked, "if a policeman happens by or even an ordinary pedestrian?"

"Under no circumstances will you let go of Attila," Hans told me.

"This isn't a plan to get Eichmann to Jerusalem," I retorted. "It's a plan to land Meir and me in a Buenos Aires jail."

On the morning of May 10—D-Day was to be May 11—we gathered for a last discussion. Isser, deep in an easy chair, faced the rest of us. His eyes were bloodshot from working nonstop on his plan to get Attila out of Argentina.

It fell to Uzi to describe the opposing plans. I wanted one of the cars, the Mercedes, positioned on Garibaldi Street, hood up as if disabled, so that Attila would pass directly by it en route home. Meir was to be on the street side of the car, obscured by the raised hood, as if working on the engine, while Hans and Uzi stayed hidden within. Strolling in the opposite direction, toward Attila, I would have no apparent connection to the vehicle. When we met, after I had subdued him, Meir would help me get him into the car. The other car would turn onto Garibaldi from 202 and take the lead position to protect us in case of a blockade.

In Hans's plan, I noted, there were too many imponderables. Aside from our being exposed to passersby, what if those waiting in the cars on 202, blinded by oncoming headlights, failed to make out what was happening? What if a cop, spotting two cars on the side of the highway, stopped to investigate?

"If Hans's plan fails—that's it, we'll never have another shot."

Isser studied me intently. "What if Attila panics when he sees the car?" he asked. "What if he runs?" It was a legitimate apprehension.

I simply didn't think it would happen, not to a proud German officer, a creature of habit and routine. "You can't run away from every suggestion of the unknown," I said. "It's impossible to live that way."

Then I added, "There's something else. If Hans's plan fails—that's it, we'll never have another shot. With my plan, even if his suspicions are aroused by the car, we simply continue to work on the engine, slam down the hood and drive away. In all likelihood, he figures he was being paranoid, and we try again later."

Isser pulled himself out of the chair, walked over to me and placed his hands on my shoulders, both a benediction and a warning. "All right. I agree. But, Peter, it's on your head."

* * *

On May 11, Meir and Uzi were up at dawn to test the cars. When they returned an hour later, Uzi was soaring. "Like we just drove them out of the showrooms!" he announced.

An hour before we were due to leave, I went to my room and lay down on the bed. I tried to think about loved ones at home, about my mother, but everything was pushed aside by a vivid, persistent image: Klement coming toward me in the dark. He was a trained soldier, a man who had survived on instinct for 15 years. The slightest mistake on my part, and he could be off. Or he could take off for no reason at all.

And, too, there remained the terrible question: Was it really Eichmann?

I went to the bathroom, splashed cold water on my face, studying it in the mirror. What does a kidnapper look like? A moment later I pulled on a wig and combed it into place; then I added a pair of glasses. Back in my room I dressed in a blue sweater and black trousers.

I also stuffed a pair of fur-lined leather gloves in my back pocket. They would of course help with the cold, but that was not the reason I brought them. The thought of placing my bare hand over the mouth that had ordered the death of millions, of feeling the hot breath and saliva on my skin, filled me with an overwhelming sense of horror.

It was 6:45 p.m. Time to go.

We were intentionally cutting it close. The 30- to 35-minute ride to San Fernando would leave approximately a quarter-hour before the usual arrival of Attila's bus; not long enough for a disabled car to arouse suspicion.

We drove in silence, arriving a little past 7:15. Swinging onto Garibaldi, we stopped 20 yards before the Klement house. Ahead, on the shoulder of 202, we could see the Chrysler, its headlights dark.

The street was deserted. The wind had picked up, and every minute or two there was thunder and a flash of lightning, but no rain. Out of the car, I walked back 40 paces, measuring the distance to the spot where I intended to meet him. Then I waited, buffeted by the wind, trying to stay warm. Ten minutes went by. Twenty.

I wandered back to the car. I tapped on the front window. Uzi's head popped up. A lightning bolt flashed, illuminating his face eerily. "It's getting late," I asked. "What do we do?"

"Maybe we missed him." It was Hans answering. "Maybe he came earlier."

I shook my head. "No, he's not here yet. You can tell by the light in the house."

"Give him 15 more minutes," Uzi decided.

I stayed by the car for a few minutes. Then off to the left, heading northeast from Buenos Aires, at once familiar and startling, the No. 203 bus came into view.

At that instant, a young man turned up Garibaldi on a bicycle, his overcoat whipping behind him like a cape. Spotting us, he yelled a friendly greeting in Spanish and started pedaling our way. A Good Samaritan!

Leave us alone. The words rang out within. *Get away!*

Smiling at his approach, Meir simply shook his head and slammed down the hood, giving it an affectionate pat for good measure. Waving, the man passed by and continued around the corner. Instantly, Meir reopened the hood. The bus was at the stop. When it pulled away, there he stood, framed in silhouette by the oncoming headlights.

As he turned onto Garibaldi, I began my leisurely stroll toward him. The lightning was flashing on all sides, the thunder booming. But still no rain. It was Judgment Day.

*　*　*

Burrowed within his coat, his collar upturned, hands in his pockets, leaning into the wind, Attila continued steadily toward me. We were 50 feet apart. I could hear his footfall, regular as the tick of a clock. Would he pause at the sight of the car? No—he didn't hesitate. Twenty-five feet between us. Fifteen.

"*Un momentito, señor.*" The simple phrase I had been practicing for weeks.

He stopped. Behind black-rimmed glasses, his eyes met mine. He took a step backward. I leaped at him.

We fell hard to the ground and tumbled into the ditch alongside the walkway. I was on my back in a couple of inches of mud, grasping him with all my strength, one hand around his throat. He was making gurgling noises. As I struggled to my feet, hoisting him with me, I eased my hold.

Suddenly he let out a piercing scream. It was the primal cry of a cornered animal. Tightening my grip, I cut it off. "It will do you no good," I told him as I dragged him to the car. "This is the end for you."

Meir appeared. He lifted the feet, and I kept hold of his shoulders and head. The back door swung open, and we stuffed him inside the car.

I slid in after, still holding fast, my hand over his mouth. Meir ran around to the front seat, and Hans put the car into gear. As we lurched forward, we gagged him and covered his eyes with goggles. Then we threw a blanket over Attila, and he lay absolutely still on the floor.

Twenty minutes later, we pulled into the courtyard of the villa. David slammed the gate behind us, rushed up to the car and peered in. "You did it!"

Uzi and I led Attila to his room, trailed by Hans. Shutting the door behind us, we studied the prisoner for the first time. He stood in the center of the room, still in his overcoat, his eyes obscured by the goggles. He was utterly rigid except for his hands, which were opening and closing spasmodically.

Months before, we had obtained a list of Eichmann's identifying characteristics from the SS files. Hans, whose primary responsibility as interrogator was to make a positive identification, knew them by heart: his height and weight, head circumference and shoe size, scars, dental work, a tattoo under his left arm listing blood type.

"*Wie heeissen Sie?*" demanded Hans sharply.

"Ricardo Klement," came the reply. His voice was weak and raspy.

Four times the question was asked and the answer repeated.

Changing to English, Hans snapped, "Take off his coat and shirt." We removed his coat, shirt, tie and shoes.

Eichmann stood before us, his hands still working. At Hans's direction, I lifted his left arm. There, where the tattoo with his blood type should have been, was a small scar. Something had been removed. But a scar on his chest was just where the records indicated.

We began silently taking measurements. All three of us buzzed around him with measuring tapes. Everything matched perfectly, except the dental information. The man before us wore dentures.

"*Wie heeissen Sie?*" Hans demanded again.

"Otto Heninger," the man said now. It was an alias he'd used after the war. It meant nothing to us.

"Your SS number," Hans spoke up, "was 45526."

There was a pause. "No," he corrected, "45326."

"Good. Now." Hans asked his question a last time. "*Wie heeissen Sie?*"

"*Ich bin Adolf Eichmann.*"

* * *

Peter Z. Malkin joined Israeli intelligence in 1950. For many years under a government order to keep silent about his work, he is now free to tell the story of his part in the capture of Adolf Eichmann. With the exceptions of Peter Malkin and Isser Harel, names of Israeli operatives have been changed for security reasons.

After Eichmann's capture, Malkin and his team spirited their prisoner out of Argentina on a plane to Israel. Eichmann stood trial, and on December 11, 1961, he was found guilty of crimes against humanity and the Jewish people, war crimes and membership in criminal associations. He was hanged on May 31, 1962.

* * *

In the spring of 1973, on assignment in Athens, I received a midnight phone call from Aharon. "Your mother is ill," he told me. "She broke her hip and is in the hospital."

I was all she had left. Yechiel had died the year before.

"Is it serious?" I asked.

"Peter, at this age you never know."

I rushed out to the airport. At that hour there were no commercial flights, but I discovered a British Airways cargo plane due to leave shortly for Jerusalem and hastily explained the situation to the captain. He was apologetic, but firm. The policy was no unauthorized personnel on board.

I offered him every reference I could think of. "Please," I said, "I'm sure they'll give you the necessary waivers." At last he agreed.

My wife was waiting for me at Lod Airport, and we raced to the hospital. It was just after dawn, hours before visiting time, and I had to make my own way in.

I Captured Adolf Eichmann

I located my mother's room, and as I did, I knew that Aharon had been right to call me. My mother was dying. Her color was bad, her breathing labored. I made my decision then. In almost 15 years, it was the first time I would ignore the Mossad's gag order.

I knelt beside her bed and took her hand. "Mama," I whispered. "Mama, it's me, Peter."

The elderly lady in the next bed turned toward me. "She doesn't talk," she said loudly in Yiddish.

"Mama, I want to tell you something. What I promised, I have done. I captured Eichmann."

There was no response. "Mama, Fruma was avenged. It was her brother who captured Adolf Eichmann."

I repeated it.

"Quiet," said the other lady, "she doesn't hear."

But suddenly her hand began to squeeze mine.

"Do you understand, Mama? I captured Eichmann."

Her eyes were open now. "Yes," she managed in a whisper. "I understand."

Originally published in the February 1991 issue of *Reader's Digest* magazine.

Israeli secret agent Peter Malkin died on March 1, 2005, in New York City. He is buried in the Kiryat Shaul Cemetery in Tel Aviv.

Some Sort of Magic

by Annette Foglino

This extraordinary horse had a rare gift for helping troubled kids.

On a crisp fall morning, Michele Davis opened the barn door to feed Mac and brush him up. As sunlight streamed through the barn, the horse was wide awake and waiting in his stall, blowing steam through his nostrils in the chilly air. "There's a little girl coming to see you," Michele told him. "And she really needs your help."

Later Teresa and Jeff Freshcorn came up the driveway toward Michele's home in West Mansfield, Ohio. With them was their four-year-old daughter, Jessika, who had withdrawn into her own impenetrable world. Her condition, delay onset autism, could not be effectively treated. But when the Freshcorns heard that Michele owned an old horse who had a special way with kids, they decided to give him a try.

You really do work some sort of magic, Michele thought as she stroked Mac's neck. Indeed the horse had touched many lives over the years—and none more than her own.

Back in 1979 Michele, then 32, was teaching Latin American literature at Ohio State University in Columbus. She often recalled how much she had enjoyed riding horses as a little girl. One day she decided to splurge on horse-jumping lessons at a local riding stable. She was paired with a black saddle horse, called Skunk for his distinctive white legs and white tail.

Again and again Michele came back to ride and jump with the horse. She loved how he'd leap over fences without ever faltering. So when Michele learned he was for sale, she was thrilled—but confused. "Why are you letting such a good horse go?" she asked the owner.

The owner explained that he guessed the horse was about 17 years old. "I want to find a good retirement home for him," he said. Michele knew that many horses don't live past 20. But the owner was asking only $1,500. Michele thought it a fair price, and bought him.

She immediately rechristened him McDougall—a name that matched his dignified demeanor—and called him Mac for his easygoing nature.

*　　*　　*

In the next few years Mac continued jumping with ease. Meanwhile, Michele was intrigued that many people in the area seemed to recognize him. "I can't believe he's still around," they would tell her. "He must be pretty old."

Michele traced Mac's birthplace to Columbus. There she found an old ranch hand who had worked at the stable where Mac was born. "It was 1948," he told her. "The owners bred that horse for color. They wanted a parade horse."

The owners named him Mr. Tie & Tail for his shiny black coat and white flourishes. Michele also learned of Mac's subsequent names: Whispering Winds, One-for-the-Road, Houdini (for his ability to get out of a locked barn, a talent Michele discovered one night when he let all her horses out) and then Skunk.

It was amazing: Mac appeared to be about 30 years old. To get a veterinarian's assessment, Michele consulted Dr. Ronald Riegel of Marysville, Ohio. When he finished with his exam, he shook his head and whistled. "This is the oldest horse I've ever seen," he said. Riegel, too, thought the horse was about 30.

Michele marveled that Mac was still standing. When she rode him as a show horse in parades, he never missed one of her signals as she steered him into formation. Mac was a walking miracle. In 1986 Michele needed her own miracle. She had lost her university job and was broke. Eventually she was forced to sell Mac.

The first two times she did, however, Mac got sick and the new owners returned him. Once back with Michele, Mac quickly got better.

When a third buyer came around and handed Michele a check for $300, Mac collapsed. "What's wrong with him?" asked the shocked buyer.

"I think he's dying," Michele said, giving the buyer back his check.

This time Mac was seriously ill. He lay sprawled in the barn, trembling and sweating with a fever.

Over the next few weeks neighborhood children would come by to check on Mac and talk to him. One little boy brushed his mane, and a little girl read to him. One afternoon when Mac heard the children coming up the driveway, he went to the window by his stall and whinnied. That's when Michele knew he was going to make it.

*　　*　　*

As Mac got better, however, Michele's problems intensified. Although she found another job at the university, she was still struggling to pay her bills. One day a neighbor phoned her at work to tell her that her barn was on fire.

One day a neighbor phoned her at work to tell her that her barn was on fire.

By the time Michele reached home, nothing remained but a pile of cinders. Rushing out into the pasture, she found her three surviving horses; among them was Mac.

"When we opened the barn door, two horses tried to run back in," a firefighter told her. "But that old horse kept pushing them out into the field."

Mac and Jessika

The fire made Michele think she was jinxed. Unable to sleep one night, she went for a walk, ending up near the makeshift barn her neighbors helped her build. As she sat lost in thought, she looked up to see Mac standing quietly at her side. "You're old reliable, aren't you?" she said. "You'd never desert me."

As Michele sat under the stars with Mac, she thought about how much he had endured. Time and again he had shown her how miraculous life could be.

Michele resolved to press on too. Pursuing an interest in natural health, Michele began to work with children who suffered from various disorders. When word about her gentle old horse got around among the parents, she invited them to bring their children to visit Mac. It was then that Mac's special skills started to blossom.

There was four-year-old Samuel, who suffered from hyperactivity. His parents found that after each visit with Mac, he would calm down for weeks. And shortly after three-year-old Payton started visiting Mac, he stopped wetting his bed. "How did you do it?" Michele asked the little boy. "I dreamed Mac told me not to," he said proudly.

*　　*　　*

Mac's best magic, however, has been worked on little Jessika. When Teresa Freshcorn first contacted Michele, she was desperate. Jessika had stopped speaking, and her eyes never met anyone's. She only slept for 20 minutes at a time, and when she awoke, she'd retreat to a corner. One of the things that hurt her parents most, however, happened when Jessika's seven-year-old brother, Tyler, would give his sister a hug: invariably she drew away.

Michele suggested that seeing Mac might help. Upon arriving at Michele's house, Jessika just stared off into the distance. "Come into the barn," Michele said to her. "There's someone who wants to meet you."

Some Sort of Magic

Despite Mac's slight swayback, the Freshcorns thought he looked quite dignified. Teresa asked Jessika, "Do you want to sit on the pretty horsey?" The child already seemed transfixed with Mac, but when her father tried to pick her up, she squirmed away.

Mac walked slowly toward Jessika and put his head way down so she could pet him. The little girl who never seemed to notice anything stared at him with wide eyes. Then Jessika's father placed her on Mac's back. She let out a squeal of delight, but Mac remained calm.

Suddenly the girl quieted down and with curiosity began looking all around. Then came the most wonderful sound the Freshcorns had ever heard. A tiny voice called out, "What is that?"

The voice came from Jessika—the same little girl who hadn't spoken a coherent sentence in over six months.

"It's . . . it's a beautiful horse," Teresa sputtered tearfully.

Jessika laid her back flat against Mac's, letting her arms dangle at his sides. That night, for the first time in over a year, she slept without waking up once. The next day she spoke two more sentences. First she asked for water, then she announced, "I want to play!"

Today Jessika visits Mac at least once a month, and her progress continues. She communicates more regularly. Recently she tested normal for her age in alphabetical and numerical skills.

One day while visiting Mac, Jessika began singing. Then noticing Tyler nearby, she motioned for him to come over and play. As he did, Tyler gave his sister a hug. This time, instead of recoiling, Jessika hugged him back.

Originally published in the August 1998 issue of *Reader's Digest* magazine.

Jessika worked with Mac until his passing in 1998. Jessika completed high school and now lives and works with her mom on the family farm. Over the years, she has continued having enriching friendships with animals including: Penny and Cardigan, a pair of miniature sheep; Calamity Jane, a miniature horse; Penelope, a rascally kitten; and Andy, her mom's standard poodle.

Humor Hall of Fame

For the second week in a row, my son and I were the only ones who showed up for his soccer team's practice. Frustrated, I told him, "Please tell your coach that we keep coming for practice but no one is ever here." My son rolled his eyes and said, "He'll just tell me the same thing he did before." "Which was?" "That practice is now on Wednesdays, not Tuesdays."

—**ANNETTE OLSEN**
LAYTON, UTAH

My young son declared, "When I grow up, I'm going to marry you, Mommy."

"You can't marry your own mother," said his older sister.

"Then I'll marry you."

"You can't marry me either."

He looked confused, so I explained, "You can't marry someone in your own family."

"You mean I have to marry a total stranger?!" he cried.

—**PHYLLIS SHOWERS** SAN DIEGO, CALIFORNIA

"He's outside setting up a tent for the kids."

Cartoon by Bill Abbott

Cartoon by Roy Delgado

"Go sit in WHAT corner?"

Whoever coined the phrase "the pitter-patter of little feet" clearly never heard a four-year-old walk.

—TWITTER@MYMOMOLOGUE

Mail from the bank was piling up for my daughter, who was away at college. So I called her. "Open one up and see what it is," she said. I unsealed an envelope. "It says your account has insufficient funds." "That's got to be a mistake," she said. "I still have plenty of checks left."

—**PATTY HAPPY** GRANVILLE, NEW YORK

Just as I got out of the shower, my three-year-old son walked into the bathroom. As I frantically grabbed for my robe, he quickly assured me, "It's OK, Mom; I won't laugh."
—**ELLA ROBBINS**
MYRTLE BEACH,
SOUTH CAROLINA

A friend knew that she'd overdone it with the gifts last Easter when her kid woke up to all the booty and shouted, "This is the best Christmas ever!"
—**CHRIS MCDONOUGH**
WILMINGTON, DELAWARE

BLUE LAUNDRY

Twenty-three years ago, I became a firefighter's wife. I was told that it was going to be tough, but no one told me about the blue laundry. Tons of blue laundry, saturated with the smell of smoke, sweat and other things. It seemed an endless cycle, year after year, he would bring home more blue shirts and blue pants and all I could say was "No! Not more blue laundry!" Then September 11th, 2001, happened. As we sat in the living room watching his firefighter brothers rushed into a flaming building, I turned to him and said, "Why would they run into that!" He turned to me and said simply, "Because that's our job." So that night as I put yet another load of blue laundry in the washing machine, I decided that maybe a little blue laundry was not such a big deal after all.

—Teri Jones *Richfield, Ohio*

THE QUALITY OF CIRCLES

Sitting on her mother's lap, reading *The Book of Shapes*, my daughter came to the triangle page. "What's this shape?" her mom asked. Wheels of cogitation began to spin (signified by a mouth scrunched to one side) and after a brief pause (and with the certainty of a jury foreman) she said, "A circle." Mom asked her, "Are you sure?" (As she did whenever an answer was incorrect.) But my daughter, sensing that something was amiss, said, "Yep," and then pausing, added, "but it's not a very good one."

—Bruce May *Smyrna, Tennessee*

My Fourteenth Summer

by W. W. Meade

*A boy thought his father's cure for
what ailed him was just a ploy.*

One evening I sat in Miami's Pro Player Stadium watching a base-ball game between the Florida Marlins and the New York Mets. During the seventh inning stretch, I noticed a teenage boy and his father one row in front of me. The father was a Mets fan, by the looks of his cap; his son's bore the Marlins' logo.

The father began ribbing his son about the Marlins, who were losing. The son's responses grew increasingly sharp. Finally, with the Marlins hopelessly behind, the boy turned to his father in a full-bore adolescent snarl. "I hate you!" he said. "You know that!" He spat the words as though they tasted as bad in his mouth as they sounded. Then he got up and took the steps two at a time toward the grandstand.

His father shook his head. In a moment he stood and squeezed out of his row of seats, looking both angry and bereft. Our eyes met. "Kids!" he said, as though that explained everything.

I sympathized—after all, I was a father now. But I knew how father and son felt. There was a time when I, too, had turned on the man who loved me most.

*   *   *

My father was a country doctor who raised Hereford cattle on our farm in southern Indiana. A white four-board fence around the property had to be scraped and painted every three years. That was to be my job the summer after my freshman year of high school. If that wasn't bad enough news, one June day my dad decided I should extend the fence.

We were sitting at the edge of the south pasture, my father thoughtfully whittling a piece of wood, as he often did. He took off his Stetson and wiped his forehead. Then he pointed to a stand of hemlocks 300 yards away. "From here to there—that's where we want our fence," he said. "Figure about 110 holes, three feet deep. Keep the digger's blades sharp and you can probably dig eight or ten a day."

In a tight voice I said I didn't see how I could finish that with all the other stuff I had to do. Besides, I'd planned a little softball and fishing. "Why don't we borrow a power auger?" I suggested.

"Power augers don't learn anything from work. And we want our fence to teach us a thing or two," he replied, slapping me on the back.

I flinched to show my resentment. What made me especially mad was the way he said "our" fence. The project was his, I told him. I was just the labor. Dad shook his head with an exasperated expression, then went back to his piece of wood.

I admired a lot about my dad, and I tried to remember those things when I felt mad at him. Once, when I'd been along on one of his house calls, I watched him tell a sick farm woman she was going to be all right before he left or he wasn't leaving. He held her hand and told her stories. He got her to laugh and then he got her out of bed. She said, "Why, Doc, I do feel better."

I asked him later how he knew she would get better. "I didn't," he said. "But if you don't push too hard and you keep their morale up, most patients will get things fixed up themselves." I wanted to ask why he didn't treat his own family that way, but I thought better of it.

*   *   *

If I wanted to be by myself, I would retreat to a river birch by the stream that fed our pond. It forked at ground level, and I'd wedge my back up against one trunk and my feet against the other. Then I would look at the sky or read or pretend.

That summer I hadn't had much time for my tree. One evening as my father and I walked past it, he said, "I remember you scrunchin' into that tree when you were a little kid."

"I don't," I said sullenly.

He looked at me sharply. "What's got into you?" he said.

Amazingly, I heard myself say, "What the hell do you care?" Then I ran off to the barn. Sitting in the tack room, I tried not to cry.

My father opened the door and sat opposite me. Finally I met his gaze.

"It's not a good idea to doctor your own family," he said. "But I guess I need to do that for you right now." He leaned forward. "Let's see. You feel strange in your own body, like it doesn't work the same way it always had. You think no one else is like you. And you think I'm too hard on you and don't appreciate what you do around here. You even wonder how you got into a family as dull as ours."

I was astonished that he knew my most treacherous night thoughts.

"The thing is, your body is changing," he continued. "And that changes your entire self. You've got a lot more male hormones in your blood. And, Son, there's not a man in this world who could handle what that does to you when you're fourteen."

I didn't know what to say. I knew I didn't like whatever was happening to me. For months I'd felt out of touch with everything. I was irritable and restless and sad for no reason. And because I couldn't talk about it, I began to feel really isolated.

"One of the things that'll help you," my dad said after a while, "is work. Hard work."

As soon as he said that, I suspected it was a ploy to keep me busy doing chores. Anger came suddenly. "Fine," I said in the rudest voice I could manage. Then I stormed out.

*   *   *

When my father said work he meant *work*. I dug post holes every morning, slamming that digger into the ground until I had tough calluses on my hands.

One morning I helped my father patch the barn roof. We worked in silence. In the careful way my father worked, I could see how he felt about himself, the barn, the whole farm. I was sure he didn't know what it was like to be on the outside looking in.

> *In the careful way my father worked, I could see how he felt about himself, the barn, the whole farm.*

Just then, he looked at me and said, "You *aren't* alone you know."

Startled, I stared at him, squatting above me with the tar bucket in his hand. How could he possibly know what I'd been thinking?

"Think about this," he said. "If you drew a line from your feet down the side of our barn to the earth and followed it any which way, it would touch every living thing in the world. So you're never alone. No one is."

I started to argue, but the notion of being connected to all of life made me feel so good that I let my thoughts quiet down.

As I worked through the summer, I began to notice my shoulders getting bigger. I was able to do more work, and I even started paying some attention to doing it well. I had hated hole-digging, but it seemed to release some knot inside me, as if the anger I felt went driving into the earth. Slowly I started to feel I could get through this rotten time.

One day near the end of the summer, I got rid of a lot of junk from my younger days. Afterward I went to sit in my tree as a kind of last visit to the world of my boyhood. I had to scuttle up eight feet to get space enough for my body. As I stretched out, I could feel the trunk beneath my feet weakening. Something had gotten at it—ants, maybe, or just plain age.

I pushed harder. Finally, the trunk gave way and fell to the ground. Then I cut up my tree for firewood.

* * *

The afternoon I finished the fence, I found my father sitting on a granite outcrop in the south pasture. "You thinking about how long this grass is going to hold out without rain?" I asked.

"Yep," he said. "How long you think we got?"

"Another week. Easy."

He turned and looked me deep in the eyes. Of course I wasn't really talking about the pasture as much as I was trying to find out if my opinion mattered to him. After a while he said, "You could be right." He paused and added, "You did a fine job on our fence."

"Thanks," I said, almost overwhelmed by the force of his approval.

"You know," he said, "you're going to turn out to be one hell of a man. But just because you're getting grown up doesn't mean you have to leave behind everything you liked when you were a boy."

I knew he was thinking about my tree. He reached into his jacket pocket and pulled out a piece of wood the size of a deck of cards. "I made this for you," he said.

It was a piece of the heartwood from the river birch. He had carved it so the tree appeared again, tall and strong. Beneath were the words "Our Tree."

Leaving the Miami stadium that day, I saw the man and the boy walking toward the parking lot. The man's arm rested comfortably on his son's shoulder. I didn't know how they'd made their peace, but it seemed worth acknowledging. As I passed, I tipped my cap—to them, and to my memories of the past.

Originally published in the July 1998 issue of *Reader's Digest* magazine.

"Please Don't Leave Me!"

by James Hutchison

*Trapped in a blazing inferno, the young girl
put her faith in a courageous firefighter.*

Let's go, Mum!" Shirley Young begged her mother. It was Thursday, August 9, 1990—late-night shopping at the Manukau City Shopping Center in South Auckland. One of the highlights of the week for the 12-year-old Maori girl was to spend a few hours at New Zealand's biggest mall with her aunt and cousin. Her mother, Gaylene, a single parent struggling to improve her job prospects, appreciated having a few hours by herself to catch up on her studies.

Gaylene drove the trio to the mall in her sister's white car, stopping at the curb on busy Wiri Station Road to drop them off. As Shirley headed across the car park to join the throng of shoppers she suddenly realized she didn't have her purse. "Wait, Mum!" she yelled, running back. "I forgot my money." Shirley opened the passenger door and leaned in.

Further back along the busy road, Buddy Marsh shifted gears on his huge Scania tanker as he headed up the rise. The 39-ton truck and trailer held more than 8,700 gallons of gasoline destined for a service station in central Auckland. A cautious driver, Marsh kept well to the left of the two-lane road but, as he neared the mall, a taxi pulled out of the car park, blocking his lane. Marsh swung his rig away. A glance in his mirrors showed the trailer just cleared the front of the taxi. Then, as he looked ahead, Marsh gasped in horror. Not 20 yards away, directly in his path, was a stationary white car.

Marsh yanked on the steering wheel and hit the air brakes, locking up several of the 14 sets of wheels. The truck slammed into the rear of the car, spinning it round like a child's toy and rupturing its fuel tank. Gasoline sprayed both vehicles, igniting them instantly. Carried on by its massive momentum, the trailer jack-knifed, reared over the curb and toppled on top of the wrecked car.

One second Gaylene was talking to her daughter; the next, she was whirling around in a vortex of crumpling metal. She sat stunned as flames poured into the car and a single, terrible thought rose in her mind. *Shirley! Where is she?* Gaylene groped frantically around in the darkness but the passenger seat was empty. *Thank God. She's made it out of here.* An excruciating pain shot up her legs; her sneakers and track pants were on fire. Gaylene struggled to open the buckled doors, but they wouldn't budge.

"Brian!" Marsh called on his two-way radio to his shift mate Brian Dixon in another truck. "I've had an accident! I'm on fire! Call emergency services!"

Marsh jumped down and ran around the front of the tanker to the burning car. Flames were licking the trailer's tanks. Worse, fuel was leaking from relief valves on the overturned trailer and spewing from a hole in its front compartment. The whole rig could blow.

Marsh reached the car just as a bystander hauled Gaylene out and smothered her flaming clothes with his own body. He and other bystanders then carried her a safe distance away.

* * *

Above the hiss of escaping compressed air and the roaring fire, Marsh heard a voice calling "Mum! Mum!" At first he couldn't see anything. Then, as he searched underneath the toppled trailer, he saw a young, dark-haired girl trapped in a tiny space between a rear wheel and the chassis. "Mum!" she cried. "Mum!" Marsh grabbed her beneath the arms. "You'll be all right. You're coming with me," he said. But he couldn't budge her: her lower body was pinned to the ground by the wheel assembly. "I want my mum!" she wailed.

A wall of fire ran the length of the tanker, threatening to sweep around under the trailer where Shirley lay. Then came a thunderous roar. An explosion tore a hole in one of the trailer's four fuel compartments. An immense fireball ballooned into the sky. Shoppers in the car park ran for their lives. Shielded by the tanker from the full force of the blast, Marsh shouted, "There's a little girl trapped under the trailer."

"Let the firefighters handle it," a policeman replied. "Clear the area now!" Truck, trailer and car were now lost in a cauldron of fire. "That poor little girl," Marsh said, holding his head in his hands. "She didn't have a chance."

With a blaze of sirens, a pumper and rescue trucks from Manukau Station arrived. Immediately the vehicles stopped, and senior firefighter Royd Kennedy pulled an armful of hose out of the locker as his partner was lugging foam containers down behind him. Driver Tod Penberthy was sprinting to connect the pump to the nearest hydrant. Waiting for the water, Royd saw his boots, fireproof overtrousers and the rubber on his breathing apparatus begin to singe. When they turned the hose on the fire, the heat was so intense that the water steamed away before it reached the flames.

The tanker was burning end to end, shooting flames 100 yards into the air.

Senior Station Officer John Hyland, in charge of the initial response, had never seen such potential for disaster in 19 years of fighting fires.

The tanker was burning end to end, shooting flames 100 yards into the air. Gasoline poured from holes and relief valves into a widening lake and a river of fire raced down the road into stormwater drains.

Only a few yards away were 550 other potential fires—the cars in the crowded car park.

Within minutes of blowing up, a great fuel/air vapor conflagration—known to firefighters as BLEVE (Boiling Liquid Expanding Vapor

Explosion)—reaches out for hundreds of yards and incinerates anything in its path. Only 100 yards from the burning tanker was the mall, packed with almost 20,000 late-night shoppers.

More fire crews arrived. "Concentrate on pushing the flames away from that tanker!" ordered Divisional Officer Ray Warby, who had arrived to take control. As if to underline his words, the fuel in another compartment exploded in a monstrous fireball, forcing Royd and his crew mates back 20 yards. The vehicles in the car park around them had begun to melt, plastic bumpers and mirrors sagging, paint bubbling.

As the firefighters readied themselves for another assault, a long, high-pitched wail cut through the night. At first, it was dismissed as the sound of expanding metal. When the eerie sound came again it raised the hair on the back of Royd's neck. *I'll be damned*, he thought. It's coming from the tanker. Shielding his eyes, Royd peered into the glare, but saw only a flaming wall 50 yards high. Then, for a split second, the flames parted. From beneath the trailer he saw something waving. It was the hand of a child.

"Cover me!" Royd shouted. He dropped his hose and ran straight into the inferno.

For ten minutes little Shirley had been slowly roasting in a sea of fire. *It's hopeless*, she told herself, *no one can hear me in here.* Giddy with pain and gas fumes, she felt her mind begin to drift and suddenly saw a vivid image of her grandfather and grand-uncle—both of whom had died years before. *They are guardian angels now*, she thought. *They'll be watching over me.* The idea gave her new strength. Straining to see through the wall of fire, Shirley glimpsed moving figures. *I've got to let them know I'm here!* Mustering every ounce of strength, she screamed louder than she had ever done in her life.

As Royd neared the flames, the heat hit him like a physical blow, stinging his face through his visor. Shielding his head with his gloved hands and fireproof jacket, he crawled under the trailer. Shirley was try-ing to hold herself up by clutching a cable over her head, but her hips and thighs were under the wheel assembly and her legs were twisted up, like a grasshopper's next to her chest.

"I'm scared. Please don't leave me," she wailed. Royd tucked his air cylinder under her shoulders to support her upper body. "Don't worry," he told her. "I'll stay, I promise you." Royd meant what he said; he had always made it a rule never to break promises to his own three kids.

"My name's Royd," he said. "We're in this together now, so we have to help each other." He reached into the tiny space and cradled the small body in his arms. Having fended for himself since his teens, he knew what it meant to be alone and afraid. "Is my mum alright?" Shirley asked. Royd replied: "She's a bit burned, but she got away. My mates will soon get us out, too."

The air was so thick with fumes that the two of them could barely breathe. Royd knew it would be only seconds before the vapor ignited.

Whooosh! The firefighter braced himself as the air exploded around them. *This is it*, he thought. *Now we're goners.* Shirley whimpered. Royd felt sick with helplessness as the flames washed over her. Then, for a moment, the fire drew back. "This is pretty rough, eh, Shirley?" he said, unstrapping his helmet. "Put this on." *At least it may help save her face*, he thought. He cinched the strap tight under her chin and flipped down the visor. As he hunkered down, he thought: *Where the hell is my cover?*

The station officer was running through the car park to the rest of their team, yelling at the top of his voice. "Royd's under the tanker. Get that hose up here!" Struggling with the water-filled hose, they took no more than a minute to get within striking distance, but it seemed an eternity.

A second wave of fire washed over Royd and Shirley. Then more explosions rocked the trailer, and Royd's heart sank. *We don't have a chance now*, he thought. He looked down at the girl's tortured body. *I won't leave you. That I promise.* Then he wrapped his arms tightly round her and waited for the final surge of flame that would surely immolate them both.

Instead of fire, they were hit by an ice-cold waterfall. "My mates are here!" yelled Royd. Divisional Officer Warby appeared through the curtain of water. "Don't worry, we'll get things moving," he told Royd, then he took quick stock. The two were shielded from the full force of the main fire above and beside them, but the burning wreckage of the car was in the way, hampering the firefighters' efforts to protect and rescue the pair.

Warby crawled out and ran to Peter Glass, the officer in charge of a rescue truck. "Get that girl out. I don't care how you do it as long as you do it fast!"

As four firefighters sprayed the life-giving water that kept fire away from Royd and Shirley, they were exposed to the full radiated heat of the main tanker blaze. It gnawed through their multi-layered bunker coats as if they were tissue paper, blistering their skin. But they didn't dare back off. If the spray wavered, fire would instantly sweep back over. Even changing crews was too risky.

Ironically, now Shirley and Royd began to shiver violently: 20 gallons of freezing water were cascading over them each second. Soon they were in the first stages of hypothermia.

"I'll get someone to relieve you," Warby yelled. "No," Royd retorted. "I must stay with her. I made a promise."

Glass brought his rescue vehicle in as close as he dared while a crewman sprinted to the car and hooked a winch cable to the windscreen pillar. The winch was not powerful enough to drag the car out so they rigged it to the rescue truck's crane and, using it like a giant fishing rod, hauled the burning wreck away.

Assistant Commander Cliff Mears, from the fire brigade headquarters, had set up a mobile command post and called in a fourth, then fifth alarm. Any vehicle in the city that could be useful was on its way to the scene. However, the firefighters were facing yet another potential catastrophe. Fed by tons of fuel, a torrent of fire was pouring into stormwater drains in the car park and on Wiri Station Road. But what route did the drains take?

The answer came with a deafening explosion. A manhole cover blasted out of the ground at the main entrance of the mall, narrowly missing a woman and flinging her shopping cart into the air. Rumbling underground explosions began lifting and blowing out manhole covers all over the complex. A mile away, stormwater drains emptying into the Puhinui Stream sparked five separate fires in the scrub on the stream's banks.

The entire shopping center was now permeated with gasoline fumes. "Evacuate the center. Quick as you can," Mears ordered.

* * *

Back at the burning rig, Warby approached a paramedic from a waiting ambulance crew. "There must be something we can do to ease the girl's pain—do you think you could make it under there?" he asked.

Biting back his fear, the paramedic donned a bunker coat and helmet and headed into the inferno. As he crawled into the tiny space where Shirley and Royd lay, he realized he wouldn't have room to get an IV drip going. He considered administering a painkiller, but decided against it: Shirley seemed to be coping and side effects such as suppression of her breathing might hamper the rescue operation. Trauma victims need to get to hospital within an hour of injury—dubbed the "golden hour" by emergency services—to have a decent chance of survival. Crawling out, he was conscious that timing was vital. Shirley had been under the tanker for more than 30 minutes. With her massive injuries, burns and now the cold, she could easily slip into shock and die.

Royd had been trying to take her mind off her predicament. "What do you watch on TV?" he asked, and they talked for a while about her favorite shows. "If you could go anywhere in the world, where would you go?"

"Disneyland," she said emphatically. "I love Mickey Mouse." *This man's so brave*, she thought. *He could get out of here any time he wants. Grandad and Uncle Vincent must have sent him.*

Whenever she was startled by a sudden noise, Royd would explain what the firefighters were doing. He tried to reassure her: "You've got a few broken bones and burns, but it's marvelous what the doctors can do." Occasionally she would let out stifled moans. "It's OK, yell all you want," he encouraged. "Bite me if it helps."

The pain from the injuries to Shirley's lower body was becoming unbearable. She cried out, burying her hands in Royd's thick hair, pulling

After she had sufficiently recovered, Shirley got her promised ride on Gilly with Royd.

hard to ease her agony. As a firefighter, Royd had seen grown men with very little wrong with them blubbering like idiots, yet here was a 12-year-old girl who had not shed a single tear.

The steady flow of water wavered for an instant. *God no*, thought Royd, *the fire can't take us now.* Shirley barely managed to move her arms as the flames rolled in. Then the water came pouring back and Royd was horrified to see several layers of skin on her arms had slid down and bunched up round her wrists. "I'm still with you, Shirley," he said. "Do you like horses?" he asked, desperate to get her talking again.

"I've never been on a horse."

"When we're out of here, I promise you a ride on my daughter's horse, Gilly."

As Royd talked, he kept a finger on Shirley's wrist to check her pulse. Now it was growing noticeably fainter and more erratic. She'd been trapped for nearly 40 minutes. *Dear God, how much more can she take?*

With the wreck out of the way, Glass was trying to lift the trailer off the girl. He faced a knife-edge decision. A hydraulic jack would be quicker, but it risked tilting the trailer, tipping out more fuel and inciner-ating the pair. "We'll use the airbags. They'll give a straight lift," Glass told his crew. Only one-and-a-half inch thick and made of rubber rein-forced with steel, the 2-foot-square bags could each lift a railway wagon 2 feet. They slid one under each set of rear wheels and began feeding in compressed air. As the trailer moved they slipped in wooden blocks to keep it on an even keel.

Royd felt Shirley's pulse flutter and she closed her eyes. "Shirley, talk to me!" he pleaded. She rallied for a couple of moments but her pulse was so faint now he could barely feel it. She lifted her head and looked into his eyes. "If I don't make it, tell Mum I love her," she whispered.

"We're losing her, Warby," Royd shouted. "Throw me an Air Viva!" He put the mask of the portable resuscitator over Shirley's face and forced air into her lungs. She stirred a little and opened her eyes. "You tell your mum yourself," he scolded. "I promised I wouldn't leave you. Now don't you leave me!"

"I'll hang on," she murmured.

*　　*　　*

The rescue team had run into trouble. Part of the trailer was on soft ground, which was sodden from all the water, and the airbag under the wheel that was trapping Shirley was sinking into the mud instead of lift-ing. They blocked one more time and inflated the bag to its maximum, but the wheels had risen only four inches. "We must have her out now," Warby told Glass.

Praying it would give them that extra few inches of lift without tipping the trailer, Glass shoved a small hydraulic ram under the chas-sis. He held his breath. The trailer lifted some more. Now he had a 6-inch gap between ground and wheels; it would have to be enough.

"Go for it!" he yelled. Royd gently, but quickly, untangled Shirley's legs from under the wheel; they were crushed so badly they were like jelly in his hands. Warby helped him juggle her crumpled body from its tiny prison. Then they carried her to the stretcher. Just before Shirley was lifted into the waiting ambulance, she smiled at him and he bent down to kiss her on the cheek.

"You've done it, Shirley," he said. Then, overcome by fumes, shock and cold, he pitched forward into the arms of a fellow firefighter.

For Shirley, the ordeal continued. As the ambulance headed for hospital, the paramedic bathed her burns in saline solution and gave her nitrous oxide to relieve her pain. *If anyone deserves to live*, he thought, *it is this girl who has fought so hard.*

Back at the mall, firefighters were able to pour foam into the tanker. Before, it would have endangered Royd and the girl; now they quenched the burning rig in just three minutes.

When Hyland revisited the scene the next morning, he saw something that will haunt him for the rest of his life. For 75 yards the top layer of tar on the road had burnt away, in places down to bare gravel—except for a patch the size of a kitchen table that was lightly scorched by fire. This was where Shirley had been lying.

"It was as if the devil was determined to take that girl," one firefighter said later, "and when she was snatched away, he just gave up."

Originally published in the August 1991 issue of *Reader's Digest* magazine.

Shirley's recovery was slow, and included a series of painful skin grafts to her legs. Orthopedic surgeons found the right calf muscle too badly damaged to repair and decided to amputate her leg below the knee. Royd Kennedy now lives in Australia and retired in June 2019 after 44 years in firefighting and emergency service work. Shirley has three children.

A BONDING MOMENT

I sat in a rocking chair holding my sleeping three-week-old son. He wasn't sleeping through the night. He was always fussy and only slept two hours at a time. I felt like I was a failure. I was sure I was doing everything wrong. Overcome with emotions, I began to cry. I looked down at my son and was surprised to see he was awake and staring at me intently. I looked down and met his gaze. We sat there for a moment gazing at each other and then simultaneously we both grinned. The wonder of the moment caused me to laugh out loud. At the sound of my laugh, his grin widened into a full open mouth smile. At that moment, I let my anxieties go and began to focus solely on the joys of being a mother.

—Rebecca Jamison *Emporia, Kansas*

AFTER YOU

Having had a total knee replacement, three weeks ago, I recently had my first outpatient visit with the surgeon. When the office visit was over, my wife went ahead of me, to get the car. I walked, cane assisted, through the lobby. As I approached the glass exit door, and started to press the automatic door button, I noticed an elderly gentleman, approaching from the other side. To be courteous, I waited for him to enter, first. Only then, did I realize I was looking at my own reflection in the door!

—Dr. Gregory Larkin *Indianapolis, Indiana*

Gone Fishin'

Although human visitors to Katmai National Park in Alaska are required to complete a "bear etiquette" orientation, the bears make no offer of their own hospitality. As the salmon in this 2017 photograph are about to find out, brown bears rule at Katmai. Around 2,200 of them roam the four-million-acre park, compared with the 60 campers allowed at the park's only established campground. *Photograph by Art Wolfe*

MAKING FRIENDS WITH MY KITCHEN

When my son's kindergarten teacher had the kids draw pictures of their moms, he drew me baking a birthday cake. A note on my refrigerator says, "Deer Mom. Yor fud is gud." (Translation: Dear Mom. Your food is good.) If you asked me what I did best, cooking would be far down on the list. I cook out of necessity. Hungry family + tight budget = being forced to become friends with my kitchen. I didn't have cash for a bakery birthday cake and the meal that inspired my son's note was made out of leftovers and random cans from my pantry. One day, after getting frustrated by a recipe that wouldn't turn out, I asked my son why he thought I was a good cook. "Because you love us," he said as he reached over to give me a kiss on the cheek. Yup. That works for me.

—Dana Hinders *Clarksville, Iowa*

THANK YOU FOR YOUR SERVICE

A group of uniformed servicemen was exiting a restaurant as I entered with a group of teacher friends wearing our school shirts. I thanked them for serving our country, and as they walked away, I heard one say, "They're the ones who work in a war zone full of runny noses, stacks of papers, and 1,000 questions a day. I prefer my job!" Coming from a military family, I was both humbled and amused by our mutual admiration.

—Stephanie A. Woodard *Missouri City, Texas*

How to Ruin
a Joke

by Andy Simmons

A classic joke goes like this: A nurse rushes into an exam room and says, "Doctor, doctor, there's an invisible man in the waiting room." The doctor says, "Tell him I can't see him."

Pretty simple, right?

Here's how I tell it: "A nurse—her name is Joyce—feels a presence in the waiting room. She looks around but sees nothing. She jumps up from her desk, carefully replaces her chair, and runs down the lavender-hued hallway to the doctor's office. She knocks on the door. No response. He's not there. Where can he be? She continues down the hall, admiring a lithograph of an 18th-century Mississippi paddleboat along the way." By this time, my audience has left, but I soldier on. "She bursts into the exam room and says, 'Doctor, doctor!' The doctor, I should mention, is a urologist with a degree from Ohio State, which is where my nephew . . ."

You get the idea I'm an embellisher. I can't leave a simple gag alone.

I'm not the only joke-challenged member of the family. My sister's worse than I am. Her problem: She can't remember them. "'A nurse rushes into an exam room and says . . .' Uh, let me start all over again. 'A nurse rushes into a waiting . . .' No, it's not the waiting room. She just came from the waiting room. Let me start all over again. 'A doctor rushes into . . .' No, wait . . ."

My uncle's different. He's guilty of taking a perfectly fine joke and selling it as the second coming of Oscar Wilde: "Okay, this is a good one. Ready? No, really, ready? Okay, fasten your seat belts. Ready? 'A nurse . . .' Got it? A nurse? Okay, ready? 'A nurse rushes into an exam room and says, "Doctor, doctor, there's an invisible man in the waiting room."' Now, this is where it gets funny. Ready?"

No one is ever ready, so they leave before he gets to the punch line.

My father's on Wall Street, so he hears all the jokes before they hit the Web.

My father's on Wall Street, so he hears all the jokes before they hit the Web. And he lets you know he knows them all by telling you all of them. He also knows that most people don't like jokes. So he slips them in under the radar: "I was chatting with Ben Bernanke the other day. You know Ben, don't you? The Fed chief? Anyway, we were reviewing the Fed's policy on long-term interest rates, and he told me it had evolved into its current iteration only after a nurse rushed into an exam room and said, 'Doctor, doctor, there's . . .' Hey, where are you going?"

My brother Mark understands that the secret to good joke telling is to know your audience. When he entertained my grandmother's mah-jongg club one evening, he made it a point to adapt the joke to them: "A stacked nurse rushes into an exam room . . ."

No one in my family has ever finished this joke.

But as bad as it is not to be able to tell a joke, there's something worse: not being able to listen to one. Take my cousin Mitch.

"Why couldn't the doctor see him?" he asked.

"Because he's invisible," I said.

"Now, I didn't get that. I thought the doctor couldn't see him because he was with a patient."

"Well, yeah, okay, but the fact that the guy was invisible . . ."

"Could the nurse see him?"

"No. She's the one who said he was invisible . . ."

"How'd she know he was there?"

"Because he . . ."

"When you say he was invisible, does that mean his clothes were invisible too?"

Here's where I tried to walk away.

"Because if his clothes weren't invisible," Mitch said, stepping between me and the exit, "then the doctor could see him, right?"

"Yeah, but . . ."

"At least his clothes."

"I guess . . ."

"Unless he was naked."

"Okay, he was naked!"

"Why would he go to his doctor naked?"

Next time you see my family and someone's telling a joke, do yourself a favor: Make yourself invisible.

Originally published in the September 2008 issue of *Reader's Digest* magazine.

Humor Hall of Fame

The note I left on my middle-school student's test said: "Please look up the meanings of suppository and depository." It was in response to a question he'd answered concerning where Lee Harvey Oswald was when he assassinated President Kennedy.

—KAREN SKOPHAMMER
FORT DODGE, IOWA

"In Franz Kafka's The Metamorphosis," I said to my sophomore English class, "a man, discontented with his life, wakes up to find he has been transformed into a large, disgusting insect." A student thrust her hand into the air and asked, "So is this fiction or nonfiction?"

—DIANE STURGEON SIOUX FALLS, SOUTH DAKOTA

Nailed Through the Heart

by Per Ola and Emily D'Aulaire

As a youth, he'd performed countless daredevil stunts. Now he needed a miracle to save him.

Sun beat down on a grateful Mike Spaulding. The 32-year-old framing contractor had a house to finish in the hills overlooking the town of Truckee, California, in the Sierra Nevada. He and carpenter Travis McMaster, 27, wanted to take advantage of the good weather before snow blanketed the Donner Pass region.

Using 3¼-inch-long spikes that fed into their powerful nail guns like bullets in a machine gun, the two men pinned rafters into place as easily as stapling sheets of paper together. A slight pull on the trigger drove a nail up to its head in the heavy timbers.

By midmorning that December 5, 1991, the temperature had climbed into the low 40s. The two men were working in their T-shirts. McMaster was holding a rafter in place while Spaulding muscled the lower end into position. Suddenly, a gust of wind caught the board and swung it toward him. The unexpected impact caused Spaulding's finger—resting on the trigger—to squeeze. The gun fired.

At first, Spaulding thought the nail had missed him—he felt no pain. Then a searing agony welled up from his chest. Glancing down, he saw the nail head buried so deep in his chest that it had pulled part of his T-shirt into his body. His mustachioed, chiseled face became contorted with pain. *Feels like someone rammed a railroad tie through my chest,* he thought.

Gasping for breath, Spaulding tugged at his shirt, trying to wrench the nail free. The fabric ripped, but the nail wouldn't budge. Frantically, he reached for his "cat's paw," a tool with a curved hook for extracting buried nails.

"Stop!" McMaster yelled, as he raced down the ladder from the ridgepole above. He remembered a cardinal rule of first aid: *never pull out an object impaled in the body.*

Whatever had been struck in Spaulding's chest, McMaster knew, the nail now acted like a finger in a dike. To remove it without surgery could cause Spaulding to bleed to death in minutes.

"We're going to the hospital," he told his boss, trying to sound calm. He steered Spaulding toward the pickup truck.

Spaulding felt himself fighting the darkness squeezing in on him as he propped his feet on the truck's dashboard and tucked his head down to minimize shock. A former professional freestyle skier, he grasped the irony of what had happened. *After all the risks I've taken for fun,* he wondered grimly, *am I going to die on a simple little job?*

At age 15 he was doing two backward somersaults on skis after soaring off a ski jump. For a movie, he'd once raced down a 50-degree slope, sailed off a 30-foot-high cliff, performed a perfect back flip over a moving freight train and landed safely on the other side of the tracks. Three skiers who had tried the stunt before him had been killed.

I got through some crazy things, he thought woozily. *But I don't know if I'm going to dance through this one.*

With flashers blinking and his hand on the horn, McMaster raced the truck down the mountain roads. "You'll be okay," he kept telling his friend. "Just hang in there."

Spaulding's eyes shut, and he started to slip into unconsciousness. "You can't die on me, Mike," McMaster bellowed. "Hang on! We're almost there!"

Struggling to stay conscious, Spaulding thought about his girlfriend, Judi Schorr, 28. He'd met the petite brunette a year earlier on a blind date. Almost immediately, he fell in love with her. After a few months he asked her to marry him. She said no—not because she didn't love him, but because she'd decided marriage wasn't for her. She'd seen too many marriages end unhappily.

"After you drop me at the emergency room," Spaulding gasped, "tell Judi what happened. Ask her to come to the hospital. I may never see her again."

*　　*　　*

Shortly after 11 a.m. at Tahoe Forest Hospital, emergency-room nurse Judy Erhardt heard a truck skid to a halt in the bay normally reserved for ambulances. Erhardt hurried outside with other staffers.

"My friend's dying," McMaster yelled, waving toward the barely conscious figure slumped in the passenger seat. Sweat poured from Spaulding's face, drenching his clothing. His lips were blue from lack of oxygen.

Inside, emergency-room physician Edward Heneveld looked at the nail head in Spaulding's chest and grimaced. Pressing on the neck artery, he could barely feel a pulse. The man's pale, sweaty appearance and deteriorating vital signs were evidence of severe shock.

The trauma team cut off Mike Spaulding's clothes, inserted I.V. lines into his arms and placed an oxygen mask over his nose and mouth. X rays and a sonogram confirmed Heneveld's worst fears: that the nail had driven straight into Spaulding's heart, allowing blood to leak into the space between the organ and its surrounding membrane, the pericardium. Each time the heart beat, more blood spurted into the space. The growing pressure of blood in the pericardium was literally strangling Spaulding's heart.

His lips were blue from lack of oxygen.

Tahoe Forest, a 72-bed district hospital, boasted a large emergency room for its size. It was not equipped for heart surgery, however. Normally, a patient with the type of injury that Spaulding had would be moved to a trauma center in Reno, 35 miles away. *He'll never make it,* Heneveld realized.

"Get Boone in here quick," he said. "We're going to lose this guy unless we open him up fast."

Across the corridor in the physicians' lounge, Dr. Howard Boone was unwinding after assisting at a hernia operation. The bearded, six-foot-four-inch surgeon favored blue jeans and cowboy boots and was a popular figure both at the hospital and in town.

Boone's patients liked him for his gentle and confident manner, as well as his skill and compassion. A colleague tells of the time Boone performed emergency stomach surgery on a 76-year-old cancer patient. "We couldn't help you," Boone told her when she came out of anesthesia. "But I promise to make you as comfortable as possible." He remained at the woman's bedside all that night and into the next afternoon, personally nursing her until she passed away.

"Dr. Boone, ER stat," the loudspeaker in the doctors' lounge crackled—hospitalese for "to the emergency room, immediately." Boone loped across the corridor and shouldered his way past the nurses and physicians surrounding Spaulding's gurney.

After a glance at the man's X rays and heart sonogram, the surgeon knew they were in deep trouble. Spaulding needed open-chest surgery immediately. The last time Boone had performed such an operation was 16 years earlier during his residency in San Francisco. Boone knew Tahoe Forest was not equipped for this type of surgery: the hospital had no heart-lung machine and no chest saw.

Without a sternal saw, he'd have to use an old Lebsche knife. This is a ten-inch-long stainless-steel bar with a handle at one end and a sharpened wedge at the other. On the back side of the wedge is a flat surface that can be banged with a mallet to drive the wedge into the bone. Before orthopedic saws, the Lebsche knife had been the standard tool that thoracic surgeons used to crack breastbones open for access to the heart and lungs.

Boone knew the hospital had one left over from earlier years.

"Prepare for an open chest," Boone directed. "We need all the usual stuff, plus the Lebsche knife, a chest jack and a blood recycler."

Travis McMaster rushed into the emergency room with Judi Schorr. After pleading to be allowed to see Spaulding, Schorr was shown into the area where he was being examined. Recognizing her, he lifted off his oxygen mask and whispered, "I love you."

A nurse steered Schorr away. "I'm afraid you have to leave," she said. Trying to prepare her for the worst, the nurse added quietly, "You might want to say good-bye. He may not make it."

Boone and Dr. Jacinto "Butch" Orozco, the general surgeon who had performed the hernia operation Boone had assisted with, were already suited up and scrubbed. Nurses rolled Spaulding, still conscious, into the operating room. They moved as rapidly as possible, for they could see the patient was dying before their eyes.

Spaulding looked up at nurse Suzanne Achey and asked weakly, "Am I going to die?"

"Not if we can help it," she answered with her most reassuring smile. "We're a very determined bunch."

Boone wanted to hold off until the last moment before giving anesthesia. He couldn't risk the patient's blood pressure plummeting further.

✳   ✳   ✳

Now, scalpel poised, Boone nodded to the anesthetist. "Aren't you going to knock me out first?" asked a frightened Spaulding.

"Put him out," Boone said as he began the chest incision. Spaulding felt a sharp sting down the center of his breastbone. As the anesthesia kicked in, a black curtain descended. Incredibly, only 20 minutes had passed since the spike had been driven into his chest.

"Lebsche knife," Boone called. The scrub nurse placed the gleaming instrument into his gloved, outstretched hand. Boone put the sharpened wedge of the Lebsche knife against the top of Spaulding's sternum. "Go ahead," he said to Orozco. "Slam it."

Orozco struck the knife's flat surface forcefully with a small stainless-steel mallet. He had expected a few whacks to drive the wedge into the patient's sternum and split it cleanly in half. But Spaulding was an athlete with stone-hard bone. Although Orozco pounded again and again, the wedge didn't move. "This guy's built like a rock," he muttered.

Anticipating the next move, the scrub nurse asked for an orthopedic tray, which would have a bigger hammer. When it arrived, she said, "Try this, Butch," and handed him a three-pound hammer.

This time, after only three blows, Spaulding's breastbone split open. Boone exhaled with relief. "Rib retractor," he ordered.

The nurse handed him a steel device like a small tire jack. Slowly, Boone cranked the chest open, careful not to dislodge the nail. He probed inside with a gloved finger. The spike had entered Spaulding's chest just off center of the breastbone. It had angled to the left before perforating the right lung; then it penetrated the right chamber of the heart. Finally, it had punctured the aorta, the garden-hose-size main artery that leads from the heart to the rest of the body. The pericardial sac around Spaulding's heart ballooned with dark, oxygen-poor blood. Equally ominous, with each feeble beat of the heart, the nail again poked at the aorta like woodpecker pounding a tree.

Boone was amazed that his patient had survived this long. *It's a one-in-a-million chance to get this kind of injury,* he thought, *and not have it be fatal.*

With surgical scissors, Boone carefully cut open the pericardium to relieve the pressure on the heart, suctioning and sponging out the pooled blood. If they could stop the heart for a few minutes, it would be much easier to work on. But for that they needed a heart-lung bypass machine. The surgeons would have to make their repairs while the heart was still beating. Working on a moving target, they would need every ounce of skill they could bring to the table.

By now Spaulding had lost perhaps a quarter of his body's blood. They didn't want to transfuse him because there hadn't been time to determine his blood type before rushing him to surgery. To compensate, three large-bore I.V.s poured more than a gallon of clear fluids into his veins. An autotransfuser recycled the blood spilling into his chest cavity and returned it to his veins.

While Boone pulled the nail back bit by bit, Orozco put his fingers over the holes it had made. At last, Boone held the nail in the air. Then he handed his trophy to a nurse. "I want to save it," he explained. "I'll probably never see a case like this again."

Over the next two hours, Boone worked to suture each hole that the nail had made. First he repaired Spaulding's damaged lung. Next, with tiny stitches, he attached a Teflon patch to seal the hole in the upper-right chamber of the heart.

He watched the patch pulsate. "This guy's strong as an ox," Boone said as he worked.

Finally he tackled what he knew would be the trickiest part of the surgery—repairing the aorta. The staff fell silent as Boone gingerly peeled back a clot covering the puncture wound. A geyser of blood spurted across the room. *My God, we could still lose him*, Boone thought. Orozco immediately put a finger over the wound.

Boone was now working blind, the hands of both surgeons deep inside Spaulding's chest. Then, while Orozco kept his finger firmly in place, Boone prepared needles for suturing. Because the puncture was located deep in a crevice where the heart and aorta meet, each surgeon placed half the suture in the part of the wound he could best reach. "I think I've got it," Boone finally announced.

To help seal the hole, Orozco held a gauze sponge in place for five more minutes. An audible sigh went up in the operating room when he slowly removed it and not a drop of blood appeared.

Between his cap and mask, Boone's eyes registered relief as they met Orozco's. "Let's close him up," Boone said. "This just wasn't his day to die."

Mike Spaulding recovered with surprising speed. Only three days after surgery, he was begging so hard to go home that Boone finally granted permission—with a warning.

"If you try anything strenuous during the next two months," the surgeon said, "your blood pressure could rise enough to blow a hole in one of our sutures. If that happens, you'll be dead. It's that simple."

Judi Schorr and Travis McMaster got Spaulding home and made sure he was comfortable. After nearly losing her man, Judi found that her thoughts about marriage had changed. Just nine days after the accident, Mike and Judi were married. By mid-March 1992, Spaulding was back at work—careful to keep his finger off the trigger of his nail gun until he was ready to fire it.

Spaulding changed in other ways. Formerly hard-driving, competitive and sometimes argumentative, he became more relaxed. "I've found I'm not as invincible as I'd thought," he says. "And I can't always do everything by myself."

Still, some of his renegade spirit remains intact. After receiving a clean bill of health from Boone, he asked if he could jump the freight train again.

Boone smiled. "Sure," he said. "Just tell me when. It's an event I wouldn't want to miss."

The nail that almost took Spaulding's life nestles in a box on Boone's desk at his office. Every once in a while, the surgeon twirls it in his fingers and marvels at the gleaming 3¼-inch-long sliver of galvanized stud. He says, "Mike definitely had an angel on his shoulder that day."

Originally published in the June 1993 issue of *Reader's Digest* magazine.

Mike Spaulding died of cancer on July 10, 2013. Dr. Howard Boone is still practicing at Tahoe Forest Hospital. Dr. Jacinto Orozco is a general surgeon in Goldendale, Washington.

WORST ENEMY

Looking across the crowd at my 40th high-school reunion, I spotted walking my way one of the persons I really had not looked forward to seeing. He had been a tormenter, a teaser, a prankster who had made me feel miserable. He grinned, called out my name, and started talking about himself and asking questions of me as warmly as the exchanges with long-lost best friends. That's when I realized he really hadn't been among my worst enemies. For the teasing and taunting had prepared me for the rough patches in life that always arise. Without him, I would not have been as prepared for adversity. He was really among my best friends. I can't wait to see him again.

—Greg Rohloff *Amarillo, Texas*

GRANDDAD'S TRUCK

I was four, out back playing in the humid Kentucky air. I saw my grandfather's truck and thought, Granddad shouldn't have to drive such an ugly truck. Then I spied a gallon of paint. Idea! I got a brush and painted white polka dots all over the truck. I was on the roof finishing the job when he walked up, looking as if he were in a trance. "Angela, that's the prettiest truck I've ever seen!" Sometimes I think adults don't stop to see things through a child's eyes. He could have crushed me. Instead, he lifted my little soul.

—Angela Bradley-Autrey *Deer Park, Washington*

PHOTO OF LASTING INTEREST

Space Equation

American scientists pose for *Life* magazine on October 10, 1957, alongside satellite orbit equations drawn up by astronomer Samuel Herrick. The photo was taken just six days after the Soviet Union had launched *Sputnik 1*—the world's first human-made satellite and a win in the earliest round of the space race. NASA was created the following October, and within months, the United States was also in orbit: On January 31, 1958, NASA launched the *Explorer 1* satellite from Cape Canaveral, Florida. *Photograph by J.R. Eyeman/Getty Images*

$$p = a(1-e)$$

$$r = \frac{1}{1+e\cos v} = a(1-e\cos E)$$

$$b = a(1-e^2)^{1/2}$$

$$X_\omega = r\cos v = A(\cos E - e)$$

$$c = ae = CF = CF_2 \,;\quad Y_\omega = r\sin v$$

$$= a\sqrt{1-e^2}\,\sin E$$

$$\mu = m_1 + m_2$$

$$n = \frac{2\pi}{P} = K\sqrt{\mu}\; a^{-3/2}$$

$$\tau = K(t-t_0)$$

$$\ddot{x} = \frac{d^2x}{d\tau^2} = -\frac{\mu x}{r^3}$$

$$\frac{d^2x}{dt^2} = -K^2\mu\,\frac{x}{r^3}$$

$$er)\sqrt{\mu/p}$$

$$s\,v + e)\sqrt{\mu/p}$$

$$a(1-e^2\cos^2 E)$$

$$\dot{x}_\omega^2 + \dot{y}_\omega^2 = r^2 + r^2 v^2 = \mu(1+2e\cos v + e^2)/p$$

$$\dot{s}^2 = \mu\left(\frac{2}{r}-\frac{1}{a}\right)$$

$$v^2 = \left(\frac{ds}{dt}\right)^2 = K^2\dot{s}^2 = K^2\mu\left(\frac{2}{r}-\frac{1}{a}\right)$$

$$\sqrt{\mu/p}$$

$$\frac{m}{s},\; s^2 = p'^2 + r^2 - 2p'\,r\cos\chi$$

$$= \Phi + \frac{1}{2}\omega^2(x_c^2 + y_c^2) + 2\omega(x_c\dot{y}_c - y_c\dot{x}_c)$$

$$\omega = \dot{\theta}_0$$

$$X_\alpha = X_f\cos\theta_0 - Y_f\sin\theta_0$$

$$Y_\alpha = X_f\sin\theta_0 + Y_f\cos\theta_0$$

$$X_f = X_\alpha\cos\theta_0 + Y_\alpha\sin\theta_0$$

$$Y_f = -X_\alpha\sin\theta_0 + Y_\alpha\cos\theta_0$$

$$\int Y_f$$

$$X_f$$

$$\ddot{X}_f + \dot{\omega}Y \quad Y_f - \omega^2 X_f$$

Raising Alexander

by Chris Turner

Alexander was a strangely motionless and silent baby, and doctors knew of fewer than 100 cases like his in the world.

For the first six months of Alexander's life, I wanted to believe he might get well on his own. I would often lie down on the floor and make faces at him, trying to tease out a smile. Sometimes, after lots of effort, it worked. But mostly, my son was motionless and silent, his eyes focused on nothing in particular.

It was fall 2009, and my wife, Ashley, and I had only just moved into a new home in downtown Calgary, Alberta. We had a vivacious four-year-old daughter named Sloane, a grouchy Siamese cat, and an infant son who was a mystery. Alexander had been born hypotonic—floppy, basically—with an abdominal hernia, a heart murmur, strange folds on his ears, and a V-shaped birthmark in the center of his forehead. The geneticist assigned to us in intensive care, Micheil Innes, knew these were markers of a genetic disorder, but he couldn't identify which one it was.

Even after Alexander was healthy enough to come home, he was undersized and underweight, hardly able to hold up his head. Amid the rush of feeding and diapers and getting Sloane to school, I could pretend he was just a little quiet and weak for his age. But the truth is, we often wondered if there was any awareness inside him at all.

The first tentative answer arrived on a dark afternoon in December. We were called to a small room at the Alberta Children's Hospital, where Innes explained that a piece of our son's genetic coding simply wasn't there. He showed us Alexander's lab results: rows of striped squiggles like some ancient alphabet and a red dot indicating the location of the missing material, near the end of the "q" branch of the ninth pair of chromosomes. The precise spot, in technical terms, was 9q34.3.

Innes then handed us a pamphlet that had been printed from a website. The document explained that "9q34.3 subtelomeric deletion syndrome" was usually an uninherited, spontaneous mutation, likely occurring at conception. The condition is also called Kleefstra syndrome, after a Dutch researcher who studies it. Innes believed there were fewer than 100 verified diagnoses worldwide at the time. Alexander's developmental problems were born of a single cause—the tiniest of wounds, duplicated in every single cell in his body, forever. Because there were so few cases, the pamphlet provided anecdotes rather than a prognosis: a series of expected obstacles—to speech, mobility, learning—that our son might overcome, if lucky, after a lifetime of hard work.

Ashley and I drove home from the hospital in devastated silence, as if some vital swatch of our family's fabric had been ripped away. We were terrified that our mute child would never walk or talk, let alone run across a playground or march up the aisle at his wedding. Later, as I watched Alexander in bed, I was too numb even to cry. I started to indulge in wishful thinking. Maybe he'll simply catch up to his peers, I thought. Maybe someone will figure out how to fix this. I was convinced, in any case, that I couldn't.

A few days after meeting the geneticist, we were having dinner when Sloane left her seat and skipped to her brother in his high chair at the other end of the table. We hadn't discussed Alexander's diagnosis with her, but Sloane's internal radar for her parents' moods had always been impeccable, and we were both far too shaken to hide it very well. My wife, usually a boisterous, no-holds-barred play fighter, had already stopped the roughhousing as the house filled with a formless, boundless anxiety.

Sloane set herself up behind Alexander, hands clutching either side of his chair, and flung herself from one side of his head to the other. With each swing, she bellowed, "Hello, Mr. Chubby Cheeks!" Alexander began to swing his head back and forth in time with her. His face erupted in a gap-mouthed grin. And then, for the first time in his life, Alexander laughed. Hard. A sudden gurgling, exuberant laugh. And then we all did.

Somewhere on the other side of the diagnosis was a boy who could feel joy. It was our job to find him.

We began where almost all parents with a special-needs child begin: monthly visits to an overworked early intervention clinic that recommended rudimentary physical therapy—exercises to encourage rolling over and sitting up, for example. The workouts seemed arbitrary and totally out of proportion to Alexander's need, like Band-Aids on broken limbs.

My wife pushed the therapists at the clinic for better ways to address Alexander's disorder. They were kind and competent, but Kleefstra syndrome was a question mark for them too. The message was to wait and see, to react once Alexander's symptoms were clearer. Had we acquiesced, the "intensive" part of my son's therapy would've started around the age of three, at the earliest.

Ashley has never accepted the default position on anything, and when it came to her fear of her son's diminished prospects, she was relentless. She used her background as a research editor and radio producer to dig deeper. Books on disability and the brain piled up on her bedside table. One title was Glenn Doman's *What to Do About Your Brain-Injured Child*. Doman—who died in 2013, at 93—was the founder of the Institutes for the Achievement of Human Potential, an unconventional teaching institute in Philadelphia. Using its methods, neurologically impaired kids learn not only to walk and talk but to read and count—often well ahead of unimpaired peers. Ashley had been begging me to look at Alexander's condition as a crisis that, though it could never be eradicated, could be treated. Here, finally, was corroborating evidence.

As a physical therapist in the 1940s, Doman was frustrated by the high failure rate of the techniques used on stroke victims and, later, children with disabilities. He and his associates at the clinic developed a new approach founded on the theory that the brain can grow and change through use—today called neuroplasticity. His clinic amassed evidence, case by case, that with enough hard work, kids like Alexander often exceeded every limitation that had been placed on them.

At that point, the simple exercises at the clinic inspired nothing but frustration from Alexander. But following specifications in a book by Doman's son, Douglas, my father and I built a "crawling track" in our living room. It was a simple ramp with low sides made of heavy plywood, like a jungle gym slide, wrapped in padding and turquoise vinyl. Following the instructions, we propped the track at an incline steep enough that Alexander's slightest wiggle would result in movement. Then, against any number of parental instincts, we placed my son at the top. He was seven months old and had never willfully moved an inch in his life. He howled in protest, squirmed in defiance—and the motion sent him skidding down the track.

Within a week, he was propelling himself, angry at first, but eventually with resolve and even joy. We reduced the incline as he improved, until it was lying flat. A few months later, he crawled right off the end of it. And then he kept right on going.

We signed up for the next available introductory session at Glenn Doman's clinic, now directed by his daughter-in-law, Rosalind. Alexander was the first diagnosed Kleefstra kid the clinic would ever treat.

In Philadelphia the following April, when Alexander was just 11 months old, we found ourselves surrounded by three dozen parents who had come from as far away as Belarus, Singapore, and India. In a week of all-day lectures, our expectations for Alexander—and for our role in his therapy—were turned upside down. The clinic's program was wildly ambitious and nearly impossible to implement fully. It involved almost constant, regimented stimulation, physical activity, and intellectual engagement: daily crawling distance targets, reading and math exercises, workouts aimed at improving breathing and

Alexander and his mother, Ashley Bristowe, at home in Calgary in late 2014

coordination—all of it done by parents themselves. As Rosalind told us at the time, "There are lots of reasonable programs out there. Trouble is, they don't work very well."

When we returned home the next week, we reorganized the main floor of our house around Alexander's therapy. We filled our living room with mats and flash cards emblazoned with words and dots for counting. As part of Alexander's physical therapy, we installed an elaborate "monkey bars" ladder apparatus. (Learning to walk while alternating hands on the rungs would help train Alexander's brain in "cross-pattern" movement, and the raised arms would encourage good posture.) Our son's diet was stripped of known allergens and inflammatories to eliminate any possible nutritional impediments to his development. His daily regimen looked like something prescribed to an Olympic athlete.

The standard approach for a developmentally delayed person is not this ambitious. But we didn't want to wait until after our child's malleable brain had stiffened into adulthood. Ashley and I now had the tools

"Alexander's progress isn't a miracle," says the author, Chris Turner (here with his wife and son). "It's the product of hard work."

to make the most of Alexander's crucial early years. We intended to use them all.

Ashley threw herself into running Alexander's therapy program full-time, and my daily routine as a work-from-home freelancer soon involved at least as much duty as a therapy assistant. The stress was enormous, and our debt grew whenever we sacrificed more work time for Alexander's sessions. For my wife, the manager of our ersatz team, administering the multiple programs meant constructing a self-made cage. Once, our professional lives had involved extended research trips, and now whole weeks could pass without either of us leaving the house except to ferry our daughter to and from school.

Still, we agreed that the strain on our family was far better than the despair of not knowing what to do. We believed, most of the time, that there was a smart little boy straining to emerge from those flapping, disorganized limbs. Alexander's program required a platoon of volunteer helpers, which meant most of our block knew all about his condition. The spring after he turned three, when he started to walk up and down the street on his own, his first trips were victory laps to cheering neighbors.

We would have to wait another year for proof that the reading and math exercises were sinking in. Day in and day out, we dutifully held up flash cards containing words and numbers, sentences and equations. But how could we know for sure how much of it was working when Alexander could speak only in fragments and monosyllables? Incontrovertible evidence came one day when we were in the car, about to pull out of a parking lot. Ashley was listing off rhyming words for Alexander to attempt to repeat. "Car," she recited. Alexander repeated it. Then they ran through *far, bar, star*.

Ashley paused, thinking the game was over. From the backseat came a thin, cheerful voice: "Guitar!" An unprompted, two-syllable rhyme. Our explosive cheer was so loud, it startled Alexander almost to tears. The kid could talk—and rhyme! Every agonizing day of his therapy had been worth it for that marvelous rhyme.

> *The kid could talk—and rhyme! Every agonizing day of his therapy had been worth it for that marvelous rhyme.*

Alexander recently turned seven, and we no longer have reason to doubt his ability to learn. His daily life is an inventory of things he wasn't expected to do—possibly ever, certainly not by now. He can tell you his name and address. He'll ask you to draw a cement truck on his whiteboard, then spell the letters with glee as you write them out. At the grocery store, he counts off the aisles from the signs overhead, calling, "Aisle five!" with particular delight. Then we stand in beloved aisle five to wait for the automated checkout kiosks. "Commpooter!" Alexander announces as I sweep our groceries over the sensor, raising his arms in excitement. Gazing out from beneath a tussle of golden hair, his deep brown eyes are magnetic—they never fail to tease a smile from the checkout attendant.

Last fall, just a year behind schedule, Alexander started kindergarten in a standard classroom. Whatever his limitations are, he is nowhere near them yet. He might never be completely self-sufficient. But I believe if he winds up anywhere near such a state, it will be because, against the advice of many experts, we maximized every moment during his early years, when his brain was most able to reorganize itself to compensate for the tiny missing sliver of gene in every cell. I want Alexander to be seen as a model of how early intervention should be done: all day, every day, as much as a distressed family can possibly cram in, from the moment anyone suspects anything is wrong.

This, I hope, is my son's lesson for all of us: Our approach to special-needs kids is completely upside down. We've only just left the dark ages when it comes to our understanding of how the human brain works. The potential waiting there is an enormous untapped resource. And, as Alexander has proved already, many of the limits we long believed were impossible to overcome fall away in the face of the right kind of hard work.

Originally published in the October 2016 issue of *Reader's Digest* magazine.

Alexander can walk, talk, swim, jump on a trampoline, and do many of the same activities as other 10-year-olds. At school, he's working hard to master reading. He goes on field trips, participates in group projects, and played a tree in a school performance.

On the Line

by Mitch Lipka

With seconds separating them from an oncoming train, one man risked everything to save a woman he'd never met.

Lisa Donath was running late. Heading down the sidewalk toward her subway stop in Manhattan's Washington Heights neighborhood, she decided to skip her usual espresso. Donath, 25, had a lot to do at work, plus visitors on the way: Her parents were coming in for Thanksgiving from her hometown of Minneapolis. But as she hustled down the stairs and through the long tunnel, she started to feel uncomfortably warm. By the time she got to the platform, Donath felt faint—maybe it hadn't been a good idea to give blood the night before, she thought. She leaned heavily against a post close to the tracks.

Several yards away, Ismael "Mel" Feneque, 43, and his girlfriend, Melina Gonzalez, found a spot close to where the front of the train would stop. Feneque, a pattern maker, had a mound of sketches waiting for him in his studio, but on this morning, women's fashion was far from his mind. He and Gonzalez were deep in discussion about a house they were thinking of buying.

But when he heard the scream, followed by someone yelling, "Oh, my God, she fell in!" Feneque didn't hesitate. Yanking off the bag he had slung across his six-three frame, he jumped down to the tracks and

Ismael Feneque and Lisa Donath

ran some 40 feet toward the body sprawled facedown on the rails.

"No! Not you!" his girlfriend screamed after him.

She was right to be alarmed. By the time Feneque reached Donath, he could "feel the vibration on the tracks and see the light coming into the tunnel," he remembers. "The train was maybe 20 seconds from the station." In that instant, Feneque gave himself a mission: I'm going to get her out, and then I'm going to get myself out, ASAP. I'm not going to let myself get killed here.

Feneque, a former high school wrestler who trains at a gym to stay in shape, grabbed Donath under her armpits. She was deadweight. "It was hard to lift her. She was just out," he says. But he managed to raise her the four feet to the platform so that bystanders could grab her arms and drag her away from the edge. That's where Donath briefly regained consciousness, felt herself being pulled along the ground, and saw someone else holding her purse.

"I thought I'd been mugged," she says. She remembers the woman who held her hand and a man who gave his shirt to help stop the blood pouring from her head. And, she says, "I remember trying to talk and I couldn't, and that's when I realized how much pain I was in." The impact of her fall had been absorbed by her face—she'd lost teeth and suffered a broken eye socket, a broken jaw, and cuts all over her head.

But as the train closed in, Feneque wasn't finished. He still had to grab and hoist up a man and a teenager who'd hopped down to the tracks and then use all the strength he had left to lift himself onto the platform. He did so just seconds before the train barreled past him and came to a stop.

Police and fire officials soon arrived, and Feneque gave his name to an officer and told him the story. "He said that it was a great thing I had done, and I thanked him," Feneque recalls. Gonzalez says her unassuming boyfriend was calm on their 40-minute train ride downtown—just as he had been seconds after the rescue.

Donath's parents joined her at her hospital bedside by the next morning and stayed in town to see her through the series of surgeries she'd need to reconstruct her face. Once Donath returned to her job, she was determined to find the man who had saved her life—the man the police had listed, incorrectly, as Feneque Ismael. "I was never really into going on TV or getting my picture put in the *New York Times*—as you can imagine, having a scarred-up face isn't fun," says Donath. "But I did so to know that I tried everything I could [to contact him]."

Feneque, for his part, couldn't stop wondering what had happened to the woman on the tracks. Several weeks later, while surfing the Internet for any new clues . . . bingo! A television station had posted an update on its website, detailing Donath's recovery and her search for her rescuer. Feneque e-mailed the address provided to say that he was that man.

When the two first met, Donath threw her arms around Feneque and wept. It was overwhelming, she says, to try to convey her feelings. "What do you say to the person who saved your life?" When they met again several months later, for this photo shoot, it felt a lot easier. "I finally had the chance to hear his side of the story in detail," she says. "He really just seems like such a sweet and humble person."

Feneque says there's no point in wondering why he was on the platform—at a different time from when he usually rides and at a station a considerable distance from his apartment—at the moment Donath needed help. "Whether it was pure coincidence or sent from above, who's to say? All I know is I was there and I'd do it again," he says.

"I have a daughter. And I said to myself, I'm going to help this person. She could be anybody's daughter."

Originally published in the November 2008 issue of *Reader's Digest* magazine.

MY WEALTHY LIFE

At 16 my guitar and I found a captive audience at the local
hospital. I went from room to room and miraculously, patients
responded with smiles and laughter. Doctors and nurses
directed me to Billy, a little boy battling cancer. I sang to him
every day for two weeks, then one day his big blue eyes closed
forever as I held his little hand. I was just a kid, but realized
that music had the power to change lives and my career path
was chosen for me. A few years ago, after performing my song
"Dreams," I was signing autographs and a frail little lady with
tears rolling down her cheeks gave me a bear hug. She told me
she had recently lost her husband of 50 years, and after hearing
the song, realized she needed a new dream. For years I thought
wealth had eluded me, I was wrong.

—Jim Moore *Chattanooga, Tennessee*

A DANCING BLESSING

My stepfather, Marlin, bought a dancing Christmas tree
in the mid-2000s as a gimmick decoration. Marlin passed
away in 2014. My sister, Stacy, had taken possession of it
along the way. Stacy got engaged to her longtime boyfriend
on Thanksgiving night (Marlin had met him). The tree was
unpacked, but had no batteries. Later that evening, with all
the ladies sitting around talking, the tree lit up and started
to dance! The empty battery pack was in hand and the only
conclusion we could reach was that Marlin was sending his
blessing and dancing a jig.

—Norman Powers *Sheffield, Alabama*

"Information Please"

by Paul Villiard

The voice of this genie-in-the-telephone
receiver had an enduring message.

W hen I was quite young my family had one of the first telephones in our neighborhood. I remember well the polished oak case fastened to the wall on the lower stair landing. The shiny receiver hung on the side of the box. I even remember the number—105. I was too little to reach the telephone, but used to listen with fascination when my mother talked to it. Once she lifted me up to speak to my father, who was away on business. Magic!

Then I discovered that somewhere inside that wonderful device lived an amazing person—her name was "Information Please" and there was nothing she did not know. My mother could ask her for anybody's number; when our clock ran down, Information Please immediately supplied the correct time.

My first personal experience with this genie-in-the-receiver came one day while my mother was visiting a neighbor. Amusing myself at the tool bench in the basement, I whacked my finger with a hammer. The pain was terrible, but there didn't seem to be much use crying because there was no one home to offer sympathy. I walked around the house sucking my throbbing finger, finally arriving at the stairway. The telephone! Quickly I ran for the footstool in the parlor and dragged it to the landing. Climbing up, I unhooked the receiver and held it to my ear. "Information Please," I said into the mouthpiece just above my head. A click or two, and a small, clear voice spoke into my ear. "Information."

"I hurt my *fing*errrr—" I wailed into the phone. The tears came readily enough, now that I had an audience.

"Isn't your mother home?" came the question.

"Nobody's home but me," I blubbered.

"Are you bleeding?"

"No," I replied. "I hit it with the hammer and it hurts."

"Can you open your icebox?" she asked. I said I could. "Then chip off a little piece of ice and hold it on your finger. That will stop the hurt. Be careful when you use the ice pick," she admonished. "And don't cry. You'll be all right."

After that, I called Information Please for everything. I asked her for help with my geography and she told me where Philadelphia was, and the Orinoco—the romantic river I was going to explore when I grew up. She helped me with my arithmetic, and she told me that my pet chipmunk—I had caught him in the park—would eat fruit and nuts.

And there was the time that Petey, our pet canary, died. I called Information Please and told her the sad story. She listened, then she said the usual things grown-ups say to soothe a child. But I was unconsoled: Why was it that birds should sing so beautifully and bring joy to whole families, only to end up as a heap of feathers, feet up, on the bottom of a cage?

She must have sensed my deep concern, for she said quietly, "Paul, always remember that there are other worlds to sing in."

Somehow I felt better.

Another day I was at the telephone. "Information," said the now familiar voice.

"How do you spell *fix*?" I asked.

"Fix something? F-i-x."

At that instant my sister, who took unholy joy in scaring me, jumped off the stairs at me with a banshee shriek—"*Yaaaaaaaaaa!*" I fell off the stool, pulling the receiver out of the box by its roots. We were both terrified—Information Please was no longer there, and I was not at all sure that I hadn't hurt her when I pulled the receiver out.

Minutes later there was a man on the porch. "I'm a telephone repairman," he said. "I was working down the street and the operator said there might be some trouble at this number." He reached for the receiver in my hand. "What happened?"

I told him.

"Well, we can fix that in a minute or two." He opened the telephone box, exposing a maze of wires and coils, and fiddled with the end of the receiver cord. He jiggled the hook up and down, then spoke into the phone. "Hi, this is Peter. Everything's under control at 105."

"The operator said there might be some trouble at this number."

He hung up, smiled, gave me a pat on the head and walked out.

* * *

All this took place in a small town in the Pacific Northwest. Then, when I was nine years old, we moved across the country to Boston—and I missed my mentor acutely. Information Please belonged in that old wooden box back home, and I somehow never thought of trying the tall, skinny new phone that sat on a small table in the hall.

Yet, as I grew into my teens, the memories of those childhood conversations never really left me; often in moments of doubt and perplexity I would recall the serene sense of security I had when I knew that I could call Information Please and get the right answer. I appreciated now how patient and kind she was to have wasted her time on a little boy.

A few years later, on my way west to college, my plane put down at Seattle. I had about half an hour between plane connections, and I spent 15 minutes or so on the phone with my sister, who lived there now, happily mellowed by marriage and motherhood. Then, really without thinking, I dialed my hometown operator and said, "Information Please."

Miraculously, I heard again the small, clear voice I knew so well: "Information."

I hadn't planned this, but I heard myself saying, "Could you tell me, please, how to spell the word 'fix'?"

There was a long pause. Then came the softly spoken answer. "I guess," said Information Please, "that your finger must have healed by now."

I laughed. "So it's really still you," I said. "I wonder if you have any idea how much you meant to me during all that time . . ."

"I wonder," she replied, "if you know how much you meant to *me?* I never had any children, and I used to look forward to your calls. Silly, wasn't it?"

It didn't seem silly, but I didn't say so. Instead, I told her how often I had thought of her over the years, and I asked if I could call her again when I came back to visit my sister after the first semester was over.

"Please do. Just ask for Sally."

"Good-bye, Sally." It sounded strange for Information Please to have a name. "If I run into any chipmunks, I'll tell them to eat fruit and nuts."

"Do that," she said. "And I expect one of these days you'll be off for the Orinoco. Well, good-bye."

*　*　*

Just three months later I was back again at the Seattle airport. A different voice answered, "Information," and I asked for Sally.

"Are you a friend?"

"Yes," I said. "An old friend."

"Then I'm sorry to have to tell you. Sally had only been working part-time in the last few years because she was ill. She died five weeks ago." But before I could hang up, she said, "Wait a minute. Did you say your name was Villiard?"

"Yes."

"Well, Sally left a message for you. She wrote it down."

"What was it?" I asked, almost knowing in advance what it would be.

"Here it is, I'll read it—'Tell him I still say there are other worlds to sing in. He'll know what I mean.' "

I thanked her and hung up. I *did* know what Sally meant.

Originally published in the June 1966 issue of *Reader's Digest* magazine.

CREDITS AND ACKNOWLEDGMENTS

"Letter in the Wallet" by Arnold Fine, *Jewish Press* (January 20, 1984), copyright © 1984 by Arnold Fine; *Reader's Digest,* September 1985

"In Over His Head" by Doug Colligan, *Reader's Digest,* April 2007
   Photographs by Gunnar Conrad

"Not a Moment to Spare" by Kevin Harter, *Reader's Digest,* October 1998

"Stowaway!" by Armando Socarras Ramirez, as told to Denis Fodor and John Reddy, *Reader's Digest,* January 1971

"To Do or Not to Do" by Mary Roach, *Reader's Digest,* June 2002

"Class Action" by Lynn Rosellini, *Reader's Digest,* April 2004
   Photograph by Kelly Laduke

"Friends for Life" by Ellen Sherman, *Reader's Digest,* March 2005
   Photograph on page 38 by Chris Cone; pages 40 and 41 right courtesy Herb Heilbrun; page 41 left courtesy John Leahr

"The Prisoner and the Encyclopedia Editor" by Daniel A. Gross, *New Yorker* (September 13, 2016), copyright © 2016 by Daniel A. Gross;

Reader's Digest, December 2017/January 2018
   Photograph courtesy Daniel A. Gross

"Killer on Call" by Max Alexander, *Reader's Digest,* November 2004
   Photograph on page 52 by Bradley C. Bower/AP/Shutterstock; page 56 Tony Kurdzuk/AP/Shutterstock

"Grizzly Attack!" by Peter Michelmore, *Reader's Digest,* June 1992

"A Five-Year-Old Teaches a Lesson in Grace" by Leslie Kendall Dye, *New York Times* (November 3, 2017), copyright © 2017 by Leslie Kendall Dye; *Reader's Digest,* March 2019

"Emergency Whistle on Block Island" by Floyd Miller, *Reader's Digest,* June 1970

"The Baby and the Battalion" by Kenneth Miller, *Reader's Digest,* May 2007
   Photographs on pages 86 and 93 by Michele McDonald/Boston Globe/Getty Images; page 89 courtesy Maureen Walsh; page 90 courtesy Captain Sean Donovan

"An Evening Drive" by Joe Posnanski, joeposnanski.substack.com (September 17, 2015), copyright © 2015

by Joe Posnanski; *Reader's Digest,* November 2016

"One Wing and a Prayer" by Penny Porter, *Reader's Digest,* September 1997
   Photograph by Roger de la Harpe/Shutterstock

"Summer's Magical Music" by Allan Sherman, *Reader's Digest,* July 1971

"When Your Best Fish Story Is About Catching a Goat" by Rick Bragg, *Garden & Gun* (June/July 2017), copyright © 2017 by Rick Bragg; *Reader's Digest,* November 2017

"Horror in the Heartland" by Henry Hurt, *Reader's Digest,* May 1996
   Photograph on page 118 by Charles H Porter Iv/AP/Shutterstock; page 128 by Bill Waugh/AP/Shutterstock

"Thank You for Caring So Much" by Peter DeMarco, *New York Times* (October 6, 2016), copyright © 2016 by Peter DeMarco; *Reader's Digest,* November 2017
   Photograph courtesy Peter DeMarco

"At the Bottom of the Bay" by Anita Bartholomew, *Reader's Digest,* January 2007
   Photographs by Kelly Laduke

"Life on the Funny Farm" by Laura Cunningham, *New York Times Magazine* (May 12, 1991), copyright © 1991 by Laura Cunningham; *Reader's Digest,* September 1991

"Stopping a Kidnapper" by Alyssa Jung, *Reader's Digest,* June 2017
    Photograph by Trevor Paulhus

"The Little Boat That Sailed Through Time" by Arnold Berwick, *Reader's Digest,* May 1993

"Buried in Mud" by Nick Heil, *Reader's Digest,* April 2014
    Photograph on page 158 courtesy Michelle Grainger; page 163 by Jeremy Papasso/Getty Images

"I've Come to Clean Your Shoes" by Madge Harrah adapted from the book *On Children and Death*, copyright © 1983 by Elisabeth Kübler-Ross, M.D., published by Touchstone, a division of Simon & Schuster, Inc.; *Reader's Digest,* December 1983

"Gandalf and the Search for the Lost Boy" by Christopher W. Davis, *Reader's Digest,* December 2007
    Photographs by Ann States

"The Curse of Sigurd the Fingerless" by Ruth Park, *Reader's Digest,* September 1984

"The Day We Planted Hope" by Conrad Kiechel, *Reader's Digest,* March 1994

"The Over-the-Hill Gang" by Mark Seal, *Vanity Fair* March 2016, copyright © 2016 by Mark Seal; *Reader's Digest,* International Editions, 2017
    Photograph on page 192 by Kjpargeter/ Shutterstock; page 194 by Shutterstock; page 198 by Metropolitan Police/AP/ Shutterstock; page 203 by Stefan Wermuth/Reuters/ stock.adobe.com

"My Mamma's Letters" by Octavia Capuzzi Locke, *Johns Hopkins Magazine* (June 1987), copyright © by Octavia Capuzzi Locke; *Reader's Digest,* June 1992

"The Stranger Who Taught Magic" by Arthur Gordon, *Reader's Digest,* June 1970, reprinted with permission of the Estate of Pamela M. Gordon

"Runaway Train" by William M. Hendry, *Reader's Digest,* March 2002
    Photograph on page 216 by Frank Cezus/ Getty Images; page 218 by Michael O'Neill

"A Miracle of Mermaids" by Margo Pfeiff, *Reader's Digest,* September 1995

"I Captured Adolf Eichmann" excerpted from the book *Eichmann in My Hands* by Peter Z. Malkin and Harry Stein, copyright © 1990 by Peter Z. Malkin and Harry Stein, published by Grand Central Publishing; *Reader's Digest,* February 1991
    Photograph on page 235 by GPO/Getty Images; page 239 by Evan Agostini/ Liaison/Getty Images

"Some Sort of Magic" by Annette Foglino, *Reader's Digest,* August 1998
    Photographs by Roger Mastroianni

"My Fourteenth Summer" by W. W. Meade, *Reader's Digest,* July 1998

"'Please Don't Leave Me!'" by James Hutchinson, *Reader's Digest,* August 1991
    Photograph on page 266 by brazzo/Getty Images; page 274 courtesy Royd Kennedy

"How to Ruin a Joke" by Andy Simmons, *Reader's Digest,* September 2008

"Nailed Through the Heart" by Per Ola and Emily D'Aulaire, *Reader's Digest,* June 1993

"Raising Alexander" by Chris Turner, *Reader's Digest,* October 2016
    Photographs by Noah Fallis

"On the Line" by Mitch Lipka, *Reader's Digest,* November 2008
    Photograph by Rudy Archuleta/Redux

"'Information Please'" by Paul Villiard, *Reader's Digest,* June 1966